Contents

Acknowledgements

A book of this nature would not have been possible without the help of many people and organisations too numerous to individually mention. I am indebted to many for providing photographs and information - first-hand and anecdotal - for this story, but in some cases it has not been possible to identify the original photographer or information source and so credits are given in the appropriate places to the immediate supplier. If any of the pictures have not been correctly credited, please accept my apologies.

I would, however, like to offer my special thanks to a small group of people for freely letting me have access to their collections of images and information, including Dr Harry Friedman, Jeff Duford, David Lee, Peter Clegg and Peter Green.

Introduction

On 8 September 1944, at around 18:45, a German V-2 rocket landed on Staveley Road, Chiswick, London, killing three people and doing considerable damage to nearby properties. This was only the second V-2 rocket to be launched operationally and the first to kill on impact. As such, Britain became the first nation to suffer casualties as a result of a ballistic missile attack. The V-2 on Chiswick resulted in three deaths: three-year-old Rosemary Clarke, who lived at number 1 Staveley Road; Ada Harrison, aged 68, of 3 Staveley Road; and Sapper Bernard Browning, who was on leave and on his way to Chiswick Station. Destruction was considerable. The V-2 blew a crater thirty feet wide and eight feet deep at the point of impact.

On 2 October 1945, after the Second World War had ended in Europe and Asia, the British launched a V-2 under experimental conditions.

So it was that in a little over twelve months, the United Kingdom went from being a victim of long-range guided missiles to a wielder of this impressive new military technology. That, however, is not the whole story. By 1948, Britain had decided not to pursue the development of an independent long-range rocket capacity any further, instead choosing to focus on jet-powered, piloted bombers as the preferred delivery method for conventional, and later atomic, payloads. As a result, most accounts of Britain's missile programme begin with the initial - and ultimately abortive - development of the Blue Streak rocket in 1955, so the initial post-war efforts, some ten years earlier, are now largely forgotten.

This book has three main objectives. The first is to challenge this conventional but incomplete narrative. While it may make sense for historians to use this in the form of a retrospective overview, only picking up the story with the first clearly-defined British missile project in the mid-1950s, they have blatantly ignored the contemporary perspectives of officials and policymakers at the end of the Second World War, who very much saw themselves as active participants in the newly-dawned missile age.

Instead, I have emphasised a key principle that guided policy in the immediate post-war period - atomic weapons would shape any future conflict and that the most effective delivery method for nuclear warheads would almost certainly be long-range ballistic missiles.

Furthermore, most historical accounts fail to mention another key principle which influenced early British plans for an independent missile programme - the assumption that the quickest and easiest way for Britain to obtain a missile capacity of its own would be to draw upon German technology and expertise once the Third Reich had collapsed.

Therefore, the second objective is to combat this omission, to locate German contributions to this process, and thus to reframe the story as transnational rather than solely Anglo-centric.

With these two objectives in mind, the aim is to show that, from the last months of the war until the independent missile programme was dropped in 1948, the United Kingdom saw itself as an active and significant competitor in the new international missile race. It believed that its chances of success hinged on the effective utilisation of German equipment and know-how as an entire, integral system. In this way, Operation Backfire - the assembly, preparation and firing of three V-2 rocket system by experienced German staff under British supervision and observation in October 1945 - can be seen as a critical moment in the UK's first foray into missile development. Some histories of this subject have dismissed the results of Backfire as being of *'limited and of little practical value'*, but those involved in the operation certainly did not see it that way. The official Backfire report noted that all relevant British ministries were unanimous that carrying out such an operation was most desirable, based on the widely-held view that it should save years of development work.

This occurred against the global backdrop of worsening relations between East and West and the increasing hostility and suspicion of the developing Cold War. Indeed, in the official predictions of future conflict, which highlighted the importance of long-range rockets, the envisaged enemy was always the Soviet Union. The crucial requirement for the most powerful ballistic missiles desired by the UK was that they would be able to hit targets in western Russia if launched from the UK or overseas bases in Cyprus or India.

The third objective is to show that the USSR was not Britain's only foreign adversary in its drive to build up a missile capacity after the Second World War, especially in the first year or so after the conflict. Instead, it soon became entangled in a fierce rivalry with its closest wartime ally, the United States of America.

Both countries - as well as the other occupiers of Germany, France and the Soviet Union - sought to make use of German expertise to build up a domestic missile arsenal. Still, the US's more significant resources and newly-minted superpower status allowed them to steamroll over their transatlantic allies. As such, the competition for the best assets of the German rocketry programme - both material and personnel - provided the British with an early and brutal realisation that they were no longer at the very top table of global politics and that they might have to be prepared to play second fiddle to the Americans moving forward.

Operation Backfire proved a particularly sensitive flashpoint, especially when the US authorities withdrew their support for what had started as an Anglo-American undertaking and threatened to scupper the whole initiative by demanding the removal of several of the most prominent German engineers involved.

So, I intend to closely examine Operation Backfire and the period immediately surrounding it to achieve the three stated objectives. I will show that for a brief time after the Second World War, Britain was fully committed to developing an independent missile capability, that it identified the utilisation of German expertise as vital to attaining this goal, and that the greatest threat posed to this scheme came from American intransigence and overriding self-interest. This short chapter of history, so often glossed over by historians, will tell us a remarkable amount about Britain, its views on new military technologies, and its relations with other countries in the earliest part of the Cold War.

This book was not easy to write and assemble on a technical and design level. The most significant contributor was the five-volume Operation Backfire Report itself, a copy of which was found in the National Archives and Records Administration (NARA) in College Park, Maryland, USA. Here was the story's What, How, Where, When and Why in minute detail - written in the driest, technical English I have ever had the pleasure of translating!

From the same team that brought you the maximum permissible pressure inside the A-Stoff Anhaenger - liquid oxygen road tank trailer - (it was 14.5 kilogrammes per square centimetre, by the way), there were literally hundreds of photographs, technical drawings and maps in this 520-page document. I just had to use what I could, but there were problems, not least because it had been microfilmed for archiving and then digitised.

Artificial Intelligence (AI) software allowed me to recover many of the images, and an old-fashioned draughting board and Rotring pens - yes, I still have a set - allowed me to recover many of the drawings. The only problem I could not beat was matching an image to the relevant associated text on something like the same page near each other - the puzzle was just too difficult, but it's impossible to win them all!

So, here is the story. As so many (American) books and web pages love to tell you - after the Germans, they were the first - they were not.

For the record, the launch dates were:

The United Kingdom: 1 October 1945

The USA: 16 April 1946

The USSR: 18 October 1947

Graham M Simons
Peterborough.
12 May 2026

Chapter One

In the Beginning

Throughout the 1930s, as the threat of another European war loomed large, people spent much time and effort attempting to imagine the next conflict. In nearly all cases, the expectation was that it would be fought to a considerable, perhaps even overwhelming, extent in the air. The fear of the bomber dominated civilian life, especially after the establishment of an Air Raid Precautions Department in 1935 and the distribution of gas masks during the Sudeten Crisis of September 1938. It significantly developed Hitler's foreign policy aims and tested Britain and France. The Sudeten Crisis focused on Sudetenland, an area of Czechoslovakia that bordered Germany. The region had German speakers who had been placed there after the break up of the empires at the end of World War One.

Czechoslovakia was led by Edvard Beneš (*b.* 28 May 1884, *d.* 3 September 1948). He was a statesman, foreign minister, President, and founder of modern Czechoslovakia.

Beneš was deeply concerned about Germany's actions after Anschluss, the annexation of Austria by Germany in 1938. Hitler had forced the resignation of the Austrian Chancellor by demanding that he admit Nazis into his cabinet. The new Chancellor, a pro-Nazi, invited German troops to enter the country on the pretext of restoring law and order. Determined to protect his country, Beneš desperately tried to work with Britain and France to ensure they would be safe from German aggression. Adolf Hitler (*b.* 20 April 1889, *d.* 30 April 1945) used similar tactics to that of Austria and got local Nazis to stir up trouble for the Czech authorities. Benes got assurances from France, Britain and the Soviet Union that they would help protect Czechoslovakia if needed. The Sudetenland was also important as this was where many Czech armament factories and defences were, so losing them would mean Czechoslovakia would be defenceless.

To help stop a war, British Prime Minister Arthur Neville Chamberlain (*b.*18 March 1869, *d.*9 November 1940) met with Hitler, who said that Germany only wanted those parts of the Sudetenland which spoke German and that they should be able to vote on it. Chamberlain believed this was a reasonable course of action and was convinced this would end it. Chamberlain, alongside the French, submitted the plan to the Czechs. However, just days later, Hitler then demanded all of the Sudetenland, not just the German-speaking parts. Hitler used the pretext that the Czechs were oppressing the Germans and that the Reich should rescue them. The Sudeten Crisis led to the Munich Agreement in September 1938.

The idea of a knock-out blow from the air maintained a central place in strategic predictions, even after the limitations of aerial bombardment had been exposed during the Spanish Civil War. In all these concepts and calculations, the place of the long-range rocket or flying bomb remained peripheral at best. The threat from these untested and essentially hypothetical weapons paled in comparison to that of fleets of manned bombers delivering massive devastation to cities with impunity.

These assumptions proved correct when the Second World War broke out in 1939. While the expected 'knock-out blow' never materialised, aerial bombardment played a key part in the Nazi military campaigns of 1939 and 1940. It was later utilised during the Blitz to try and bomb Britain into submission. The long-range rocket was nowhere to be seen.

However, it did not entirely disappear from the minds of military strategists and intelligence experts. The Nazi menace was seen to be closely entwined with science, and as such, a clearer picture of German work on long-range rockets began to emerge.

Creating a liquid-fuelled rocket with a greater range than any conventional artillery fell to the scientists and engineers at Kummersdorf. The team progressed through increasingly complex rocket designs, designated the 'A' series for 'Aggregat', meaning aggregate or assembly. The A-1 was four and one-half feet long, one foot in diameter, and generated six hundred and sixty pounds of thrust. Although it was never launched, the A-1 led to the redesigned A-2, with a better motor and increased stability. The A-2 was launched successfully in December 1934. The much-advanced A-3 was twenty-five feet tall and incorporated technological improvements in pressurisation, control systems, and fuel valves. Problems with the guidance system necessitated changes that were incorporated into the A-5. The production of an A-5 rocket was not envisioned initially but became necessary to resolve unforeseen problems with the A-3 before the team could progress to the already planned, much larger A-4.

The A-4 missile went into production for use against Britain and other European targets, and the German Propaganda Minister, Paul Joseph Goebbels (*b.* 29 October 1897, *d.* 1 May 1945), renamed the missile the V-2 - Vergeltungswaffe Drei, or in English, Vengeance Weapon 2. It was meant as retaliation for Allied bombing attacks on Germany.

An Intelligence star.

A key, but in many ways unsung hero of British Intelligence was Professor Reginald Victor Jones. He was a British physicist and scientific and military intelligence expert who played a massive role in the defence of Britain in World War Two by solving scientific and technical problems and by the extensive use of deception throughout the war to confuse the Germans.

In 1936, Professor Jones took up a post at the Royal Aircraft Establishment (RAE), Farnborough, a part of the Air Ministry. Here he worked on the problems associated with defending Britain from an air attack and later in support of the liberation of Europe from the Nazis. More generally, he was fond of practical jokes and describes how he used that skill to deceive the Germans in his book *Most Secret War*. His extensive use of deception to deceive the Germans is consistent with the modern term 'disinformation', which is defined as the deliberate planting of false information and physical evidence to lead an opponent astray.

In September 1939, the British decided to assign a scientist to the Intelligence section of the Air Ministry. No scientist had previously worked for an intelligence service, but Jones quickly rose to become ADI - Assistant Director of Intelligence (Science) - there. He was closely involved with the scientific assessment of enemy technology and developing offensive and countermeasures technology. He solved several challenging scientific and technical intelligence problems and is generally known today as the 'father of Scientific and Technical Intelligence'.

Jones was briefly based at Bletchley Park in September 1939 but returned to London (Broadway) in November, leaving behind a small specialised team in Hut 3, who reported any decrypts of a scientific or technological nature to 'ADI Science'.

Bletchley Park is an English country house and estate in Bletchley, Buckinghamshire, that became the principal centre of Allied code-breaking during the Second World War. The mansion was constructed in the years following 1883 for the financier and politician Herbert Leon in Victorian Gothic, Tudor, and Dutch Baroque styles on the site of older buildings on the same estate.

During the Second World War, the estate housed the Government Code and Cypher School (GC&CS), which regularly

Professor R V Jones (*b,* 29 September 1911, *d.* 17 December 1997).

penetrated the secret communications of the Axis Powers – most notably the German Enigma and Lorenz cyphers. The GC&CS team of codebreakers included John Tiltman, Dilwyn Knox, Alan Turing, Harry Golombek, Gordon Welchman, Hugh Alexander, Donald Michie, Bill Tutte and Stuart Milner-Barry.

According to the official historian of British Intelligence, it was estimated that the 'Ultra' intelligence produced at Bletchley shortened the war by two to four years, and without it, the war's outcome would have been uncertain. The team at Bletchley Park devised automatic machinery to help with decryption, culminating in the development of Colossus, the world's first programmable digital electronic computer.

Frederick William Winterbotham CBE was an RAF officer who supervised the distribution of Ultra intelligence. He passed to Jones the Oslo Report in 1939, which had come from an anti-Nazi German scientist. Jones decided that it was genuine and largely reliable, though the three service ministries regarded it as a 'plant' and discarded their copies: Jones was later quoted as saying *'... in the few dull moments of the War, I used to look up the Oslo report to see what should be coming along next.'*

Jones' first job was to study 'new German weapons' real or potential. The first was a radio navigation system called Knickebein by the Germans. Jones soon determined that the Lorenz blind landing system was developed to enable an aircraft to fly along a chosen heading with useful accuracy.

At Jones's urging, Churchill ordered an RAF search aircraft on the night of 21 June 1940, and the aircraft found the Knickebein radio signals in the frequency range Jones had predicted. With this knowledge, the British were able to build jammers whose effect was to 'bend' the Knickebein beams so that German bombers spent months scattering their bomb loads over the British countryside.

So began the 'Battle of the Beams' with

Left: Frederick William Winterbotham CBE (*b.* 16 April 1897, *d.* 28 January 1990) seen in his RFC uniform.

Right: Frederick Alexander Lindemann, 1st Viscount Cherwell (*b.*5 April 1886 *d,* 3 July 1957)

the Germans developing new radio navigation systems and the British developing the required countermeasures. Jones frequently had to battle against entrenched interests within the armed forces, but, in addition to enjoying Churchill's confidence, Jones had strong support from, among others, Churchill's scientific advisor Frederick Alexander Lindemann, 1st Viscount Cherwell, CH, PC, FRS and the Chief of the Air Staff Charles Frederick Algernon Portal, 1st Viscount Portal of Hungerford, KG, GCB, OM, DSO & Bar, MC, DL.

Charles Frederick Algernon Portal, 1st Viscount Portal of Hungerford, KG, GCB, OM, DSO & Bar, MC, DL *(b.* 21 May 1893, *d.* 22 April 1971).

As early as 1937, Jones had suggested that a piece of metal foil falling through the air might create radar echoes. He, together with Joan Curran, was later instrumental in the deployment of 'Window': strips of metal foil cut to a length appropriate to the radar's wavelength and dropped in bundles from aircraft, which then appeared on enemy radar screens as 'false bombers'. This technology is now known as chaff and, contrary to popular belief, was also known to the Germans at the time. Both parties were reluctant to use it, fearing their enemy would do the same. The fear delayed its deployment for almost two years.

As we shall see, Jones also served as an A-4/V-2 rocket expert on the Cabinet Defence Committee (Operations) and headed a German long-range weapons targeting deception under the Double-Cross System.

The system was a World War Two counter-espionage and deception operation of the British Security Service (MI5). The Twenty Committee oversaw its operations under the chairmanship of John Cecil Masterman and took its name from the

The Bletchley Park complex near Milton Keynes in Buckinghamshire, as seen from the air.

number twenty in Roman numerals: 'XX' (that is, a 'double cross'). Nazi agents in Britain – real and false – were captured, turned themselves in or announced themselves, and were then used by the British to broadcast mainly disinformation to their Nazi controllers.

The policy of MI5 during the war was initially to use the system for counter-espionage. It was only later that its potential for deception purposes was realised. Of the agents from the German intelligence services, Abwehr and Sicherheitsdienst (SD), while many who reached British shores turned themselves in to the authorities, others were apprehended after they made elementary mistakes during their operations. In addition, some were false agents who had tricked the Germans into believing they would spy for them if they helped them reach England.

Later, agents were instructed to contact agents unknown to the Abwehr and controlled by the British. The Abwehr and SD sent agents over by parachute drop, submarine, or travel via neutral countries. The last route was most commonly used, with agents often impersonating refugees. After the war, it was discovered that all the agents Germany sent to Britain had given themselves up or had been captured, with the possible exception of one who committed suicide.

British investigations into German rocketry expanded and accelerated considerably. On 11 April 1943, the Chiefs of Staff received a report from the Vice Chief of the Imperial General Staff, Lieutenant-General Sir Archibald Edward Nye who, summarised the existing intelligence on the long-range rocket threat. The report predicted, amongst other things, that each rocket might carry an amount of explosive at least equal to that carried by the German one thousand kilogramme bomb, that the extreme range would seem to be about one hundred and thirty miles, and that 'an attack could fall without any warning'. While not all the details in Nye's report were accurate, it had the desired effect. Senior policymakers responded to his call to action: *'Even though we have no proof or even indication of action to employ these rockets against us, so far, it is considered that the indications are sufficient to justify taking certain actions given the powerful moral and surprise effect of such weapons'.*

Lieutenant-General Sir Archibald Edward Nye
(*b.* 23 April 1895, *d.* 13 November 1967)

Four days later, General Hastings Lionel 'Pug' Ismay, 1st Baron Ismay, who was Winston Churchill's chief military advisor, relayed the thoughts of the Chiefs of Staff to the Prime Minister. They were 'of the opinion that no time should be lost in establishing the facts and, if the evidence proves reliable, in devising countermeasures, and recommended Duncan Sandys, Member of Parliament for Norwood, Financial Secretary to the War Office, and Churchill's son-in-law after he married Diana Bailey, Churchill's eldest daughter. Sandys went on

Duncan Edwin Duncan-Sandys, (*b.*24 January 1908, *d.* 6 November 1987),

The famous photograph that revealed the existence of the German A-4 rocket, showing the elliptical earthwork at Peenemunde, Germany where the rockets were tested. Shown are A-4/V-2 (A), crane (B), assembly shop (C).

to head the investigative committee, and Churchill signalled his agreement by scribbling *'So Proceed'* at the bottom of the memo.

Duncan Edwin Duncan-Sandys, Baron Duncan-Sandys CH, PC, was a British politician and minister in successive Conservative governments in the 1950s and 1960s

During the war, Sandys fought with the 51st (London) Heavy Anti-Aircraft Regiment in the Norwegian campaign. He was incapacitated in 1941 by leg injuries he received in an automobile accident in Wales. Confronted with the option of amputation, he instead chose to undergo a series of operations that kept his feet intact but left him in near-constant pain and forced him to walk with a pronounced limp for the rest of his life.

His father-in-law gave him his first ministerial post as Financial Secretary to the War Office from 1941 to 1944 during the wartime coalition government. Sandys had been the wartime Parliamentary Secretary to the Ministry of Supply.

From 1944 to 1945, he served as Minister of Works for the remainder of the coalition and in the Churchill Caretaker Ministry. While a minister, he was chairman of a War Cabinet Committee for defence against German flying bombs and rockets, on which he frequently clashed with the scientist and intelligence expert Professor R. V. Jones.

The British intelligence services - the Secret Intelligence Service (SIS) and Air Ministry's Scientific Intelligence Office (SIO) - were monitoring German rocket artillery research, and information received by bugging high-ranking German prisoners-of-war increased focus on activities at Peenemünde.

Jones and his small team at the Scientific Intelligence Office (SIO) of the Air Ministry had been aware of the A-4/V-2 since the early days of testing at Peenemünde and the Baltic trials.

Since the attack of 17/18 August 1943 on Peenemünde by the RAF, the long-range rocket seemed to have been eclipsed by the flying bomb. The ringside seat at the Baltic trials enjoyed by the SIO had shown that, although there was an occasional attempt to plot the track of a rocket, the 'Establishment' was almost entirely concerned with flying bombs. In recommending the attack on Peenemünde, Jones had offered: *'Intelligence would be prepared to take the risk of the work being re-started elsewhere',* which is precisely what happened. The raid did not drive all the experimental work from Peenemünde. Still, some of it did move eastwards along the Baltic coast to Brüster Ort, and what appeared to be an out-station of Peenemünde was set up at an Schutzstaffel (SS) camp known as 'Heidelager' at Blizna near Debice, 170 miles south of Warsaw. The Air Ministry first got on to its track via some Ultra traffic from Bletchley Park, and it seemed to be primarily concerned with flying bomb trials overland. Since the Scientific Intelligence Office already knew so much about the flying bomb, studies of the activity in Poland could add little to their knowledge. Still, the message's features could not be explained.

General Hastings Lionel 'Pug' Ismay, 1st Baron Ismay (*b.* 21 June 1887, *d.* 17 December 1965)

In March 1944. the Polish Intelligence Service reported that trials were being conducted at Blizna of a missile with a range of ten kilometres, which made a large crater, and that railway tank cars thought to contain liquid air were entering the establishment. Finally, there was one item from the Ultra traffic from Bletchley Park which could not be accounted for either by the flying bomb or a short-range missile because one of the stafi at Blizna was interested in a crater near Sidlice, one hundred and sixty miles away to north-east, which was beyond the range of the flying bomb.

In response to discussions by the vice chiefs of staff on German long-range rocket developments in April 1943, Duncan Sandys was responsible for investigating how far Germany had progressed. Under the codename Bodyline, investigations by SIS, the Combined Services Detailed Interrogation Centre, and the Photographic Reconnaissance Unit were able to confirm the existence of rocketry activities at Peenemünde, and Sandys reported his findings to the Chiefs of Staff that the almost certainly well-advanced and that countermeasures should be studied.

The Bodyline Scientific Committee, which was composed of nineteen members, including Duncan Sandys, Edward Victor Appleton, John Cockcroft, and Robert Watson-Watt, was formed in September 1943 regarding the suspected A-4/V-2 rocket. After the 1944 crash of a test A-4/V-2 in Sweden, *'transmitters to jam the rocket's guidance system' were prepared. A British sound-ranging system provided 'trajectory'* [data] *from which the general launching area could be determined, and the microphone(s) in East Kent reported the times of the first A-4/V-2 strikes on 8 September 1944: 18:40:52 and 18:41:08.'*

In November 1943, the Bodyline committee handed over the tasks to the Air Ministry as the extent of the issue became apparent.

Jones then requested photographic reconnaissance of the Blizna area, and on 5

An A-4/V-2 in the process of being set up ready to fire. It is thought that the location is Peenemünde sometime towards the end of 1943. As the reader looks though this book it will become clear that there was a myriad of different versions of the rocket and 'support bands' around it, it's mounting and launch towers. *(Photo: NARA)*

May 1944, this was done. The photographs went to Medmenham, where a flying bomb ramp was immediately recognised. Still, none of the other installations previously seen at Peenemünde were thought to be associated with the rocket.

Since it was known that the photographic coverage of the area was far from complete, there must have been another compound in which the rocket activity was taking place, so R V Jones requested further cover of the whole area.

SIO subsequently learned from the British Air Attache in Stockholm of an experimental hybrid consisting of a genuine A4 rocket fitted with an extremely elaborate radio guidance system primarily designed for a smaller rocket known as 'Wasserfall', which was being developed for anti-aircraft purposes. General Dornberger, in his book

'V-2' provided something of an explanation. He stated that shortly after the missile was launched, the control officer had tried to change its direction by eye and lost contact with it when it unexpectedly moved sideways into a low cloud. It then flew on an unintended northerly course to Sweden.

It was arranged for two Air Technical Intelligence Officers, Squadron Leaders Border and Wilkinson, to go to Sweden with a request to the Swedish General Staff that they be allowed to inspect the debris. Their first report to the Air Ministry expressed surprise at the amount of electronic control equipment incorporated in the rocket. It gave their opinion that such expensive complexity would only be justified if the warhead weighed at least ten thousand pounds. So here seemed evidence for a warhead as large as British experts feared.

Additional confirmation of a large warhead seemed to come from the aerial photograph of Blizna, which showed a large crater a few kilometres from the SS camp, and Charles Ellis, the Scientific Advisor to the War Ofiice, stated that his explosives experts had estimated that it would have needed about five tons of explosives to make such a crater.

During the first half of 1944, the production series of A-4/V-2s were almost constantly exploding in flight, and the

A chilling image of what could literally be just over the horizon. A trio of A-4/V-2s in the process of being set up ready to fire. It was pictures like this and the threat it represented that made the Operation Backfire team determined to learn all they could about the German weapons system. *(Photo: NARA)*

The British government initially attempted to conceal the cause of the explosions by blaming them on defective gas mains. The public therefore began referring to the A-4/V-2s as 'flying gas pipes'. This was March 1945: Farringdon St Market, London the day after a V-2 rocket landed killing 380 people.

engineers could not determine the reason. Peenemünde engineers sought to recover - and indeed did - thirty per cent of the missiles for detailed examination. It showed that re-entry heating did not weaken the missile's structure. There was no scorching of the 0.6 mm thick paint applied to the interior of the missile. Only the outer paint showed signs of scorching. The rocket still suffered in-flight explosion, attributed to the re-entry heating of 480 degrees Celcius and residual propellant vapours that escaped despite the better sealing. Dornberger thought the liquid oxygen tank was the problem, while von Braun suspected the alcohol tank. In trying to determine the cause, five A-4/V-2s were shot with the engine running until all of the alcohol was depleted. These were followed by six shots with improved glass wool insulation of the liquid oxygen tank, over the objections of Walther Johannes Riedel (*b.* 23 January 1903, *d.* 16 November 1974) the head of manufacturing at Peenemünde. Three of these shots were made one morning, and all went off course. These were, in turn, followed by a series of highly instrumented launches from Peenemünde. The improvements developed from these tests immediately improved the missile reliability from thirty to seventy per cent. Then, the reliability slowly increased to eighty per cent as additional changes were made. Only in the last months of the war was it found that the forward part of the outer hull was failing in flight. Once strengthened with a sheet metal belt, the A-4/V-2 achieved nearly one hundred per cent reliability.

This entire process continued while production was ramping up at the underground facility at Mittelwerk. Pressure from the highest quarters to get the missile

The aftermath of a A-4/V-2 strike in London.

A A-4/V-2 rocket is being prepared for launch. 1944. *[Photo: NARA]*

Ello, ello, ello, wots going on 'ere den? A British policeman examines the remarkably intact remains of an A-4/ V-2 combustion chamber. *[Photo: authors collection]*

out in the field and attacks on England underway meant that every change resulting from these tests and research meant that the production line at Mittelwerk had to be stopped and retrofits made to undelivered missiles.

Polish escapades.
The Poles were providing much evidence: they had set up an organisation for beating the Germans to the scenes of crashed missiles, and they had analysed the liquid recovered from one incident and found it to be highly concentrated hydrogen peroxide.

By 27 June 1944, the Poles had reported that the missile was about forty feet long and six feet in diameter, which matched the dimensions measured in the Peenemünde photographs. They also found pieces of radio equipment, including a transmitter on a wavelength of about 7 metres and a receiver for about 14 metres; these were investigated by Professor Janusz Groszkowski, later the President of the Polish Academy of Science. Shortly afterwards, they reported on the construction of the main jet, and from the dimensions they gave, this was identical to the rocket unit that had fallen in Sweden.

Professor R V Jones had received information from Polish intelligence regarding the A-4/V-2. It may sound absurd now, but because the location of the research facility was known, the Allies asked the Polish Home Army to steal one and ship it to Britain - a task that most certainly would have sounded easier said than done. Patience

Due to the very nature of the task they had to do, A-4/V-2 combustion chambers had to be strong, so it is not really surprising that they were one component that survived the explosion. Here one is examined in the Limehouse area of London. *[Photo: author's collection]*

and luck were on the side of the Poles, though. In early 1944, an A-4 rocket crashed onto a muddy bank of the River Bug near the testing ground at Sarnacki, not far from the village of Mezenin, which was near Klimczyce. And remarkably, it did not blow up. The Polish underground, waiting for such a situation, rushed to the rocket and disguised it with bulrushes and an osier bed, an area or osiery where historically willows were planted and coppiced to produce withies, which were used for basket making, fish traps, and other purposes. The Germans, desperate to retrieve the missile, quickly organised an aerial and ground-based search mission but failed to locate the now-camouflaged rocket.

After the week-long German search ended, the Poles returned to the site. This time, they brought four Polish scientists, who carefully disassembled it and packed the pieces into empty barrels. The parts were shipped to a barn in Holowczyce, just a few miles away.

The Polish Home Army then contacted London to let them know that they had a virtually complete rocket disassembled and hidden away. Eager to get their hands on the pieces, the Allies organised Operation Most III (Polish for Bridge III) or Operation Wildhorn III (as it appeared in British documents), a mission to retrieve the disassembled rocket by aircraft and bring it back to Britain. Parts of the missile were secured by the Armia Krajowa and analysed at its secret laboratories in Warsaw. The analysis was performed by Professor Janusz Groszkowski (radio and guidance), Marceli Struszyński (fuel), Bogdan Stefanowski (engine), Antoni Kocjan, and others.

On the night of 25 July 1944, just past 22:00, an RAF Dakota - their name for the ubiquitous Douglas C-47 - carrying the serial KG477 of 267 Squadron lifted off from Brindisi in southern Italy bound for an abandoned airfield in Poland near the village of Wał-Ruda, codenamed Motyl. On the outgoing flight from Brindisi, the aircraft had four passengers: Kazimierz Bilski, Jan Nowak-Jeziorański, Leszek Starzyński and Bogusław Wolniak. The Dakota, which had been fitted with additional fuel tanks for a flight endurance of up to eighteen hours, was piloted by a New Zealander, Flight Lieutenant Stanley Guy Culliford, and co-piloted by a Polish native, Flight Lieutenant Kazimierz Szrajer, who also acted as translator. Other crew members were Flying Officer J P Williams as Navigator and radio operator Flight Sgt J. Appleby.

Armia Krajowa group Urban, which included Adam Gondek 'Kruk', provided security for the operation. Captain Wladyslaw Kabat 'Brzechwa' was the security commander of the Motyl landing site. Other participants were Kpr. Franciszek Nowak 'Pomidor', Dr Jan Deszcz 'Wacek', Kpr. Pchor. Władysław Bysiek 'Morena', Józef Lupa 'Czarny Sęp', Ppor. Franciszek Kuczek 'Deska', Ppor. Mieczysław Czech 'Jurand', Ppor. Paweł Chwała 'Skory', Ppor. Jan Gomoła 'Jawor'.

The plan was to land the aircraft in territory surrounded by German military units retreating westward under pressure by the Soviet Army and obtain the A-4/V-2 missile components. At just past midnight, the Dakota circled above the landing location and the partisans - who had been previously informed through encrypted codes over BBC radio - recognised the sound of the transport aircraft. Upon the aircraft's landing, the partisans emerged from the woods nearby, pulling carts with key A-4/V-2 components. Once the cargo was loaded, the pilots attempted to take off, but the wheels of the heavily overloaded Dakota were lodged in the muddy ground. Everything had to be offloaded. The Polish partisans desperately tried to free the aircraft. The mud was shovelled away, and another attempt was made to take off, but the wheels sank even deeper into the mud. Attempts to lodge sticks under the wheels were unsuccessful. Some partisans began digging around the wheels with their bare hands, while others found wooden slats in the nearby woods that were subsequently wedged underneath the wheels. Co-pilot Kazimierz 'Paddy' Szrajer then decided that the parking brake must be stuck, so the hydraulic pipes supplying the brakes were cut. But that didn't work, either; the aircraft still failed to move.

After two failed attempts to take off, and with Nazi automobile lights off in the distance, Culliford considered blowing up the plane and burning all the evidence. The crew decided to make one last attempt.

Finally, the Dakota was able to take off and stagger into the air with the A-4/V-2 components on board. The remaining Poles scattered into the night to avoid any run-ins with Nazi patrols. On the return flight, Jerzy Chmielewski, Józef Retinger, Tomasz Arciszewski, Tadeusz Chciuk, and Czesław Miciński were ferried from occupied Poland to Brindisi, Italy. It was intended that Antoni Kocjan (who had personally studied parts of A-4/V-2 missiles) would take part, but the Gestapo arrested him and, therefore, was replaced by Jerzy Chmielewski.

The flight over Hungary and Yugoslavia took five hours. When landing at Brindisi, the pilots had to land on an emergency runway without brakes.

In his book *'Most Secret War'* Professor R V Jones reveals an interesting aftermath to the adventure: *'The rocket parts with the courageous Pole arrived at Hendon on 28 July, but he could speak no English, and he refused to let anyone see the parts until he had authority from one of the only two Polish officers in Britain whom he knew. One was General Bot and the other was a Polish colonel. He sat on his sack and drew a knife whenever one of our Intelligence officers made any move towards it. This scene continued for hours, reaching peaks of embarrassment whenever he wished to fulfil one of his natural functions while we searched for the General and the Colonel.*

One of them, I think that it was the Colonel, was either ill or out of London, and finally, we had to get the General to come along and tell our gallant Pole that it was alright for him to talk to us and show us his treasures.'

The rocket components were later flown to England, where the crew was presented with gallantry medals by the Polish Government in Exile, and with Szrajer received the Cross of Valour and the squadron was praised for the 'courage, determination and coolness with which they carried out what must be one of the outstanding and epic flights of the war by an unarmed transport aircraft.'

British scientists began devising a way to interfere with the guidance of the A-4/V-2 missile using radio waves. However, it was discovered that the A-4/V-2 mechanism was designed not to 'react to countermeasures by radio.'

Defensive measures

On 21 March 1945, the 'Engagement of Long Range Rockets with AA Gunfire' plan, which called for anti-aircraft units to fire into radar-predicted airspace to intercept the A-4/V-2, was ready. Still, the plan was not used due to the danger of shells falling on Greater London.

Unlike the V-1, which had a speed similar to the fastest available fighter aircraft, the velocity and trajectory of an A-4/V-2 made aircraft interception an impossibility.

Under Sandys' leadership, the so-called Crossbow Committee worked to gather intelligence on the rocket threat and find ways to counter it. Their work became increasingly vital as the tide of war turned in favour of the Allies, and fears grew of a new German secret weapon which could theoretically undo their hard-earned

Trophy of war! A A-4/V-2 is displayed on an RAF 'Queen Mary' trailer in central London, 1945. *[Photo: NARA]*

progress. In December 1943, the Chiefs of Staff worried that if rockets were used against 'port facilities in southern England before the summer of 1944, it could seriously jeopardise Operation Overlord, the planned Allied invasion of Europe.'

The US formed its own Crossbow Committee on 29 December 1943 under General Stephen Henry (New Developments Division), and the US subsequently developed bombing techniques for ski sites in February and March 1944 at the Air Corps Proving Ground.

A mid-1944 plan for US Marine Corps aircraft to attack V-1 launch sites from aircraft carriers fell victim to inter-service rivalry – opposed by the Army. A-4/V-2 facilities were also bombed in 1944, including smaller facilities such as A-4/V-2 storage depots and liquid oxygen plants, such as the Mery-sur-Oise A-4/V-2 storage depot on 4 August 1944, and by the Eighth Air Force, which bombed five cryogenic liquid oxygen plants in Belgium on 25 August 1944 but aborted the next day's attack on plants at La Louviere, Torte and Willebroeck, Belgium due to cloud.

Indeed, after the war, Dwight Eisenhower, the commander of Overlord, wrote that '*if the German had succeeded in perfecting and using these new weapons six months earlier than he did, our invasion of Europe would have proved exceedingly difficult, perhaps impossible!*'

The issue was perhaps best expressed by the military head of the German A-4/V-2 project, Lieutenant General Walter Dornberger, in his post-war memoir: *'Only one thing can be said with absolute certainty: the use of the A-4/V-2 may be aptly summed up in the two words: 'too late'.*

Of course, this appraisal is only possible in hindsight, and the fact that the A-4/V-2s would go on to have only a limited impact on the course of the war was a cold comfort to the citizens of London (and Paris and Antwerp) when the rocket bombardment began in September 1944. Over the next seven months, some 1,115 A-4/V-2 rockets fell on Britain, resulting in 2,855 fatalities. In addition, 20,000 houses were destroyed, and 580,000 were damaged.

When compared with the impact of conventional bombing during the Blitz, which claimed the lives of over 51,000 Britons, and with the preceding and simultaneous V-1 attacks, which killed 6,184 people, these statistics seem somewhat less impressive. In terms of morale, the effect is more challenging to judge - some responded to this new threat with little more than disinterest, confident that the advancing Allied armies would soon eradicate it. In contrast, others found the prospect of an explosive arriving without warning terrifying, for the A-4/V-2 travelled faster than the speed of sound. The Allied leadership were not unduly worried that this new weapon would turn the tide of war against them but, taken with the failure of Operation Market Garden and other German technological advances, such as jet aircraft and the submarine Schnorkel system, the start of the A-4/V-2 campaign did shake the confidence the British had that the end of the war in sight in the autumn of 1944. Moreover, the British preoccupation with rocketry during this period was not only about looking for a way to neutralise this technology but also seeking to obtain it for their use.

Conversely, it has been argued that the A-4/V-2 was a poor use of resources for the Third

Sir Alwyn Douglas Crow CBE FInstP
(*b.* 10 May 1894, *d.*5 February 1965)

Sir Henry Thomas Tizard GCB AFC FRS
(*b.* 23 August 1885, *d.* 9 October 1959)

Reich, as it was extremely costly to produce while its impact was relatively small. The money diverted to the long-range rocket programme would have been far better spent on anti-aircraft defences and fighter production, though there was a severe shortage of fuel and aircraft in the latter case. That said, Hitler and the Nazi leadership felt they needed to offer a visible response to the enormous and almost ceaseless Allied aerial bombardment of Germany - hence the designation of Vergeltungswaffe Drei, translated as Vengeance Weapon 2, and to give the German people hope that these new technological marvels could turn the fortunes of the war.

The generally unimpressive record of the A-4/V-2 during the war presents an interesting paradox - if long-range rockets were such an ineffective weapon, why did all the victorious Allies rush to gather German technology and expertise in this field once the war had ended? The answer can be summarised in a single word: potential. As the British Director of Guided Projectiles, Sir Alwyn Douglas Crow CBE FInstP put it: '*As might be expected, the first two weapons - the V-1 and A-4/V-2 - are crude...*', but, he went on, '*further development may be expected considerably to improve the accuracy, to simplify the use and to increase the applications!*' In short, the A-4/V-2 was the primitive prototype for a new era in which much more advanced missiles, equipped with more sophisticated

One of the entrances to the Mittlewerk tunnels, after the Germans had abandoned them. *[Photo: NARA]*

An A-4/V-2 rocket in the the factory at Kleinbodungen, Germany, 1945. *[Photo: NARA]*

guidance systems and armed with more powerful (perhaps nuclear) payloads, would decisively shape the future of warfare.

British military planners certainly internalised this notion. On 16 June 1945, with the war in the Pacific still ongoing, a committee headed by the esteemed chemist and senior British military science advisor, Sir Henry Thomas Tizard GCB AFC FRS, was an English chemist, inventor and Rector of Imperial College, who developed the modern 'octane rating' used to classify petrol, helped develop radar in World War Two.

Acting under the instruction of the British Chiefs of Staff, Tizard produced a report entitled *'Future Development in Weapons and Methods of War'*. He noted, '*In its most revolutionary form, that of long-range rocket bombardment, the rocket has appeared too late to have a decisive effect. In all its forms, we believe its use will be great significance in a future war.'* It even went on to speculate *that 'it may contribute to render the strategic bomber obsolete'.*

After the United States entered the war in December 1941, the British and Americans had worked increasingly closely on almost all aspects of the war effort, their shared identity and purpose even seeming to erode traditional state sovereignty on occasion. The scientific and technological collaboration had long been a cornerstone of this alliance, as shown by the Tizard Mission, headed by Sir Henry Tizard, which saw an unprecedented sharing of military and scientific secrets between the two countries in 1940, even before they became formal allies. One device that Tizard took with him as a gift for the Americans was a cavity magnetron, which was vital for airborne radar. One American expert later described it as 'the most valuable cargo ever brought to our shores'. An even more straightforward example would be the Manhattan Project - the Allied atomic bomb project, which was based in and resourced by the United States but utilised British expertise and was acknowledged in the early days as a combined effort.

Even as early as November 1944, Duncan Sandys, predicted that *'in future, the possession of superiority in long-distance rocket artillery may well count for nearly as much as superiority in naval or air power!'* This thinking motivated the British and the other Allies to try and learn as much as they could about German rocketry. The expertise of their former enemy was seen as a vital shortcut to achieving their post-war technological superiority.

This attitude did not merely apply to rocketry. In the last year of the war, and even more so once it had ended, all the Allies embarked on major schemes to exploit the science and technology of the Third Reich. However, rocketry occupied a significant place in Allied exploitation from the beginning of this initiative. Any material or personnel in this critical field were considered among the most valuable spoils of war. British exploitation of German science and technology began on an Anglo-American basis under the auspices of the Combined Intelligence Objectives Sub-Committee (CIOS). When this organisation first drew up its 'Black List' of high-priority topics in August 1944, 'rockets' were the fourth item. Ten days later, the first team of CIOS investigators travelled to Europe, arriving in Paris just three days after it had been liberated.

CIOS was a committee formed under the auspices of the combined chiefs of staff, which were directly under G-2, Supreme Headquarters, Allied Force headquarters, to coordinate the exploitation of all scientific intelligence targets in Germany, which generally would not be covered by regular technical intelligence teams. Before 1 April, very few official, CIOS missions had been undertaken, but it was apparent that soon

Below: A US Military Policeman inspects a A-4/V-2 rocket on a transport trolley in one of the Mittlewerk tunnels, after the Germans had abandoned them.

Opposite page: Slave labour works on splinter camoflage patterened tail sections of the A-4/V-2 in the Mittelwerk tunnels near Nordhausen. *[Photos: NARA]*

A German crew use a Strabo crane to manipulate an A-4/V-2 rocket onto a road trailer. *[Photo: NARA]*

considerable numbers of establishments of intelligence interest would be available for examination. Initially, two officers were sent to Cologne. This was the first regular CIOS mission in Germany.

The committee was set up with several sub-departments: Radio Countermeasures Branch, Technical Intelligence Branch, Operations Section, Evaluation Section...

The first report that CIOS sent back to the London headquarters was titled *'Radar and Guided Missiles'* and detailed work which had been done on these subjects by French experts and in French facilities during the German occupation. Then, in November, CIOS operatives travelled to the Netherlands to gather intelligence on the A-4/V-2 launching procedure, a task which was motivated as much by the need to prevent the rockets from raining down on London as it was by the desire to learn more about this new technology. In the course of these investigations, CIOS agents were told by a Dutch Resistance fighter that one German soldier died of severe burns for each A-4/V-2 that was launched and that some of the warheads used contained anthrax. These strange and ultimately false claims give some sense of the rumour and conjecture with which exploitation investigators had to contend when researching rocketry." The British demand for knowledge on missiles continued into early 1945: in February, Colonel Terence Sanders of the Ministry of Supply led a four-man mission to northern France to investigate the seven so-called 'heavy' A-4/V-2 launch sites.

In September 1944, Lieutenant Colonel Stuart McClintock, one of the United States Army Air Force oficers attached to Air Intelligence, asked Professor R V Jones if he would write an article for the Eighth Air Force magazine *Stars and Stripes* on the future of the long-range rockets because he thought that the United States Air Force ought to be alerted to their possibilities. This piece needs several things taken into consideration, given the passage of time. It shows the depth of knowledge then, even though much of it was informed conjecture. It also shows the thinking of the day, although, remember, this was just what was cleared for publication; it is not all that was known or considered. It was a large article, but as Professor Jones put in his conclusions:

'There can be no doubt that with the A4 the rocket has come to stay for a long time, if only for its non-military applications; in no other way can we get free of the Earth's atmosphere, with all that this freedom may mean to astrophysical studies. The attainment of the upper atmosphere will in itself be a major factor in experimental meteorology, and sooner or later someone will seriously try to reach the moon - and succeed. Military applications are bound to be made, whatever the limits imposed by treaties, and we should do well to keep an eye on the possibilities. If we were to allow ourselves more liberty of conjecture, we might consider using atomic fuels to drive an exhaust of hydrogen molecules, or perhaps lighter particles, giving an entirely different order of performance.

It is an often-stated requirement that a weapon of war should have a probable error comparable with its radius of destruction, so that a few shots would ensure the obliteration of the target. Practical weapons seldom approach this ideal, although 'in the future it may be attainable through homing devices. With a very long-range rocket we may have to accept errors, and it may be easier to increase the radius of destruction by the use of new types of explosives based on the fission of the uranium atomic nucleus. If such an explosive becomes practicable, it will probably have a radius of destruction of the order of miles, and on this account alone it might best be carried in some unmanned projectile, of which the rocket would be a particularly suitable type by virtue of its relative immunity from interception and of its potentially better accuracy at long ranges compared with pilotless aircraft. Speculation of this kind is fascinating but can well wait for a paper at a later time when it is nearer realization.

Reviewing therefore what we have seen to be reasonable extrapolation from present practice, a two-stage rocket of about 150 tons starting weight could deliver a one-ton warhead to nearly 3,000 miles range, with a probable error of 10 miles in range and 3 miles in line. This might be a feasible weapon for delivering a uranium bomb, should such a bomb become practicable. It would be almost hopeless to counter attacks

The two major leaders in the development of the V-2 rocket share a personal moment. General Walter Dornberger (left) oversaw the military logistics and financing of the rocket programme. SS Major Dr. Wernher von Braun (right) led its technological development.

on the ground organization because the increased range would allow an almost unlimited choice of firing site, while the trajectory could be so varied that the firing point could not be deduced without sufficient accuracy for countermeasures. Production would probably take place underground. At the moment, such a rocket could not be intercepted, but by the time it becomes a serious possibility, it may itself be a target for smaller defence rockets fitted with predictors and homing devices: but these would depend upon adequate warning, and a salvo of long-range rockets might also saturate the defences.

The protagonists for the development of very long-range rockets would probably have, in Britain at any rate, to meet the criticism that it would not be worth the effort expended. The A4 has already shown us that our enemies are not restrained by such considerations and have thereby made themselves leaders in a technique which sooner or later will be regarded as one of the masterpieces of human endeavour when it comes to be applied to the exploration of Space.

As it is mainly with our enemies that Intelligence is concerned, rather than with our own views on military economics, it suffices that the long range rocket can be developed much further. In the light of this fact, we must watch.

Once the borders of the Third Reich were breached in the early part of 1945, the real spoils of war became available to Allied exploitation teams, who continued to operate under the Anglo-American auspices of CIOS in London and the Supreme Headquarters Allied Expeditionary Force (SHAEF) in the field.

The basic authority for taking custody of property in Germany was contained in Joint Chiefs of Staff (JCS) Directive 1067/6, which directed the US Zone Commander to 'impound or block' certain specified categories of property, including those of the German Reich; the Nazi Party and affiliated organisations and their prominent members; and absentee owners of non-German nationality, including United Nations and neutral governments and individuals. It turned out to be a broad directive that the Americans could use - and bent to suit whatever purpose - to take pretty much whatever they wanted. The American Zone Commander was also required to impound all property that was transferred under duress or through wrongful acts of confiscation, disposition, or spoliation and to block the relocation of works of art and cultural

A-4/V-2 tail sections being moved by train to the port at Antwerp on their way to their final destination at White Sands Proving Ground, New Mexico. *[Photo: NARA].*

An A-4/V-2 rocket, minus warhead, sits on a US low-loader for shipment back to the USA. *[Photo: NARA]*

material of value or importance, regardless of its ownership. When the US Army entered Germany in September 1944, provisions were made for the seizure of all categories of property, including that of the Nazi Party organisation.

At the cessation of hostilities in May 1945, several temporary collecting points were set up by the 12th Army Group to store all cultural objects found in the US zone in need of preservation or suspected of having been looted by the Germans. The seized property was turned over to the custody of the Office of Military Government, US Zone (Germany) [OMGUS], when it became the successor to the US Group Control Council, Germany (USGCC) on 1 October 1945. OMGUS was responsible for administering the US zone of occupation and US sector of Berlin, and for functioning as the US element of organisations comprising the Allied Control Authority, the name given to the four-power occupation control system.

The race to discover and capture the secrets of the German missile began even before the hostilities in Europe ended. On 10 April 1945, the spearhead of the advancing American troops, Combat Command B (CCB) of the US Third Armored Division, entered Nordhausen. Here CCB was to pause and link up with the US 104th Infantry 'Timberwolf' Division before continuing its drive to the east. Several miles further, as they approached the foothills of the Harz Mountains, American troops discovered Dora and the entrances to the Mittelwerk tunnels.

The KZ (Konzentrationslager, i.e., Concentration Camp) Dora-Mittelbau was built in central Germany near Nordhausen, by which name the entire camp complex is now commonly, but erroneously, known. The blandly named Mittelbau (translated as 'central construction') camp was initially established as a sub-camp of KZ Buchenwald when the SS sent a detail of one hundred and twenty slave labourers to expand a large underground Wehrmacht fuel depot to produce A-4/V-2 ballistic missiles after the existing production sites became the target of Allied bombers.

When the main A-4/V-2 effort shifted from Peenemünde to Mittelbau, the site became an independent concentration camp in late October 1944, eventually encompassing more than forty subcamps of its own, spread out over the immediate area. The first inmates who built the facilities were initially kept underground in the dark, unventilated tunnels, referred to as 'Dora' in official documents of 'Mittelbau GmbH', the business unit set up by Armaments Minister Albert Speer's vast empire, which oversaw the production site. The main factory area inside the tunnels was often referred to as Mittelwerk ('middle works.'). The SS ran all

A pair of jubilant former prisoners of Nordhausen poses in front of an assembly destined for the A-4/V-2 missile. *[Photo: NARA]*

the camps, provided the slave labour at very reasonable negotiated rates, and had a supply that was constantly 'replenished'.

When walking into the first long tunnel, the Americans were stunned to see railway freight cars loaded with A-4/V-2s and thousands of finished and unfinished parts and assemblies.

The US military had already begun to develop and implement plans for utilising not only captured German technology but the brains behind it as well. As the American troops advanced, the Army and the Navy dispatched several teams of American experts and officers to quietly locate and acquire information, hardware, and people.

When word came of the incredible find, US Colonel Holgar Toftoy, Chief of Army Ordinance Technical Intelligence, immediately began arranging for 'Special Mission A-4/V-2' from his office in Paris on what appears to have been his own initiative. Its purpose would be to evacuate one hundred complete A-4/V-2s and specialised parts back to Las Cruces, New Mexico. The A-4/V-2s were to be fired from the newly created White Sands Proving Ground in New Mexico and were to be part of the US Army Ordnance Department's Project Hermes, which began in 1944 and was not completed until 1952. Under this project, the army contracted with General Electric to develop surface-to-surface missiles. Fort Bliss, Texas was contiguous to White Sands and was the sub-office headquarters for Army rocket research under the Ordnance Department.

Major General Holger Nelson Toftoy (*b.* 31 October 1902, *d* 19 April 1967). *[Photo: NARA]*

The declared aim was to obtain experience in the handling and firing of large missiles. The A-4/V-2 missiles offered opportunities not only for the training of military personnel but also for obtaining experience which would be of value in the design of ground equipments for future missiles.

The intention was to provide vehicles for experiments directly concerned with the design of future missiles: to provide vehicles for

A pair of erections in Trafalgar Square, London.

An A-4/V-2 missile is displayed alonside Nelson's Column. *[Photo: NARA]*

Liquid oxygen transfer at Peenemünde to fuel a A-4/V-2. *[Photo: NARA]*

operational tests of components for future missiles and to obtain ballistics data.

The A-4/V-2 missiles offered opportunities not only for obtaining ballistics data for high altitude trajectories but also for developing and proving various means for tracking and measuring these trajectories. Finally, the plan was to provide vehicles for upper atmosphere research projects:

At the time this programme was initiated the A-4/V-2 was the only rocket in existence capable of carrying heavy payloads to a high altitude. This high-load capacity offered agencies the advantage of being able to conduct many related high-altitude experiments simultaneously. Since the V-2 provided many cubic feet of space for experimental apparatus, it was not necessary for the experimental agencies to expend the time and effort necessary to reduce the size of their apparatus to meet the dimensions of smaller missiles.

To support his mission, Toftoy organised special rapid-response Ordinance Technical Intelligence teams for each Army group. These teams organised the available specialists in the field to quickly address the task given to them.

These teams were equipped with cameras, radios, transport trucks, and qualified personnel whose job it was to ferret out interesting weapons technology and record it. The team designated to investigate the Mittelwerk was headed by Major James P Hamill of Ordinance Technical Intelligence. He was assisted by Major William Bromley in charge of technical operations and by Dr. Louis Woodruff, an of the Massachusetts Institute of Technology, who was an electrical engineering professor, as special advisor. The team was headquartered in Fulda, about eighty miles southwest of Nordhausen.

After rounding up captured German rolling stock and clearing a path into the tunnels, the Special Mission succeeded in loading up and sending off its first forty-waggon trainload of A-4/V-2 parts and machine equipment on 22 May 1945. Nine days later, the last of the three hundred and forty-one railway wagons left the Mittelwerk bound for Antwerp. Although the British properly protested that by prior agreement, half the captured A-4/V-2s were to be turned over to them, the Americans blithely ignored these protests. A number of Liberty ships, bearing the components for one hundred A-4/V-2 rockets, finally sailed from Antwerp, destined for New Orleans and then eventually White Sands in New Mexico. Hamill was not told that the factory would be in the Soviet zone of occupation. Consequently, quite a number of missile parts were left for the Soviets to discover.

Meanwhile, as the war in Europe drew to a close in early 1945, the rocket team at Peenemünde began to plan for their future. They knew the Russians were getting close. Having received conflicting orders from the leadership in Berlin to stay put and evacuate southward into the German interior, they decided to leave. During February, thousands of the Peenemünde employees and their families moved south to Bleicherode. The team received orders to hide their technical data, select the four hundred and fifty most crucial people for the programme, and move to Bavaria. This core group lived in Bavaria for the remainder of the war. The German war effort nearly collapsed in late April, and the Allies advanced rapidly across German territory. The rocket team decided to cast their lot with the Americans rather than the Russians, thinking this might give them a better chance to continue their rocket research.

Major Robert Staver from the Rocket Section of the Research and Development branch of the Ordinance Office was tasked in directing the effort to find and interrogate the German rocket specialists who had built the A-4/V-2. Since 30 April he had been in the Nordhausen area searching the smaller laboratories for A-4/V-2 technicians. On 12 May, Staver located his first A-4/V-2 engineer, Karl Otto Fleisher, who began to put him in touch with other Mittelwerk engineers who had not been

Two views, one formal, one not so of German rocket scientist Wernher von Braun - in a civilian suit - seen with other German officers at Peenemünde. *[Photos: NARA]*

A test launch of an A-4 rocket at Peenemünde. *[Photo: NARA]*

part of SS Major Wernher von Braun's caravan to Bavaria. On 14 May, Staver found Walther 'Papa' Riedel, (*b.* 5 December 1902, *d.* 15 May 1968) head of the Peenemünde rocket motor and structural design section, who urged the Americans to import perhaps forty of the top A-4/V-2 engineers to America. After their surrender to US forces in Bavaria, Wernher von Braun's A-4/V-2 specialists were moved to a prisoner enclosure in Garmisch-Partenkirchen, where a variety of Allied interrogators questioned them. At this point the Americans had the missiles, they had the top scientists, but they were still missing the all-important Peenemünde documentation. Peenemünde engineer Dieter Huzel had hidden fourteen tons of Peenemünde documents in an abandoned iron mine in the isolated village of Dörnten in early April.

Ten days after the hoard of A-4/V-2 items was discovered - on 22 April - Colonel Holger Toftoy of the US Ordnance Department gleefully reported that Allied troops had captured *'two trainloads of substantially complete A-4/V-2 German long-range rockets'*, as well as *'a third trainload of warheads and fuses'*. With palpable excitement, Toftoy noted that *'the capture of these rockets is of considerable interest and importance since this is the first time that undamaged specimens have been recovered and an opportunity afforded for their examination'*, and stated his belief that *'this capture will result in a considerably improved knowledge of the rockets'*.

Less than two weeks later, SHAEF issued a directive to all Army Groups and Air Forces operating in the European theatre. It stated: *'Immediate steps will be taken to ensure that all captured A-4/V-2s, associated launching and control equipment are carefully preserved for examinations and possible future use, and are not tampered with in any way.'*

The Americans interviewed thousands of German scientists and engineers during the immediate aftermath of the war. As the rocket team was undergoing several weeks of interrogation, the Americans were developing plans for offering the German scientists short-term contracts for employment in the United States. The code name for the project to bring the rocket specialists to America was 'Operation Overcast'. This name and project were later incorporated into 'Operation Paperclip', a much broader programme that brought 642 German and Austrian technical specialists in many fields to America between May 1945 and December 1952. The code name resulted from the technique used by some agencies involved to identify specialists accepted for participation – their folders were marked with a paperclip. The United States rocket programme could begin where Germany had ended through this concurrent acquisition of hardware, documentation, and personnel. It saved the US military and defence industries time and money, both of which would shortly become essential elements of the ensuing arms race with the Soviet Union.

Wernher Magnus Maximilian Freiherr von Braun (b. 23 March 1912, d. 16 June 1977) was a German aerospace engineer and space architect. He was a member of the Nazi Party and Allgemeine SS, the leading figure in the development of rocket technology in Nazi Germany. He began as an Untersturmführer (Second lieutenant) and was promoted three times by Hienrich Himmler, the last time in June 1943 to SS-Sturmbannführer (Major).

News of von Braun's capture was released to the Press by HQ US 7th Army on 6 May 1945 as shown in the surviving poor quality carbon copy: *'A smiling, pink-cheeked, young German scientist sat down in a 44th Infantry Division command post and said that if he had been given two more years the A-4/V-2 rocket bomb he invented could have won the war for Germany.'*

Professor Wernher von Braun, 33, said that he formed the basic idea for his deadly weapon in his student days in Berlin. When he received his degree in aeronautics in 1933, the Nazis, already planning world conquest, set him up in a laboratory and, in the years that followed, spent $250,000,000 on his invention.

Von Braun surrendered on 2 May, along with his brother Magnus von Braun, Major General Walther Dornberger of the German General Staff, who supervised the work at Pennemunde, where the bomb was completed, Lt. Col. Herbert Axster also of the General Staff and Bernhard Tossman, Hans Lindenberg and Dieter Huzel, German scientists who helped him at Pennemunde.

The surrender of the group was arranged by the brother Magnus, who drove into the 44th Division's lines and was halted by Anti-Tank Company, 324th Infantry. Magnus asked for an interpreter and Pfc. Fred Schnoikort, 2535 South Street Shoboygan, Wisc. obliged.

'I'm the brother of the inventor of the V-2...', Magnus said *'My brother and the*

Wernher von Braun and his group of scientsts with American troops after their surrender in Bavaria.

scientists who work under him are in the next town and would like to surrender'. Schnoikort listened, then yelled to his non-com, Cpl. Frank Miller, 237 West 7th Street, Mt. Carmel, Pa.' Hey Frank, I got a nut here. What should I do with him?

Magnus was sent back and late in the evening returned with Wernher and the rest of the party. The entire group spoke freely of their work at Peenemünde and of their hopes of meeting American scientists who have been doing experimental work with rockets.

Wernher von Braun with his arm in a cast following a car accident, along with his brother Magnus after their surrender in Bavaria.

Von Braun said that if Germany had been able to produce two hundred A-4/V-2s a day it was quite conceivable that the course of the war would have been changed. He said that given two more years in which to improve the gyroscope which guided the rocket, he could have made it into a weapon of pin-point accuracy.

Von Braun said three special battalions of German soldiers were trained at Peenemünde in the launching of the V-2 but that he and his group continued their research and that he had nothing to do with selecting targets for the weapon.

Je said that the great Allied bombing raid on Peenemünde on 17 August, 1943 did far less damage than the Allies believed he said. When news reports which said that the laboratories were destroyed were mentioned, the entire group denied that their work had been interupted in any great way. It was Germany's lack of industrial power, Dornberger said, which prevented the maximum use of the V-2.

The first successful V-2 rocket was fired 3 October, 1942 into the Baltic Sea. Immediately afterwards, Hitler and Goebbels began to make extravagant claims about the 'Secret Weapon' and the first V-2 was fired against England on 6 September 1944.

Major von Braun had ordered the documents hidden to prevent their destruction by SS General Kammler, and to also use them as a bargaining chip in negotiating the group's fate with the Allies. As it happened, Karl Otto Fleisher was the only person remaining in the Nordhausen area who was aware of the general location of the A-4/V-2 documents hidden by von Braun's group. Staver tricked him into revealing the location of the papers on 20 May. In less than a week, the Dörnten area was scheduled to fall into the hands of the British. A frantic scramble then ensued to transport the documents back to Nordhausen, where they were quickly shipped to Paris, and then to the Aberdeen Proving Ground in Maryland.

At the beginning of June, Staver requested that some of von Braun's senior engineers be sent to the area of Nordhausen to help identify which of the thousands of German technicians should be offered evacuation to the American zone before the scheduled handover of Nordhausen to the Soviets on 21 June, 1945. On 20 June, around one thousand German A-4/V-2 personnel and their families were selected and gathered up, then placed aboard a long

Opposite page: The Headquarters Seventh Army Public Relations Office press release announcing the capture - or as it says 'surrender' - of the Werner von Braun group on 2 May 1945.

HEADQUARTERS SEVENTH ARMY
Public Relations Office
APO 758 US Army

SPECIAL RELEASE NO. 542

6 MAY 1945

For Immediate Release:

EXCLUSIVE TO PRESS CAMP

WITH THE 44TH INFANTRY DIVISION OF THE AMERICAN SEVENTH ARMY IN GERMANY -- A smiling, pink-cheeked, young German scientist sat down in a 44th Infantry Division command post and said that if he had been given two more years the V-2 rocket bomb he invented could have won the war for Germany.

Professor Wernher von Braun, 33, said that he formed the basic idea for his deadly weapon in his student days in Berlin. When he received his degree in aeronautics in 1933, the Nazis, already planning world conquest, set him up in a laboratory and in the years that followed spent $250,000,000 on his invention.

Von Braun surrendered May 2, along with his brother, Magnus von Braun, Major General Walther Dornberger, of the German General Staff, who supervised the work at Peenemunde, where the bomb was completed, Lt. Col. Herbert Axster, also of the General Staff and Bernhard Tessman, Hans Lindenberg and Dieter Huzel, German scientists who helped with the work at Peenemunde.

The surrender of the group was arranged by the brother, Magnus, who drove into the 44th Division's lines and was halted by Anti-Tank Company, 324th Infantry. Magnus asked for an interpreter and Pfc. Fred Schneikert, 2535 South 7th Street, Sheboygan, Wisc., obliged.

"I'm the brother of the inventor of V-2", Magnus said. "My brother and the scientists who work under him are in the next town and would like to surrender". Schneikert listened, then yelled to his non-com., Cpl. Frank Miller, 237 West 7th Street, Mt. Carmel, Pa., "Hey, Frank, I've got a nut here. What should I do with him?"

Magnus was sent back and late in the evening returned with Wernher and the rest of the party. The entire group spoke freely of their work at Peenemunde and of their hopes of meeting American scientists who have been doing experimental work with rockets.

Von Braun said that if Germany had been able to produce 200 V-2's a day, it was quite conceivable that the course of the war would have been changed. He said that given two more years in which to improve the gyroscope which guides the rocket, he could have made it a weapon of pin-point accuracy.

He said three special battalions of German soldiers were trained at Peenemunde in the launching of V-2 but that he and his group continued their research and had nothing to do with selecting targets for the weapon.

The great Allied bombing raid on Peenemunde on August 17, 1943, did far less damage than the Allies believed, he said. When news reports which said that the laboratories were destroyed were mentioned, the entire group denied that their work had been interrupted. It was Germany's lack of industrial power, Dornberger said, which prevented the maximum use of V-2.

The first successful V-2 rocket was fired October 3, 1942, into the Baltic Sea. Immediately afterwards Hitler and Goebbels began to make extravagant claims about the "secret weapon" and the first V-2 was fired against England Sept. 6, 1944.

Von Braun looked like a typical German farmer or soldier -- the very opposite of the imagined German scientist. He said that if he had lived in

(more)

Major James P Hamill with Wernher von Braun in 1946. *[Photo: NARA]*

train, which eventually made its way to the small town of Witzenhausen, some forty miles to the southwest and just inside the American zone.

Von Braun and his team were heavily interrogated and jealously protected from Russian agents. Dornberger later told British interrogators, '*The Russians sent one of my former engineers to me when I was with the Americans, who told me he had an offer to make on behalf of the Russians. We were to go back to Peenemünde and it would be rebuilt, along with a parallel factory in Russia, and they offered to pay us double what the Americans were offering us. We also could move our families with us, etc. We turned it down flat. Afterward, in the town Witzenhausen, they tried to kidnap our leading men such as Dr. Wernher von Braun. They appeared at night as British soldiers in uniforms; I guess they didn't realise it was the American zone. Somehow they had obtained a proper pass, but the Americans quickly realised what was happening and sent them away. That's how those Russians operated, real kidnapping, they had no scruples at all.*

Captured V-2 launching crews and technical personnel will be kept together and not disposed of until clearance is obtained [from this Headquarters].'

It is clear, therefore, that investigations into German long-range rocketry were a top priority for the British and Americans, even while the war was still being fought. The next step was to decide how best to conduct those investigations moving forward under the more favourable peacetime conditions.

Chapter Two

The Origins of Backfire

The origins of Operation Backfire lay in a memorandum prepared by General Dwight D Eisenhower, as the head of SHAEF, and transmitted to the Combined Chiefs of Staff (of Britain and the US) on 15 May 1945, one week after the German surrender. Finally, the Allies could study everything about the A-4/V-2, piecing together everything instead of just seeing the fragments they knew, or suspected already.

It did not take the Allies - and especially the British - long to realise that what Operation Backfire had to study was a complete, integrated weapons system, not an individual, stand-alone weapon. The A-4/V-2 could only 'work' when every aspect was in place and operating in the correct sequence.

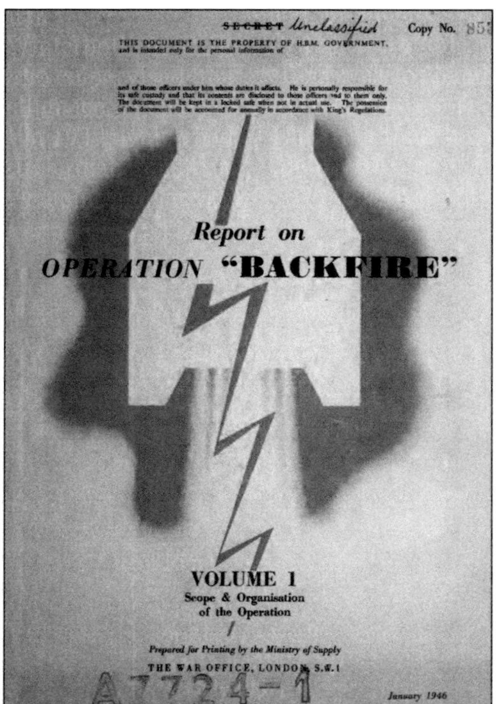

It meant that Backfire would have to be multi-faceted - the first two phases, running parallel to each other, was the acquisition of knowledge at the same time as gathering together as much hardware as possible. From those things, the Allies could then build rockets and finally fire them.

The memo from Eisenhower suggested the value to the Allies of firing trials of captured A-4/V-2s and justified it in the following terms:

a) Such a trial will save years of development work by the Allies and enable them to 'cash in' on the years of work which the Germans have devoted to this development.

b) The firing of captured A-4/V-2s now would ensure that no vital piece of equipment or operation would be kept from our knowledge.

c) The launching and control of rockets is obviously a complicated and intricate process and unless the Allies get enemy technicians to demonstrate their technique now their skill will deteriorate and before long will be lost to them. Delays which would be caused by moving personnel and equipment out of theatre therefore not acceptable'.

It went on to stipulate that any such trials would be held under SHAEF auspices as they were of equal interest to both the British and the Americans, that approximately thirty rockets would be fired, and that the results of the firings would be collated and made available to both countries. The British Chiefs of Staff considered this memo over the next two days and then asked the War Office to investigate further. Two days later, under pressure from the US Chiefs of Staff to give their assent, they requested further information on the number of complete A-4/V-2s available in Germany, stating that *'it is obviously undesirable that all or even almost all available should be expended during [the] proposed trial.'* Britain and the US had requested one hundred each and there were 'other claimants', assumed to be the Soviets and the French.

Reassured that Eisenhower *'...has at least 300, and possibly as many as 500, rockets in his possession'* and that he *'only visualises using thirty rockets in the trials',* the Chiefs of Staff gave their approval for Backfire to go ahead on 24 May 1945.

With the full backing of the relevant authorities in both London and Washington, DC, Operation Backfire began in earnest. Eisenhower named Major General Alexander Cameron, the Chief of Air Defence for SHAEF, as the head of the new Special Projectile Operations Group (SPOG), responsible for Backfire, and an establishment of some 100 officers and 900 other ranks was agreed. The site chosen for the test launches was the Altenwalde Naval Gun Testing Ground of the German armament manufacturers, Krupp, near Cuxhaven in Lower Saxony, on the North Sea coast at the mouth of the River Elbe.

The specific objective of the operation, as dictated to Cameron, was *'to obtain, while the German technical staff originally employed on long range rockets are still available and the details are still fresh in their minds:*

a) information on the testing, assembly and filling of the German A-4 rocket.
b) detailed knowledge and experience of the German technique for launching long-range rockets.'

Backfire was essentially an Allied military Operation - carried out as a race against time - and inspired, organised, and conducted by the armies on the Continent. Because it took place in the British Zone, the organisation was predominantly British. Germans carried out the actual work of building and launching A-4 rockets. The United States and the United Kingdom were invited to provide equal technical officers to participate in the opcration. The United States could not do more than provide observers, but the British Ministry of Supply loaned some six technical officers. To the military and technical officers of the Backfire organisation, credit is due for such success.

During the last month of the campaign on the Continent, a large number of German A-4 personnel fell into the hands of the Allies, and there were indications that a considerable quantity of A-4 rockets, ancillary equipment and documentation would also be captured.

Early in May 1945, therefore, an investigation was carried out to see if it was desirable and feasible to use German personnel to fire captured A-4 rockets in Germany. A staff Officer of the Air Defence Division, Supreme Headquarters, Allied Expeditionary Force, was dispatched to the United Kingdom on 7 May to discuss the project with interested authorities.

At the War Office, he saw the Scientific Adviser to the Army Council, the Deputy Chief of the Imperial General Staff and the Assistant Chief of the Imperial General Staff (Weapons); at the Ministry of Supply, he saw the Director General of Munitions Production and the Controller of Projectile Development. They were unanimous that carrying out such an operation was most desirable. They stated that it might save years of development work, and they agreed that the launching and control of rockets was a complicated operation, which the German technicians needed to demonstrate as soon as possible before they lost their skill. They also considered that unless some captured rockets were fired, it might be discovered later that certain technical information essential to rocket operation was missing. The Supreme Commander therefore directed that the operation be put in hand as a joint United States and British military operation under

TRAJECTORY OF THE ROCKET (RANGE 300 KM/185 MILES

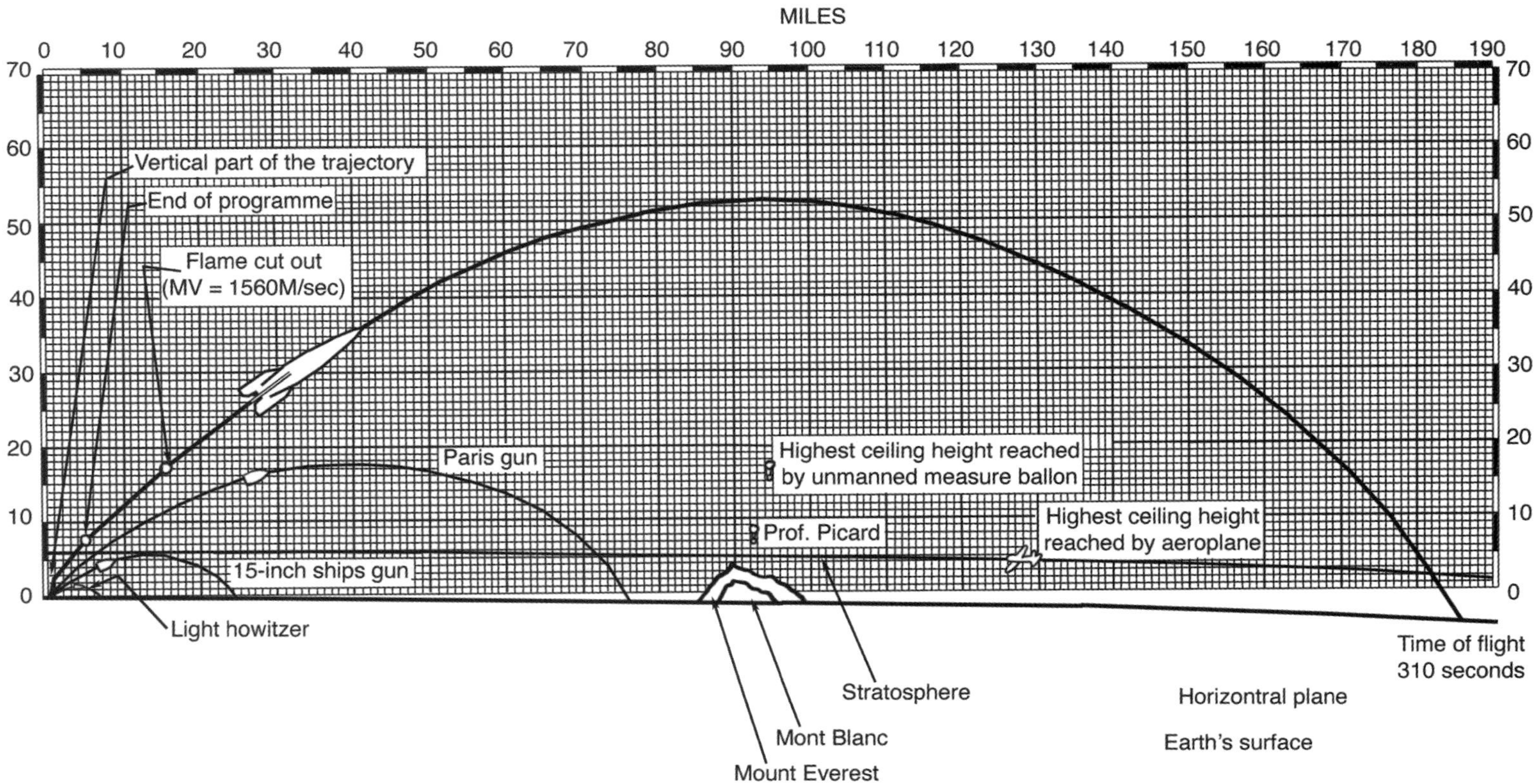

A contemporary comparison of a flight of the A-4/V-2 rocket against those of artillery shells, geographic information and other high-altitude attempts.

VELOCITY CURVE OVER TIME OF FLIGHT

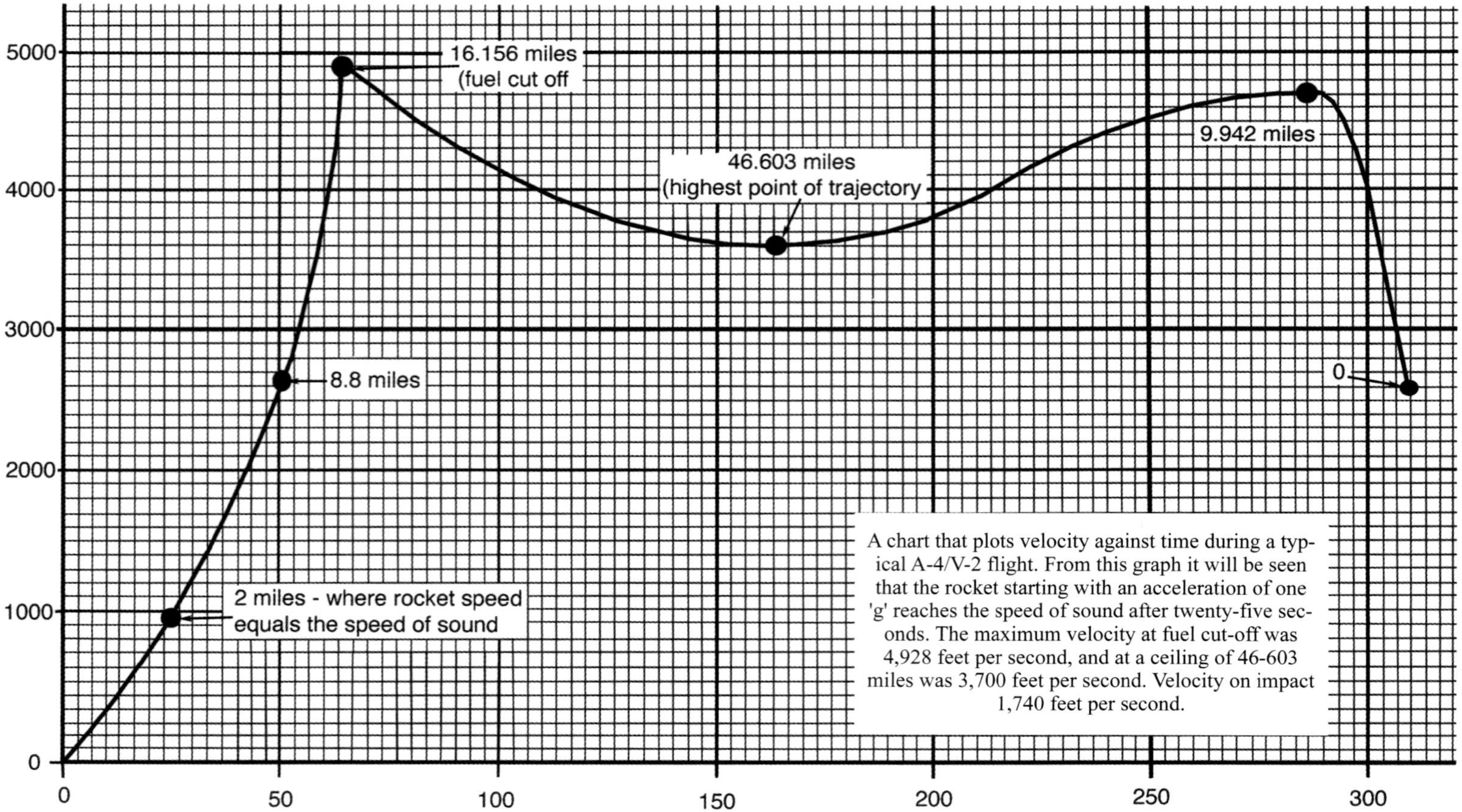

A chart that plots velocity against time during a typical A-4/V-2 flight. From this graph it will be seen that the rocket starting with an acceleration of one 'g' reaches the speed of sound after twenty-five seconds. The maximum velocity at fuel cut-off was 4,928 feet per second, and at a ceiling of 46-603 miles was 3,700 feet per second. Velocity on impact 1,740 feet per second.

Lieutenant General Alexander Maurice Cameron, (*b.* 30 May 1898, *d.* 25 December 1986. *[Photo: NARA]*

the control of Supreme Headquarters, Allied Expeditionary Force, and obtained the approval of the Combined Chiefs of Staff. He also directed that it should be completed as soon as possible.

The method of attaining what 'Backfire' had been established to do was to collect component parts and damaged rockets from fields, ditches, railway yards, canals, from factories, and then employ Germans to clean them, repair them, test them, and assemble them into complete rockets. Eight rockets were built and tested as fit to fire. In proof of the correctness of the work, three of these were set up for firing, and all three were successfully launched.

Command Structure

The Supreme Commander delegated to the Chief, Air Defense Division, Supreme Headquarters, Allied Expeditionary Force, Lieutenant General Sir Alexander Maurice Cameron KBE CB MC responsibility for the organisation and conduct of Operation Backfire. This officer and his staff were part of Supreme Headquarters. It was necessary to nominate a subordinate headquarters, which would open up the required establishment for the firing of rockets and take command of all activities at the site. It was essential to fire over the sea, so it was decided to operate in the British Zone. To simplify administration, it was planned to have a primarily British organisation, with the attachment of such United States advisers, staff officers, and technicians as the United States desired.

On 22 May, Headquarters 21 Army Group were asked to place a Brigade Headquarters under the operational control of Supreme Headquarters, Allied Expeditionary Force. Four days later, on 26 May 1945, they nominated Headquarters, 307 Infantry Brigade, under Brigadier Leslie Keith Lockhart MC. Brigadier Lockhart's functions were to inspect and select a suitable site for the operation; to arrange for the allocation or construction of the necessary workshop and firing facilities; to command all troops assigned to the operation; to administer all Germans employed on the operation; and to receive the rocket components and equipment.

On the dissolution of the Supreme Headquarters, Allied Expeditionary Force on 14 July 1945, provision had to be made for the continuity of the higher direction of the operation previously exercised by the Supreme Commander through his Air Defense Division. Therefore, the Combined Chiefs of Staff placed the responsibility on the War Office, who reconstituted the British Air Defence Division component as an independent formation headquarters. On the 15 July, this component moved from Frankfurt to Cuxhaven, the site selected for the operation, and reopened their office as Headquarters, SPOG.

The British 21 Army Group provided all the administrative units required for the conduct of the operation. They were under the command of Headquarters, 307 Infantry Brigade, and comprised:

- 1 Light Anti-Aircraft/Searchlight Battery, Royal Artillery.
- I77 Light Anti-Aircraft Battery, Royal Artillery.
- Detachment 952 Railway Operating Company, Royal Engineers.
- 307 Infantry Brigade Signals Section, Royal Signals.
- 1685 Artillery Platoon, Royal Army Service Corps.
- 1689 Light Anti-Aircraft/Searchlight

Section, Royal Army Service Corps.
- Detachment 17 Canadian Field Ambulance Section, Royal Canadian Army Medical Corps.
- 101 Anti-Aircraft Brigade Workshop, Corps of the Royal Electrical and Mechanical Engineers.
- 1 Light Anti-Aircraft/Searchlight Workshop, Corps of the Royal Electrical and Mechanical Engineers.
- 76 FCF Brigade, AFS.
- 6 Canadian Field Security Reserve Detaclnnent.
- 736 German Labour Company.

Certain other units of 20 Army Group, though not placed under command, were employed on various work in connection with the operation, chiefly construction. They comprised :
- 593 Army Troops Company, Royal Engineers.
- 670 Artizan Works Company, Royal Engineers.
- 1 Platoon, 113 Road Construction Company, Royal Engineers.
- 2 Platoons, 700 Artizan Works Company, Royal Engineers.
- 23 Mechanical Equipment Platoon, Royal Engineers
- 145 Pioneer Company, Pioneer Corps.

Three operational units and an Army Film Unit were found by the War Office:
- X Special Anti-Aircraft Radar Battery, Royal Artillery.
- 20 Special Survey Detachment, Royal Artillery.
- 2 Anti-Aircraft (ATS.) Kine-Theodolite Detachment.
- 355 A.K.S. Detachment, Royal Army Observer Corps

21 Army Group also provided a Westex Recording Unit, Royal Artillery, and No. 1 Independent Administrative Company, Royal Signals.

Although the work of assembling and testing rockets was to be carried out by German scientists and technicians, it was early appreciated that British technical officers would be required. Their role was to supervise the German technical activities, to

The Backfire team found A-4/V-2 rockets in a whole different range of conditions.... *[Photo: NARA]*

...and moved them to Cuxhaven by whatever means came to hand. Slightly overhanging load - not a problem!
[Photo: NARA]

ensure so far as possible that there was no deception by the Germans, and above all, to record technical information of value. They should, if possible, be experts in long-range rocket matters, but the officers who were eventually nominated did not have this experience.

On 22 May, the Ministry of Supply were approached. On 24 May, a signal was sent asking for a senior officer as technical adviser to General Cameron and an officer with knowledge of rocket construction to supervise the collection of components to ensure the correctness of assembly', and to inspect the completed rockets.

On 3 June, a liaison officer from the Ministry of Supply was appointed, but the oflicer to supervise construction, Colonel C W Raby, did not arrive till 9 July, and he had then also to assume the functions of chief technical adviser. Colonel Raby brought with him an Assistant Superintendent and an expert on fuels. Three more technical offioers from the Ministry of Supply had reported for duty by the 2 August. On 10 September, just three weeks before the first launch, Brigadier W. H. Wheeler was added to the staff of SPOG, but the technical direction remained in the hands of Colonel Raby.

On 28 May, the Headquarters European Theatre of Operations, United States Army, was asked for a senior United States officer to advise and assist in the setting up of the appropriate organisation but replied that no officer was available. A similar request was made to the War Department, Washington DC, on 2 June they replied suggesting one of two officers who were already in the theatre. Eventually, on 4 July, Colonel W I Wilson, United States Army Ordnance Department, reported for duty as senior United States officer, with the role of watching the United States interests and assisting SPOG by procuring from United States sources such personnel and material as might be required. Colonel Wilson was accompanied by two other officers and was succeeded on 14 August by Colonel J H Weber, United States Army Ordnance Department.

A voyage of Discovery...

Now that Allied scientists and engineers could finally get their hands on a number of A-4/V-2s, they could study both the hardware and all the procedures in detail under Operation Backfire.

The A-4/V-2 rocket was a liquid-fuelled design, intended to carry a one-ton payload over a distance of two hundred miles. Its overall length was forty-six feet one inch, and its maximum diameter was five feet five inches.

The rocket was made up of these main

THE ANATOMY OF A A-4

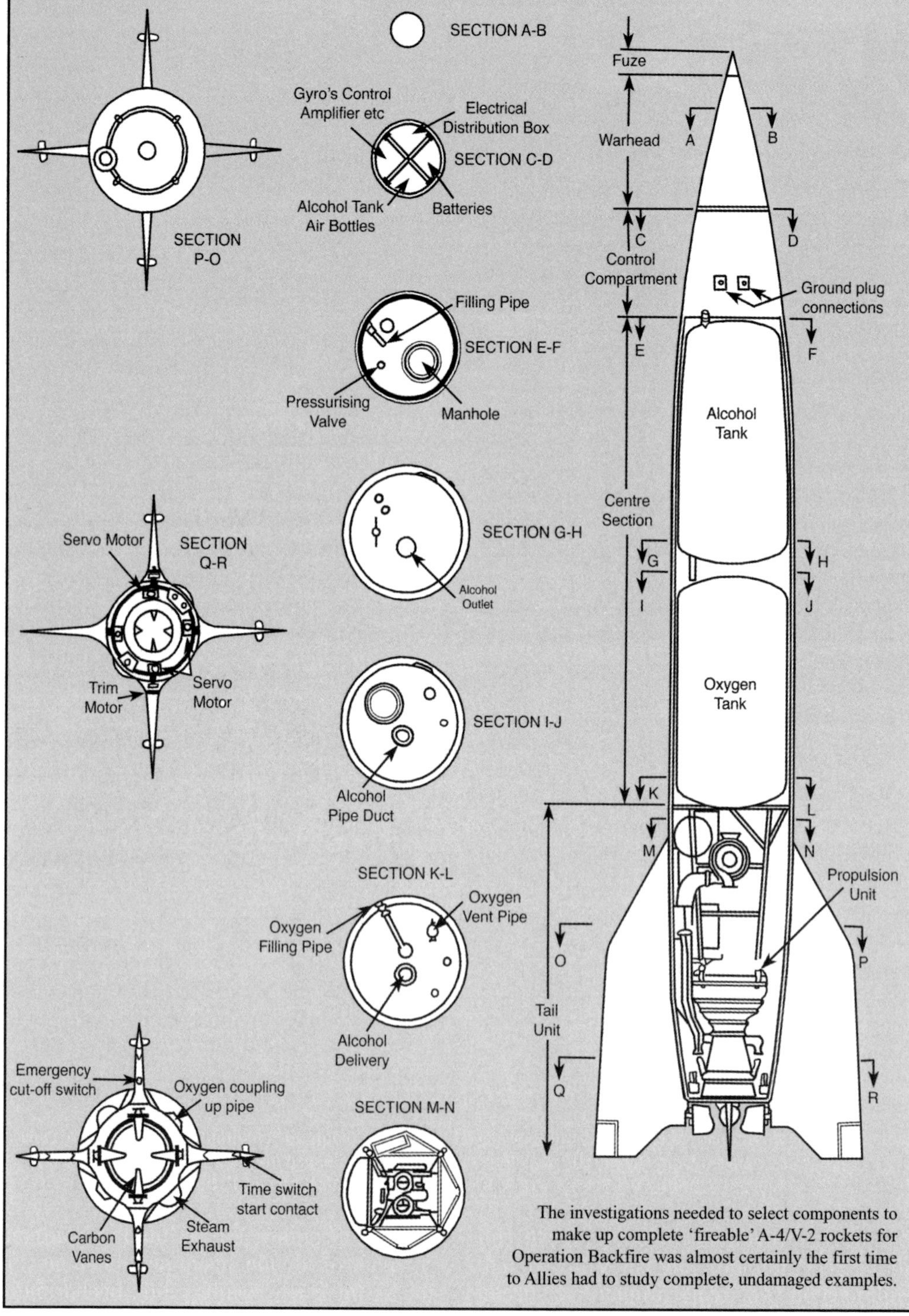

The investigations needed to select components to make up complete 'fireable' A-4/V-2 rockets for Operation Backfire was almost certainly the first time to Allies had to study complete, undamaged examples.

components:

- The ballistic nose and warhead.
- The control compartment.
- The centre section or fuel tank bay.
- The auxiliary motor unit and fuel pumps.
- The rocket motor and venturi.
- The tail unit and thrust ring.

The projectile's weight without the warhead was just under three tons. The warhead weighed 2190 pounds, giving a total weight of about four tons without fuel. When fuelled, the rocket weighed a little over twelve tons.

The warhead was a sharply pointed cone, five feet seven inches long. The side casing was of mild steel plate braced internally by struts. At the rear end, the casing was welded to a steel ring, which also welded a circular end plate with a central hole for filling. About three feet from the nose, a hole led to an internal pipe that ran through the warhead and the control compartment to the top of the alcohol tank to pressurise this tank for the first forty seconds of flight of the projectile.

Two diametrically opposite slinging points were provided in the side casing of the warhead, and two more were in the end plate itself. The warhead was attached to the control compartment using bolts, and this junction formed one of the two transport joints of the rocket when on the meilerwagen.

A central exploder tube with electrical fuses at each forward and rear ran through the warhead. Each fuse had two inertia switches, so they operated whatever the angle of impact. In addition, the nose fuse had a nose switch mounted on a steel tube that projected beyond the nose housing.

The control compartment was situated immediately in the rear of the warhead. It was a truncated cone four feet seven and a half inches long divided into four equal sections by radial plywood sheets relative to the plane of any two of the stabilising fins of the rocket. The plywood sheets were orientated at forty-five degrees.

Forced Labour, or slave workers inside one of the tunnels at Mittelwerk. The assembly lines included both detainees, German workers and supervisors, in the ratio of about two prisoners to one worker. The Engineers who ran the various workshops and production crews were German civilians and Wehrmacht soldiers who were wounded or sick would also be sent to Mittelwerk for duty as parts or process inspectors. *[Photo: NARA]*

In Compartment One was;

- Ortler or Verdoppler - radio equipment for velocity measurement. It was used to determine point of fuel cut-off when fuel cut-off was radio controlled from the ground.
- Honef or Kommandoempsfaenger - radio equipment for receiving fuel cut-off signal. Also only installed when fuel cut-off is radio controlled from the ground.
- Not-Brennschluss - Emergency fuel cut - off equipment. This enabled the fuel supply to be cut-off in an emergency. Operated by ground control up to the moment the rocket leaves the table.
- Bordbatterie - Two 16v. batteries. The main electrical DC supply for operation of gyros, control amplifier, solenoid valves, etc.

Compartment Two contained:

- Hauptverteiler - the main electrical distribution box and Bordautomat - the distribution box safety switch.
- Stotz Stecker - Ground connector plug sockets. These for ground power supply and connections between the Feuerleitpanzer - the fire control vehicle and the rocket.

Compartment Three contained:

- Sterg - the Fuse Arming Unit. This Arms fuses in warhead approximately two minutes after take off.
- Automatic pilot comprising two gyros, one for roll and yaw (Vertikant), the other for pitch (Horizont), mounted on base plate (Richtgeberplatte). It provided c-control of line and pitch of the rocket.
- I-Geraet - Integrating accelerometer. This was automatic fuel cut-off equipment and was alternative to radio equipment for fuel cut-off listed under Compartment 1.
- Zeitschaltwerk - Time switch. This governed sequence of events after take-off on a time basis.
- Mischgeraet - Control amplifier. It amplified signals received from gyros so that they would operate servo motors and rudder motors which control moveable vanes and rudders in tail unit.
- One Kemmandogeberbatterie - a 50v.

A-4 ROCKET - POSITION OF HATCHES

A Hatch for distribution box safety switch.
B Spring hatch for Stotz Plugs.
C Hatch for alcohol drainage.
D Hatch for leads for alcohol outlet valve.
E Hatch for turbine centrefugal switch.
F Hatch for alcohol main valve,
G Hatch for hydrogen peroxide fuelling inlet.
H Hatch for pressure reducing valve & auxilliary motor unit
I Hatch for hydrogen peroxide drainage and vent.
J Hatch for oxygen fuelling inlet.
K Hatch for sodium permanganate fuelling inlet.
L Hatch for sodium permanganate vent.
M Hatch for sodium permanganate drainage.
N Cowling for oxygen topping up valve.
O Turbine exhaust cowling.
P Cowling for five-way coupling.
Q Cowling for oxygen tank overflow and turbine exhaust.
R Hatches for servo potentiometers.

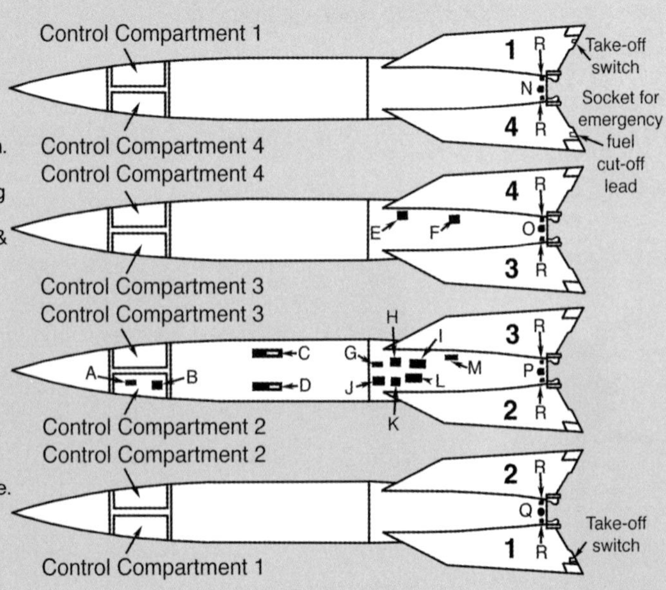

Control Compartments 1 & 4
1. Ortler. 2. 16v Batteries. 3. Emergency fuel cut-off. 4. Honef. 5. Compressed air bottles. 6. High pressure valve. 7. Leitstrahl

Control Compartments 2 & 3
1. Main electrical distnbution box. 2. Ground connector plug sockets. 3. Alcohol fuel tank inlet. 4. Base plate. 5 Automatic pilot. 6. Alternator. 7.Control amplifier. 8.Alcohol tank pressurising pipes. 9. Plywood sheet. *[Photos: NARA]*

H.T. nickel iron battery that supplied current for gyro signals.

- Umformer mit Regler Alternator with regulator that supplied A.C. three phase supply at 500 cycles per second to gyros. D.C. supply received from two 16v. batteries.
- Alcohol fuel tank inlet for alcohol fuelling.
- Alcohol tank pressurising pipe for pressurising alcohol tank from atmosphere for first forty seconds of flight.
- Handabsperrventil und manometer - hand operated stop cock and pressure gauge for filling and testing pressure in alcohol tank pressurising bottles.

Compartment Four contained:

- Leitstrahl - Receiver for radio control for line.
- Zusatzbeluftung - Three compressed air bottles for pressurising alcohol tank after fuel cut-off.
- Three alternators with regulators. This was A.C. three phase supply, 500 cycles for control amplifier and radio equipment (when installed).
- Hochdruckventil - High pressure valve. Safety valve for three compressed air bottles.

It should be noted that a literal translation of many of the German terms employed does not make sense. On the other hand, it may be difficult to make a sensible translation concise. For instance, the term Fremdkonunandotafel (literally translated 'Enemy Command Table') is, in fact, a 'panel on which there are switches for simulating gyroscopic signals during horizontal tests.' At first, therefore, common sense names were used, and owing to lack of time for correction, it has been necessary to adhere to them, although in some cases, better translations have since come to hand.

For ease of reference when using German equipment, German names, and in some cases German words of command, are also given throughout.

The centre section was twenty feet three and a half inches long, housing the alcohol and oxygen tanks. The former was forward (or above) the latter. The shell structure around the tanks was constructed in two halves made from steel reinforced by longitudinal and circumferential stringers.

The alcohol tank was constructed from a light alloy sheet and tapered towards the rocket's forward end. The top of the tank was fitted with an inspection cover, a fuelling inlet, and an electrically operated pressure valve on the pipe running through the control compartment and the warhead. A pressure-operated outlet valve and a drainage valve were at the tank's base. The outlet valve led via bellows - to allow for expansion and contraction - to a delivery pipe which ran through the oxygen tank to the alcohol pump. Access to the alcohol drainage valve was using a hatch in the side of the shell between fins two and three. The capacity of the alcohol tank was approximately 9200 pounds by weight or 183 cubic feet. Its contents, ethyl alcohol, contained twenty-five per cent water by weight, the mixture having a specific gravity of 0.85 at fifteen per cent. It was vitally important that no solid impurities were present, for any would clog the jets in the combustion chamber nozzles.

Factories producing ethanol were numerous; the raw material from which the bulk of the spirit was distilled came from potatoes, which usually yielded ten gallons of alcohol per ton of potatoes.

The oxygen tank was also constructed out of light alloy. It was filled using a fuelling connection with a hand-operated valve fitted to the tank outlet. An internal stack pipe which reached down to the top of the tank led via a valve to a vent on the tail unit of the rocket. This pipe allowed for venting of the tank during fuelling. Access to the oxygen-fuelling inlet is using a panel in the shell structure of the tail unit. The tank held about 12,200 pounds of oxygen by weight, or 170 cubic feet by volume. The tank and alcohol pipe were both heavily insulated with glass wool.

The liquid oxygen used in the A-4/V-2 was to have a purity of not less than ninety-eight per cent, the impurity being mainly nitrogen. It was vitally important to be free from all traces of oil, for this would produce explosions in the pumps. Technically, the oxygen had a specific gravity of 1.12 and boiled at minus 183 degrees centigrade at standard atmospheric pressure.

The demand for liquid oxygen created by the A-4/V-2 project could not be met by existing facilities, forcing the construction of factories solely for the purpose of supplying the A-4/V-2 requirements. One of these was at Saar, which could provide one hundred and twenty tons a day, with the facility at Thuringa producing one hundred and sixty tons a day. The Germans had also planned to convert ammonia plants in the Rhur to produce liquid oxygen.

Oxygen was extracted from the air by liquefication and subsequent rectification of the liquid by compressing the air to at least one hundred and sixty atmospheres, a process that placed a considerable demand on power supplies.

Safety procedures in handling the items were very strict. No naked flames or glowing materials could be anywhere near it, and asbestos clothing had to be worn when handling the liquid or its pipework as any contact with the body caused severe burns. At the time, the dangers of asbestosis was unknown.

The missile was fitted with an auxiliary motor and fuel pump, which provided steam for the turbine, which drove the alcohol and oxygen pumps that supplied fuel to the rocket's main combustion chambers.

The auxiliary motor unit, turbine, and pumps were mounted on a braced steel framework bolted to the rear of the tank bay. The framework also supported seven compressed air bottles, which pressurised the sodium permanganate and hydrogen peroxide tanks and operated various valves, which controlled the flow of fuels.

The hydrogen peroxide, the quality known as TSS, which contained as stabilisers twenty-five milligrammes per litre of phosphoric acid and two milligrammes per litre of ortho-oxy-quinoline.

Concentrated hydrogen peroxide was not a normal industrial demand and so to meet the requirements of the A-4/V-2 project and other war programmes, a special plant had to be built. This factory was built at Bag Lauterberg in the Hars district and was capable of producing over thirty-five tons per day. A second factory was in the course of construction nearby.

In contact with inorganic matter, concentrated hydrogen peroxide decomposed rapidly with an evolution of heat, giving an oxygen-rich atmosphere. The heat evolved was sufficient to ignite combustible materials, especially clothing. Peroxide burned the skin and blistered rapidly; protective clothing, gloves, and goggles had to be worn, preferably made of mipolam, a trade name for vinyl, or pure rubber.

No sand, soil or pieces of metal should be introduced into the peroxide. These were liable to start decomposition of the concentrate, which could lead to an

Two views of the alcohol tank, with oxygen tank behind is seen on a special railcar in the assembly building. The top of the tank was fitted with an inspection cover, a fuelling inlet, and an electrically operated pressure valve on the pipe running through the control compartment and the warhead. The tanks are sitting in a half-shell that makes up the exterior of the rocket. *[Photos: NARA]*

explosion if the temperature rose high enough. Storage of the peroxide was safer in large containers than in smaller ones.

The steam was generated for the turbine by the chemical reaction of concentrated hydrogen peroxide and the catalyst sodium permanganate. The fuels were stored in tanks, which were filled through hatches in the main tail unit of the rocket. The hydrogen peroxide tank had a capacity of three hundred and seventy-nine pounds or one hundred and twenty-six litres. The sodium permanganate tank was much smaller, with a capacity of twenty-nine pounds, or eleven litres.

The German procedure was for all fuel supplies to leave their relevant manufacturing factories by rail and be delivered to a central store area, from whence they were delivered by road vehicles to the launch site. The alcohol tankers carried 2,900 litres, with each rocket needing two tankers. The Oxygen tankers held 6,000 litres, one tanker being required per rocket. The hydrogen peroxide tanker held 2,100 litres, enough for sixteen rocket launches. Sodium permanganate came in eleven-litre cans; each can enough for one missile.

Above left: The A-4 rocket's combustion Chamber.

Left: The Combusion Camber sitting on the alignment rig, about to have the tubular framework for carrying the turbine pump unit and other equipment fitted.

Above: Oxygen pipework between the turbine pump unit and the roses atop the combustion chamber. *[Photos: NARA]*

Once required, the special vehicles were carried or towed as accessories, as was the necessary equipment for transferring the fluids from the tankers to the rocket tanks.

The alcohol was transferred through a power pumping set mounted on a trailer, which was equipped with a flowmeter. It took about twenty minutes to fill the rocket tank, the pump's suction side, and twin connections were drawn from two tankers simultaneously.

Liquid oxygen was transferred by means of a power-driven centrifugal pump, which was hung on the frame of the oxygen tanker. Once the pump had cooled down, the rocket tank was filled in about twelve minutes.

The hydrogen peroxide was filled into the Meilerwagen tank using a semi-rotary hand pump, and it took up to five minutes. From the meilerwagen tank, it gravitated to the rocket tank. A power pump was fitted in the peroxide tanker, but the German troops seldom used it.

In cold weather - below about minus ten degrees centigrade - the peroxide had to be heated to prevent freezing and this was done in a special preheating tank assembled on a trailer. This tank held enough for one charge. The sodium permanganate was poured on into the rocket tank from a container through a funnel. Before pouring, the permanganate was heated slightly to remove the presence of any crystals and to ensure the desired even decomposition of the peroxide. This heating was done simply by leaving it near a running engine.

What goes in - may have to come out!
Provision was made for the drainage of the fuel tanks if, for any reason, fuel had to be removed from the rocket. Steam produced from the auxiliary combustion chamber drove the turbine, to which were connected

Right: two views of the propulsion unit. The steam production unit to power the turbine pump is yet to be installed. *[Photos: NARA]*

the alcohol and oxygen pumps.

Exhaust from the turbine was led via the heat exchanger into the missile's rear, escaping through cowlings in the tail unit. The heat exchanger vaporised some of the liquid oxygen, which was then used for pressurising the oxygen unit tank. Oxygen was then pumped from the oxygen tank through the oxygen main valve and subsequently by eighteen pipes to eighteen roses in the main combustion chamber. Two pipes, each pumping alcohol, subsequently became three to the venturi base, passing between the venturi walls for cooling purposes to the jet in the combustion chamber.

The combustion chamber and the venturi was one welded steel assembly. The combustion chamber had eighteen open-ended cups, called 'roses', facing rearwards. The oxygen was fed to the roses directly from the oxygen main valve. Alcohol pumped to the venturi's base travelled between the venturi's walls in the alcohol main valve which operated under pressure to allow alcohol to pass to the jets in the burners. The venturi had rows of holes spaced throughout its length, these allowed alcohol to pass to the venturi for additional cooling purposes.

The tail unit of the missile was part of the shell structure that enclosed the rocket motor and auxiliary motor units. The tail unit did not transmit thrust loads; it acted as a fairing for the motor unit and as a support for the stabilising fins and the thrust ring at the rocket's base. At its forward end, the tail unit was supported by a circular rolled steel angle frame bolted to the tank bay's rear, forming the second transport joint for the complete rocket.

The four stabilising fins were fixed at right angles to each other. Two are in the same plane as the plane of rotation of the turbine rotor: numbered One and Three and aligned to the target immediately before launching.

Fins Two and Four were at right angles to the plane of rotation of the turbine motor and are consequently at right angles to the plane of the when the rocket is in flight. At the rear of each fin is an outer vane.

The tail unit had numerous hatches which were used for fuelling and to give access to various valves, servomotors and potentiometers. At the base of the rocket between fins Two and Three, here was a five way coupling which formed the connection between the rocket and the valve box. The fiveway coupling was protected by a cowling.

Between the fins One and Two and fins Three and Four respectively were vanes for the exhaust of the steam turbine. The cowlings between fins One and Two contained the valve which could be used for topping up the oxygen tank if there had been a wastage since main fuelling was

Not the best of images, but it does show the assembly shop for the simultaneous construction of four rockets. *[Photo: NARA]*

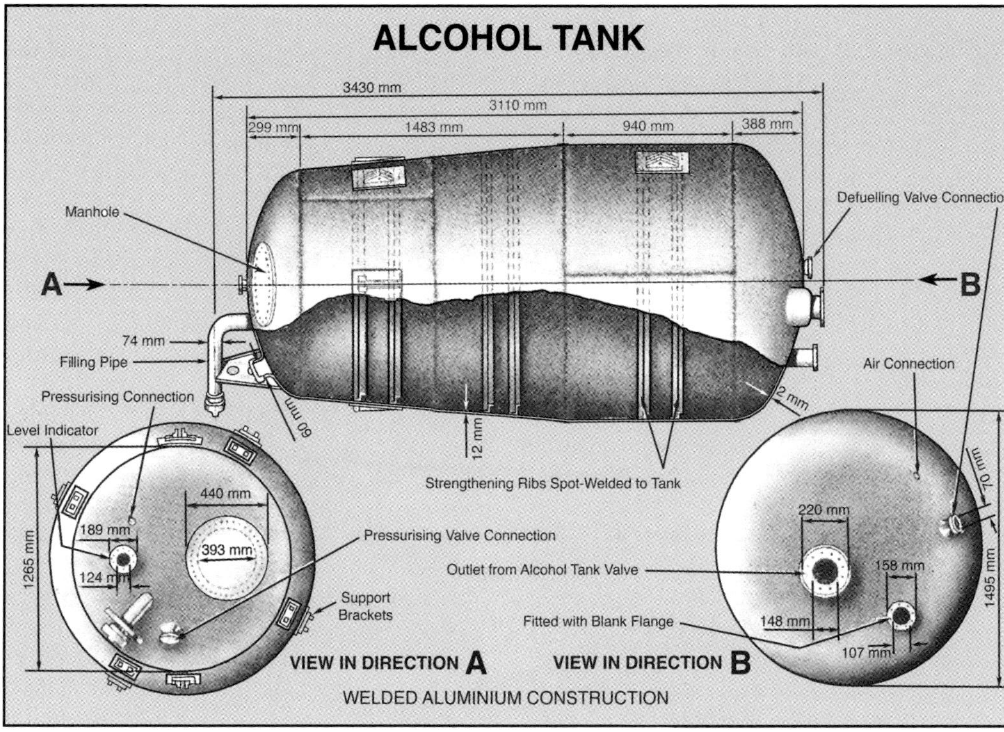
ALCOHOL TANK
3430 mm
3110 mm
299 mm
1483 mm
940 mm
388 mm
Manhole
Defuelling Valve Connection
A
B
74 mm
Filling Pipe
Pressurising Connection
60 mm
12 mm
2 mm
Air Connection
Level Indicator
Strengthening Ribs Spot-Welded to Tank
440 mm
189 mm
393 mm
124 mm
1265 mm
Pressurising Valve Connection
Outlet from Alcohol Tank Valve
Support Brackets
Fitted with Blank Flange
220 mm
70 mm
158 mm
148 mm
107 mm
1495 mm
VIEW IN DIRECTION A
VIEW IN DIRECTION B
WELDED ALUMINIUM CONSTRUCTION

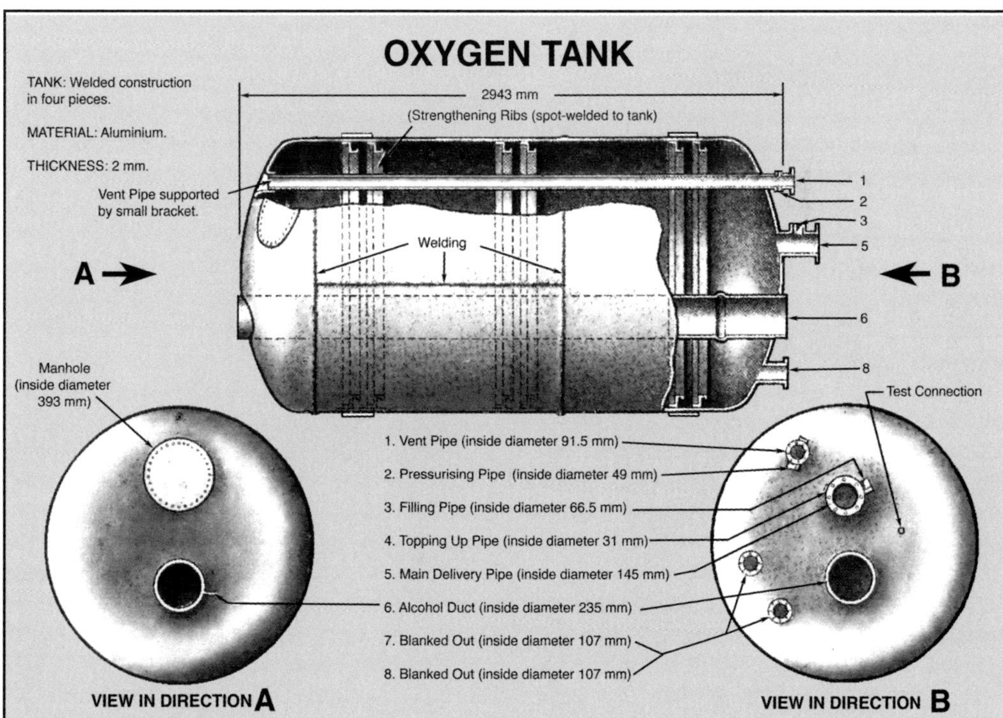
OXYGEN TANK
TANK: Welded construction in four pieces.
MATERIAL: Aluminium.
THICKNESS: 2 mm.
2943 mm
(Strengthening Ribs (spot-welded to tank)
Vent Pipe supported by small bracket.
Welding
A
B
1
2
3
5
6
8
Manhole (inside diameter 393 mm)
Test Connection
1. Vent Pipe (inside diameter 91.5 mm)
2. Pressurising Pipe (inside diameter 49 mm)
3. Filling Pipe (inside diameter 66.5 mm)
4. Topping Up Pipe (inside diameter 31 mm)
5. Main Delivery Pipe (inside diameter 145 mm)
6. Alcohol Duct (inside diameter 235 mm)
7. Blanked Out (inside diameter 107 mm)
8. Blanked Out (inside diameter 107 mm)
VIEW IN DIRECTION A
VIEW IN DIRECTION B

COMBUSTION CHAMBER

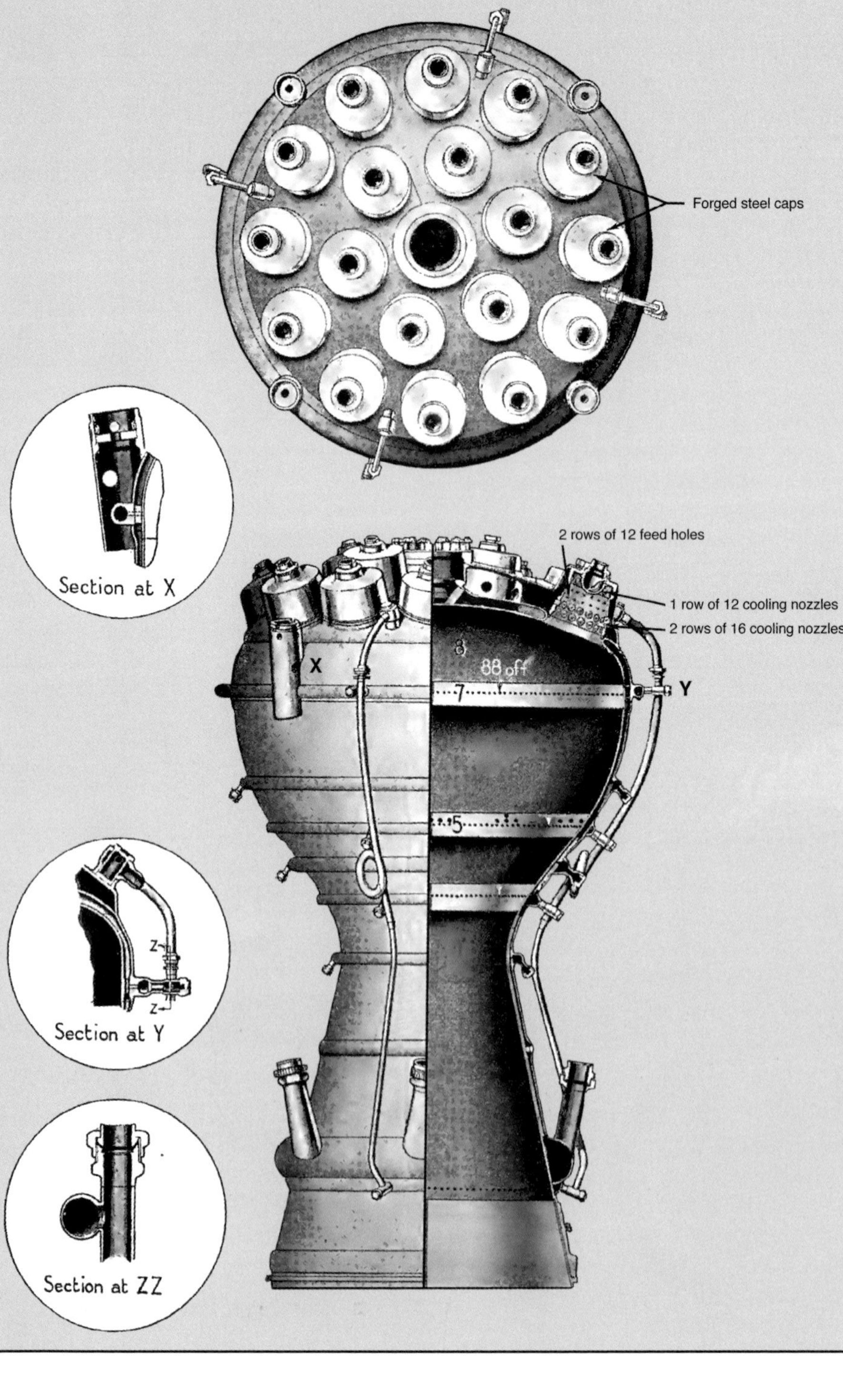

completed. In the base of fin Four was a socket for the emergency fuel cut-off line while fin One was fitted with an Abhebekontakt, or spring loaded take off switch.

The thrust ring at the base of the tail unit was a cast light alloy channel ring which mounted the four supports and brackets for the carbon rudders. These rudders, together with the four outer vanes on the fins were used to control in the rocket in flight up to the fuel cut-off point the vanes and rudders were actuated by hydraulic servo motors mounted inside the tail unit on the thrust ring. Two of the delicate carbon rudders, together with their corresponding outer vanes which were geared to them controlled the rocket for line, and counteract any tendancy of the rocket to roll or yaw. Any such tendency was detected by the roll/yaw gyro which operated the servo units through the control amplifier in the control compartment and the potentiometer on the thrust ring. The remaining two carbon rudders and associated vanes were directed by the pitch giro in a similar manner.

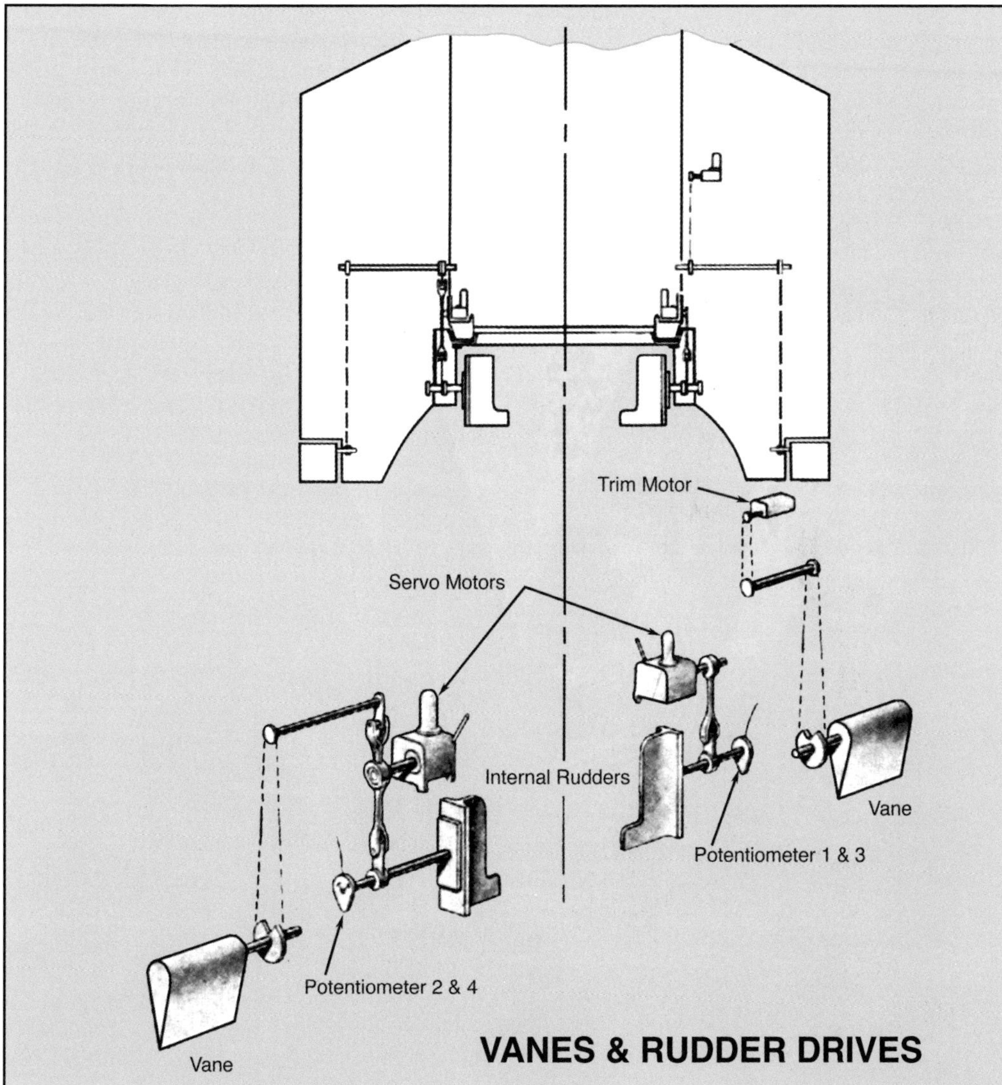

VANES & RUDDER DRIVES

A Study of targetting and Performance

From their research the Allies knew that the trajectory of the A-4/V-2 rocket was divided into two parts: from launch until fuel cut-off, and then from fuel cut-off until fall of shot. During the period before the fuel cut-off, the flight of the rocket was controlled; after the fuel cut-off, the missile is uncontrolled.

When the rocket left the launching table, it first climbed vertically for four seconds. It was then made to pitch in the direction of the target by a predetermined programme, which is put into effect by a time switch. The pitch programme lasts for approximately forty-three seconds; at the end of this time, the rocket is at an inclination of forty-seven degrees to the vertical. Thereafter, until fuel cut-off, approximately sixty-five seconds after launch, depending on the range to the target, the rocket was held at a constant inclination, and the trajectory is almost straight. After fuel cut-off, the rocket followed the typical parabolic trajectory of a free projectile, attaining a maximum height of seventy to eighty kilometres.

The initial acceleration of the rocket relative to the ground was 1 G'. The acceleration increased during burning as the rocket's weight and the atmosphere's resistance decreased until it was approximately 5 'G'. at fuel cut-off.

Conversely, air resistance, encountered as the projectile descended back into the atmosphere again, caused retardation. The maximum velocity attainable by the rocket is 5,000 ft. per second, falling to a terminal velocity of 2,500 ft. per second.

The three axes of the rocket (pitch, roll and yaw) were controlled gyroscopically during burning. The purpose of these controls, together with the thrust of the rocket motor, was to bring the rocket to a pre-determined point in space so that it had a pre-determined orientation and velocity. When this point was reached, the fuel supply to the rocket motor was shut off (Brennschluss) and control over the flight path was relinquished. Thereafter, the projectile's behaviour was similar to that of a normal shell, the velocity attained at the fuel cut-off being comparable with the muzzle velocity.

The trajectory up to the fuel cut-off was assumed constant for all rockets. To fire at a given range, it was only necessary to calculate the required velocity at fuel cut-off and set the integrating accelerometer or sequence switch (or radio fuel cut-off devices) accordingly. The setting values were read from a pre-determined set of range tables. The rocket, as used by the Germans, was fired entirely according to these range tables.

Captured A-4/V-2 rocket components and associated equipment sitting in a railway yard. *[Photo: NARA]*

What is thought to be the same A-4/V-2 rocket as the previous image. It shows the open control compartment doors, and the segmented interior. The mounting holes for the warhead in the carriage ring can also be seen.
[Photo: NARA]

Corrections were made to both lines of fire and range to allow for the effect of the earth's rotation. These corrections varied according to latitude, range of employment and direction of the line of fire. For example, for a range of five hundred kilometres or two hundred miles and a line of fire due north at latitude fifty-four degrees, the line correction is of the order of fifty-four minutes left and the range correction is approximately plus or minus two kilometres. These corrections could be read directly from the range tables. No corrections were made either for meteorological conditions or for variations between rockets. Variation in thrust performance was already allowed for in the rocket as a result of factory tests.

With methyl alcohol and no fuel cut-off - that is, all the fuel consumed meant that the mean range achieved by the rocket was two hundred and ninety-five kilometres, or one hundred and eighty-three miles with a so-called one hundred per cent zone of plus or minus thirty-five kilometres. Thus, although it was possible to reach a range of three hundred and thirty kilometres, or two hundred and five miles, it was not advisable to engage targets at ranges exceeding two hundred and sixty kilometres, or one hundred and sixty-two miles, which was the maximum effective operational range when methyl alcohol was employed. At ranges more significant than that, an increasing proportion of rounds would exhaust their fuel stocks before attaining the velocity required to take them to the target. The minimum operational range is eighty kilometres or fifty miles, governed by the time switch's limitations, which prohibited fuel cut-olf before forty-five seconds of burning.

From captured German data incorporated into known impact records, Operation Backfire discovered that missiles set up for firing suffered one of three fates:

- They failed to take off due to some technical fault.
- They took off, but failed to behave normally, also due to some technical failure.

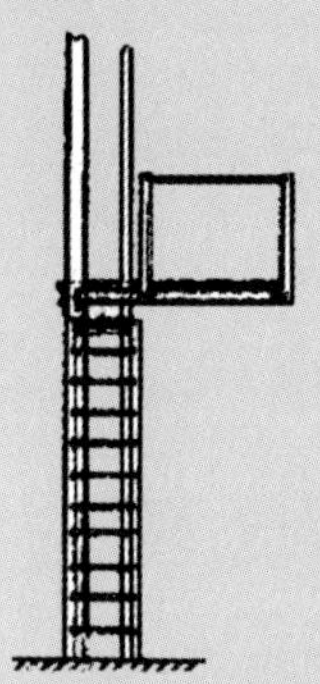

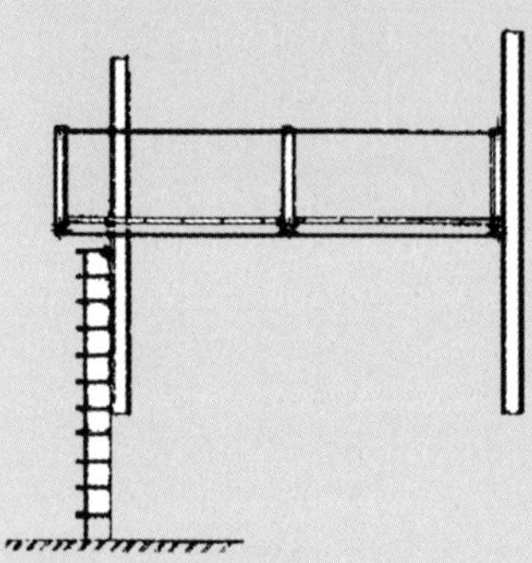

Two views of the Test Deck

LAYOUT OF MAIN ASSEMBLY HALL AT CUXHAVEN

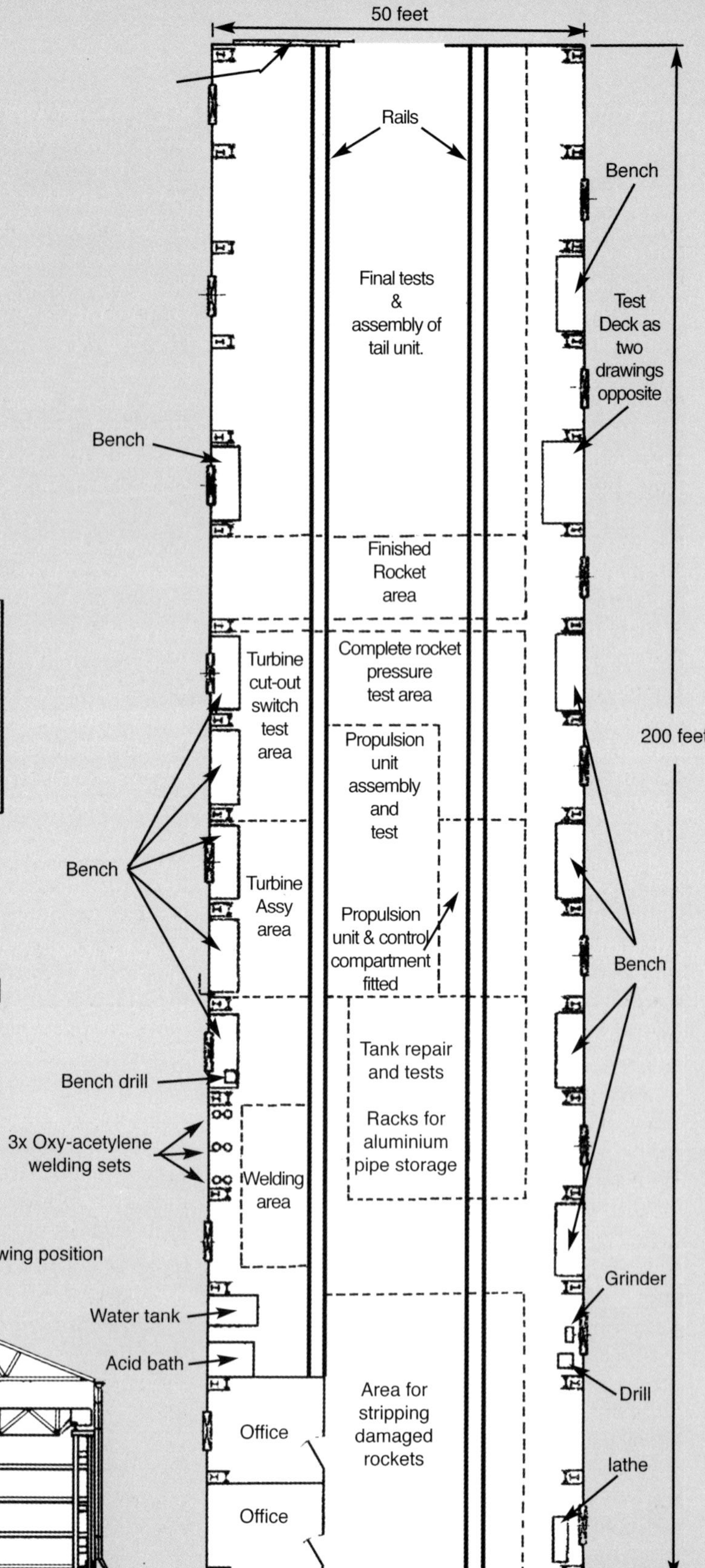

End view of Marsdon shelter showing position of travelling overhead crane

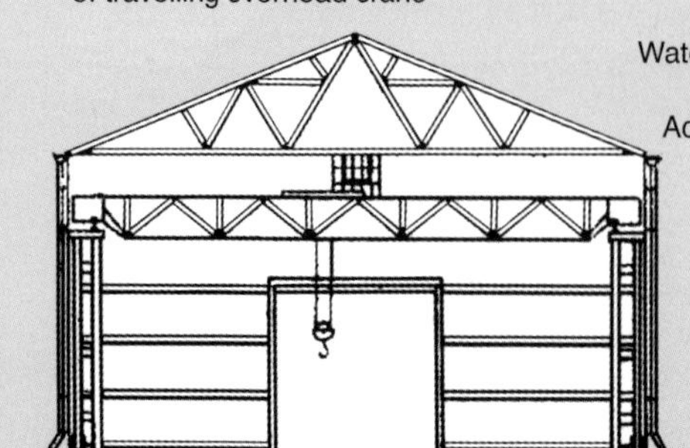

- They behaved as expected and fell in the vicinity of the target.

During the bombardment of Antwerp by the Germans, from December 1944 to March 1945, the proportion of missiles falling into these three categories was seventeen per cent, eighteen per cent and sixty-five per cent, respectively.

Of the sixty-five percent that behaved normally, the scatter of the fall of shot about the mean point of impact (MPI) varies according to the method of control employed.

It was known that after the bombing of Peenemünde by the Royal Air Force in September 1943, the Germans had transferred their experimental V-I and A-4/V-2 establishments elsewhere and that the former had fetched up in the vicinity of Cuxhaven; it was therefore thought that this might prove a suitable place to carry out Operation Backfire. Reconnaissance confirmed this view, and the Krupps gun proving grounds were taken over for the operation. Not only did this site provide some useful facilities in the way of workshops, offices, roads and railway sidings, but it was so located that the whole trajectory of the rocket could be over the sea, and yet close enough to the shores of Schleswig and Denmark for both the upward and downward portions to be plotted by radar.

June was devoted to clearing the site and constructing the additional facilities required. The chief of these was an Assembly Shop for the simultaneous assembly of four rockets, consisting of a modular Marston shelter two hundred feet long, forty-five feet wide and seventeen feet nine inches from the floor to the hook of the overhead ten-ton gantry.

After the German A-4 Division surrendered at the end of April 1945, some of its officers and men had been selected for interrogation. They were chosen from among those with the longest practical experience and the most knowledge of improvements and simplifications in launching methods. They included officers who held important operational, administrative and technical appointments in the Division. At the end of May, the party was taken over for Operation Backfire. They were segregated in a camp near Brussels and interrogated intensively, not only with a view to finding out what additional personnel would be required but also to locate rocket equipment abandoned by the Division.

By the beginning of July, the party had been increased to one hundred and thirty-seven in all and was removed to Altenwalde near Cuxhaven. A prisoner-of-war Labour Company for routine tasks was also moved there.

As soon as it became apparent that the building of rockets would be a complicated and tricky business, it was decided to supplement this party of soldiers with civilian scientists and other technicians. Permission was therefore obtained to select seventy-nine technicians from amongst those whom the United States had concentrated at Garmisch Partenkirchen, and they arrived at Cuxhaven at the end of July.

The original conception was that several complete rockets would be captured in a fit state to fire, together with the necessary ancillary equipment. In addition to studying the technique of launching, it was proposed to use and study the three methods of control in flight which the Germans had employed, and to aim at three successful launches by each method. A total of thirty rockets were considered necessary because some fifty per cent of the attempted launches might be unsuccessful and the rocket damaged past repair, and because a number of rockets were likely to be received in such a battered condition that they could never be made fit to launch.

In reality, no complete, undamaged and serviceable rockets were found. It was, therefore, necessary to collect component parts and set up an assembly shop where German personnel could put these together.

The idea of studying the various German control methods had to be abandoned because none of the ground equipment for remote control was uncovered. Instead, a simple adaption was made to the existing onboard equipment to ensure that the rocket would fall within a given area of sea. Efforts were then focused on producing only eight rockets fit to fire, out of which it was hoped that four would fire successfully.

The failure to obtain any complete rockets produced a whole range of complications. Testing the sub-assemblies and the completed rocket became necessary before it could be accepted as fit to fire. The proper test apparatus was not forthcoming, so designing and building an apparatus was required, especially for this operation. The importance of the time factor was also enhanced. It became apparent that the operation would drag on if the ordinary routine delays were accepted. Therefore, a high priority for the operation and permission to short-circuit the normal channels were obtained.

Major General Walter Dornberger (*b.* 6 September 1895, *d.* 26 June 1980) taken during his period of captivity, 1945. *[Photo: NARA]*

By the middle of August 1945, the operation had crystallised itself into two parts: the first, the production of the completed rockets and recording all the technical lessons which gradually came to light in doing so, and the second, the field operation of handling the completed rocket, setting it up on it's firing site, launching it and recording so far as possible it's behaviour in flight.

To obtain such records as were possible of the rocket in flight, the initial part of the trajectory was photographed by kine-theodolites and plotted by radar stations, and one radar station was deployed to Denmark to plot the full fall of shot.

It is perhaps worthy of note that when the Germans were first assembled, they clamoured for some guarantee of compensation in the event of injury or death resulting from an accident. Yet, from the first day until the last launch, not one man, British or German, was even injured.

Understanding the Organisation

Not only did Operation Backfire need to understand the technology and concepts that went into the A-4/V-2, but they also investigated and recorded the complete field organisational structure and backup Establishments the Germans put in place.

As expected, the interrogation of personnel involved 'in the field' revealed a myriad of differences that evolved in practice for the relatively sterile plans laid out in the Official War Establishment plans.

Top of the pile, as it were, was Div 2V, the V-2 Rocket Division. There followed the Regiment, commanded by an Oberst Lt (Lieutenant-Colonel). It consisted of a Headquarters with various Troops and three Batteries.

Within the Regiment was the Gruppe Feuhrer (HQ), which was responsible for inter-battery and Regimental HQ communications, a Medical Section, a Salvage Section, and a Supply column for the Regimental HQ.

A Wekstatt Zug, or Workshop Platoon, also carried out repairs on Motor Transport and Special Vehicles. The Kraftfahrkompanie (MT Company) was responsible for transporting fuel other than rocket fuel and oils. One of the four Regiments that made up the Rocket Division had a fourth battery under command. It comprised members of the Schutzstaffel (SS) personnel and contained an Anti-Aircraft Troop.

Two Flakvatterien, or Flak Batteries: the troops here were armed with quadruple 20mm cannons, allocated to the batteries to protect launching positions and vulnerable points.

Each Abteilung or Battery, almost operated autonomously. It had its own HQ, HQ Troop, HQ Launching Troop, Technical Troop, Fuel and Rocket Troop.

The HQ Troop contained an HQ Section, a Signals Platoon for communications within the battery, a Survey Detachment, a Medical Section, a Weapons Maintenance Section, a Light MT Repair Platoon, a Supply Column for HW Supplies and a Battery Rations Section which dealt with accounts.

Moving down one level, there was the Schiessende Batterie, or Launching Troop - responsible for the preparation for action and launching og the rocket. With this sub-unit was the Gruppe Fuehrer, or HQ Section, consisting of a Troop Commander, usually a captain, and four ingenieur, or engineers, usually of lieutenant rank. These were specialists on various branches of the rocket: a Troop Engineer who understood the rocket and particularly the rocket motor, a Control Engineer who specialised in the steering unit, an Electrical and a Wireless Engineer.

The Rechen-und-Auswertetrupp, or Computing Section, made all the calculations connected with the line-of-fire and range. The Nachschub-und-Zuhehoerstaffel (The Rocket Supply and Accessories Column) was equipped with nine Meilerwagens for transporting the rockets, taking over the rockets and accessories from the Technical Troop at the unloading point and delivering them to the Launching Platoons. They also worked the compressor and provided fire services.

The Fernsprechbetriebstrupp und Leichte Fernsprechbautrupp (Telephone Section and Light Telephone Construction Section) were responsible for the layout and maintenance of all telephonic communications within the troop.

Then came the Tross, or Supply Column

ORGANISATION OF GERMAN LONG RANGE ROCKET LAUNCHING TROOP
APRIL 1945

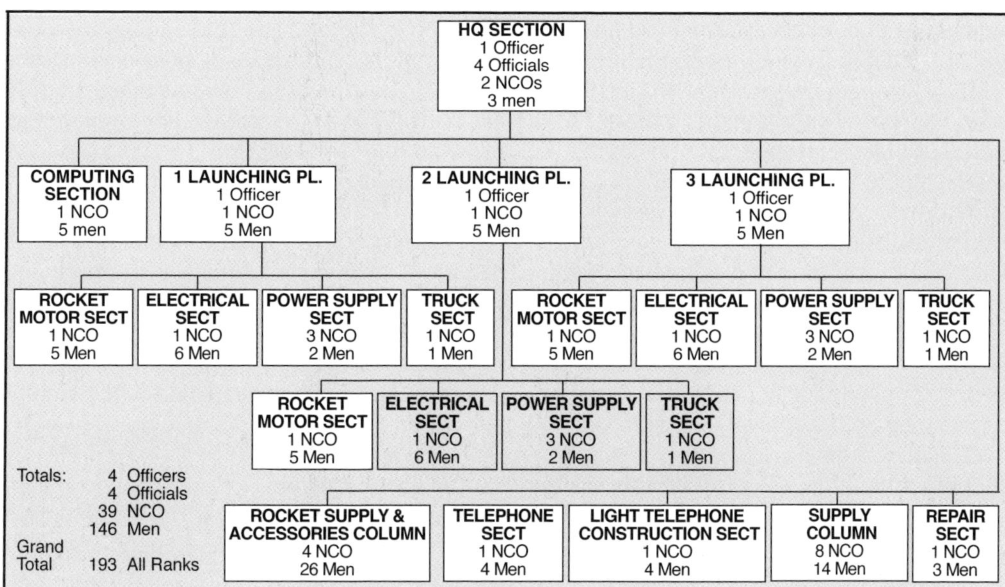

ORGANISATION OF GERMAN LONG RANGE ROCKET TECHNICAL TROOP APRIL 1945

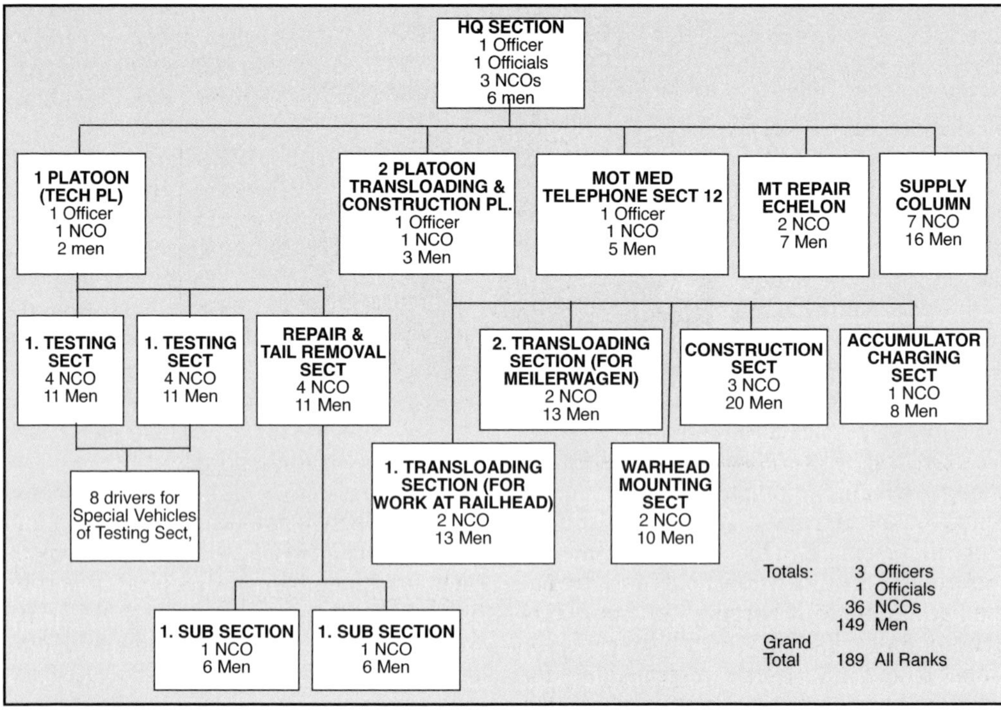

and the J Trupp (Repair Section). They were respectively responsible for non-technical supplies and minor repairs to equipment within the troop.

The next sub-unit was the Schiesszug or Launching Platoon. As normal, there was a Gruppe Fuehrer - HQ Section - with a Platoon Commander, usually of Lieutenant rank, the second-in-command was an NCO, with three layers, responsible for laying the rockets in the correct line of fire.

Within this group was the Triebwerkstrupp, or Rocket Motor Section. This group prepared and tested the rocket motor prior to launching. Then there was the Elektrotrupp and the Energieversorsungtrupp the Electrical and Power Suppy Section that were responsible for the electrical condition of elements in the control compartment and steering mechanism and the power supply to the rocket and Fire Control Vehicle via the external generator respectively. All of the Launching Platoon was supported by the Wagentrupp which operated the Meilerwagen and erected the missile on to the launch table.

The TechnischeBatterie (Technical Troop). Again, there was a Gruppe Fuehrer - HQ Section - with one hundred and eighty-eight staff. As normal, there was a Gruppe Fuehrer - HQ Section - with a Commander who was a techical expert, a second-in-command who was an engineer assisted by various clerks and draughtsmen.

The Mittl Fernsprechtrupp (MOT) which translated as Motorised Medium Telephone Section, was responsible for all telephone communications within the Technical Troop There was also a KFK-J-Staffel, MT Repair Echelon for vehicle repair and a Tross - Supply Section - responsible for the supply of rations, clothing and non-technical stores.

1 Zug, No.1 Platoon of the Technical Troop, had an officer in charge, a HQ Section, two Testing Sections and a Repair and Tail Removal Section.

The Prueftrupps, two identical testing sections were responsible for the testing of the rocket in the horizontal position.

The J-u Heckabzugtrupp - Repair and Tail Removal Section carried out minor repairs.

2 Zug, No. 2 Platoon of the Technical Troop, had an officer in charge, with two transloading sections - one for unloading the missile at the railhead, and the other for moving the rocket on the Vitalwagen (Testing Troop Trailer) and on to the Meilerwagen. A Spitzenmontsgetropp, (warhead loading section) then insalled the warhead before the rocket was sent to the transloading point and the Accumulator Charging Section. This platoon even had it's own Bautrupp, or Construction Section, responsible for building or modifying access roads to the launch point by the Techical and other troops.

Lieutenant-Colonel Wolfgang Weber, who commanded AVKO - Altenwalde VersuCha Kommando. *[Photo: NARA]*

As with all the other Troops, the Triebstoff-u-Gereat Batterie - Fuel and Rocket Troop - had it's own HQ Section, Repair Section, Supply column and three Platoons.

No.1 Platoon (A-Stoff) (Liquid Oxygen) was divided into three sections, Nos 1 and 2 each having five road trailers to transport oxygen from the railhead to the launch positions. the third section remained at the railhead for unloading and checking.

No.2 Platoon (B und T Stoff) (Alcohol and Hydrogen Peroxide) was divided into five sections. - Nos 1 and 2 with five tankers each, No.3 with four tankers for transporting from the railhead to the launch platforms. No.4 remained at the railhead for unloading anc checking while No.5 transported the hydrogen peroxide in three road tankers.

No.3 Platoon (Geraet) (Rocket Transport) had three sections, No.1 and 2 with eight

ORGANISATION OF GERMAN FUEL AND ROCKET TROOP APRIL 1945

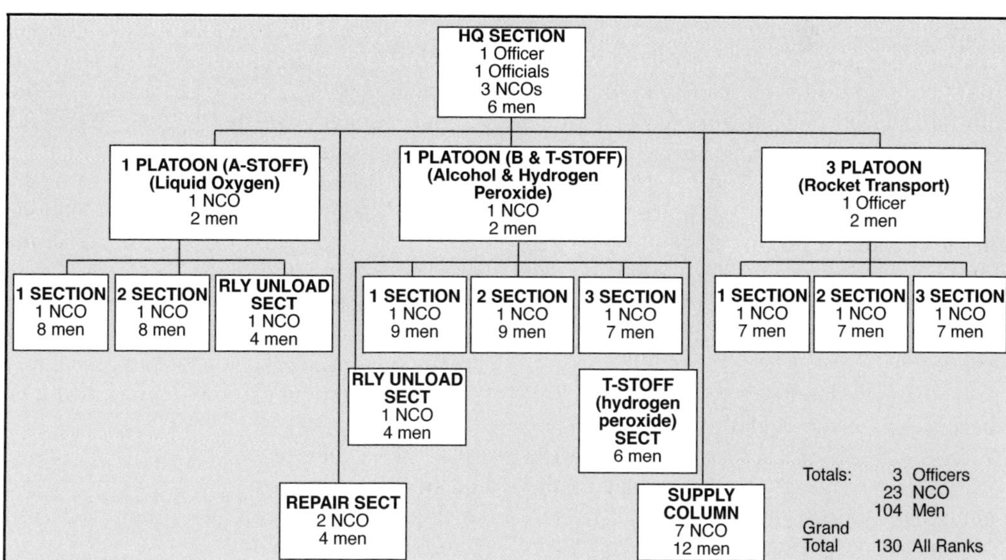

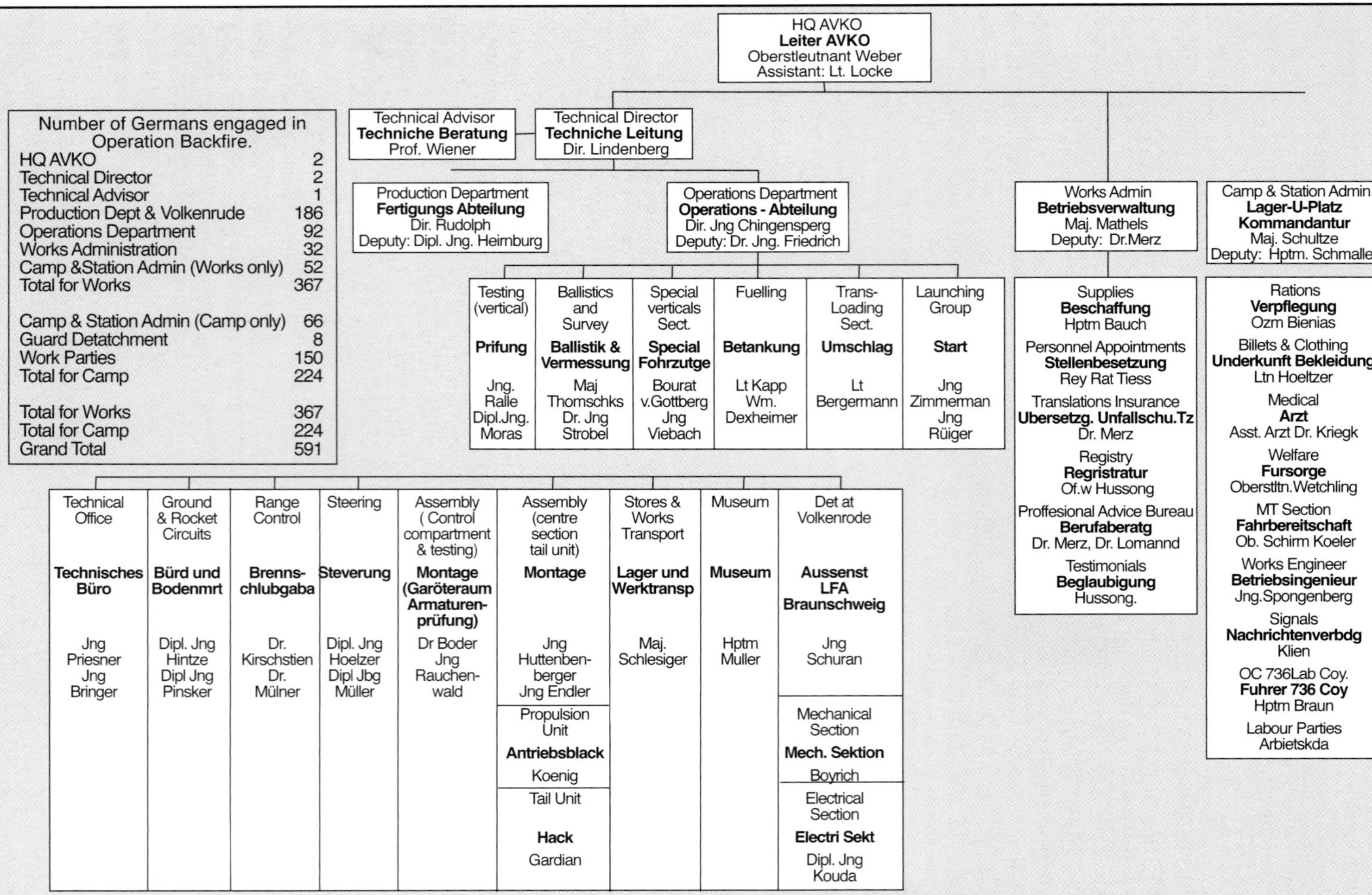

The German Organisation for Operation Backfire

Vitalwagens each that transported rockets from the railhead to the Technical Troop. No.3 Sectionm with two eight-ton lorries unloaded the warheads and Sodium Permanganate (Z-Stoff) at the railhead and transported them to the Technical Troop.

Handling the Germans - and Operation Paperclip.

It was realised from the beginning that the handling of the Germans would be a delicate matter. The problem was very different from standard interrogation. If the dificulties of building rockets were to be overcome, and the launching procedure learnt, active cooperation rather than passive obedience was essential. At the same time, there was uncertainty as to how far their apparent willingness to co-operate could be trusted. In the end it was decided to organise them into two parties; all soldiers and civilians required to work in the shops and launching unit were organised into a military unit under the command of the senior German officer, Lieutenant Colonel Wolfgang Weber, who had commanded an A-4/V-2 Regiment, and had previously been in command of the A-4 experimental battery. This unit was called AVKO - Altenwalde VersuChaKommando. The second party, comprising civilian experts, was kept in a separate camp in the village of Brockeswvalde for interrogation purposes. It was hoped by this means to ensure that information provided by one party could be cross-checked against information provided by the other party.

Lieutenant General Walter Dornberger had also been brought to Cuxhaven and he was kept separate from both parties as it was feared that his considerable influence might be embarrassing. After some weeks, no further use for him was found, and he was sent to England.

The British kept Dornberger on a short leash, away from the test firing and always under a watchful eye. The British had alternative plans for Walter Dornberger. They were not interested in the knowledge

An A-4/V-2 is moved into position by a half-track troop carrier. The picture is thought to have been taken at Peenemünde. *[Photo: NARA]*

A German team carefully remove an A-4/V-2 from its canvas camouflage cocoon.*[Photo: NARA]*

Dornberger possessed. They wanted to try him for war crimes based on his role in the indiscrimate rocket bombing of London and the surrounding area. He would not be returned to the Americans as the British had originally promised.

'The British pulled a sneaky on us,' explained Major Staver, who attended Operation Backfire. The Americans were not permitted to take Dornberger back after the operation; instead, Dornberger was declared 'on loan' and was taken to England. There, he and von Braun were interrogated for a week by the British and then kept behind barbed wire in Wimbledon for four and one-half weeks while waiting to be picked up by the Americans. Eventually, von Braun was returned but General Dornberger was not. Instead, he was issued a brown jumpsuit with the letters 'PW' for Prisoner of War stencilled on the back. Under armed guard, he was taken to the London District Cage for interrogation. From there, General Dornberger was transferred first to a castle in Wales and then to Special Camp XI in Island Farm, South Wales, where he was an

British and American scavenger groups were sometimes lucky in finding almost complete rockets...

extremely unpopular prisoner.

'Walter Dornberger was the most hated man in the camp,' Sergeant Ron Williams, a prison guard, recalled. *'Even his own people hated him. He never went out to the local farms to work like other prisoners.'* Wherever General Dornberger went while he was at Special Camp XI, he required an escort. The British feared that other prisoners pf war might kill him.

Along with some other German rocket scientists, Dornberger was released and taken to the United States under the auspices of Operation Paperclip and worked for the United States Air Force for three years, developing guided missiles.

Details of Operation Paperclip have become widely known in recent years. The media made much of a secret directive circulated on 3 September 1946, after President Truman officially approved Operation Paperclip and expanded it to include many German scientists under what was termed 'temporary, limited military custody'.

... and at others they were forced to rummage through the detritus of war.

A-4/V-2 missiles were usually transported by rail from the manufacturing centres to the launch areas - these became regular targets for ground-strafing Allied aircraft. *[Photos: NARA]*

With the collapse of the Third Reich, A-4/V-2 rocket trains were discovered abandoned in railway sidings all over Germany. *[Photo: NARA]*

This was a secret United States intelligence programme in which more than 1,600 German scientists, engineers, and technicians were taken from former Nazi Germany to the US for government employment after the end of World War Two in Europe, between 1945 and 1959; more than a few were confirmed to be former members of the Nazi Party, including the SS or the SA.

What is not so widely known is that Paperclip was an evolution of a number of other programmes to spirit away German scientists and technicians to the USA to exploit their knowledge and experience. As early as February 1945, SHAEF set up T-Force, or Special Sections Subdivision, which grew to over 2,000 personnel by June. T-Force examined 5,000 German targets, seeking expertise in synthetic rubber and oil catalysts, new designs in armoured equipment, A-4/V-2 rocket weapons, jet and rocket propelled aircraft, naval equipment, field radios, secret writing chemicals, aero

Some A-4/V-2 items were found damaged, others were untouched. *[Photo: NARA]*

medicine research, gliders, and 'scientific and industrial personalities'. When large numbers of German scientists began to be discovered by the advancing Allied forces in late April 1945, the Special Sections Subdivision set up the Enemy Personnel Exploitation Section to manage and interrogate them. The Enemy Personnel Exploitation Section established a detention centre, Camp Dustbin, first near Paris and later in Kransberg Castle outside Frankfurt. The US Joint Chiefs of Staff established the first secret recruitment programme called Operation Overcast, on 20 July, 1945, initially *'to assist in shortening the Japanese war and to aid our postwar military research'* The term 'Overcast' was the name first given by the German scientists' family members for the housing camp where they were held in Bavaria. In late summer 1945, the JCS established the Joint Intelligence Objectives Agency (JIOA), a subcommittee of the Joint Intelligence Community, to directly oversee Operation Overcast and later Operation Paperclip. The JIOA representatives included the army's director of intelligence, the chief of naval intelligence, the assistant chief of Air Staff-2 (Air Force Intelligence), and a representative from the State Department. In November 1945, Operation Overcast was renamed Operation Paperclip by Ordnance Corps officers.

To keep the Germans in a cooperative

Some of the A-4/V-2 missiles were discovered in more or less complete, undamaged condition. Others had received a lot of damage, leaving Allied soldiers to puzzle over what they had found. The soldier on the left is peering into the badly damaged control compartment of this missile. *[Photos: NARA]*

A-4/V-2 detritus scattered around the Krupps site at Cuxhaven. *[Photo: NARA]*

frame of mind, it was thought desirable to ameliorate their lot to some extent. Permission was therefore obtained to increase their pay and rations, and towards the end of the operation, a bonus, pro rota according to responsibility and technical efficiency.

As the new Chief of the Rocket Division in the Office of Research and Development Service of the Office of the Chief of Ordnance, Toftoy was responsible for deciding which team members to hire. It was essential to select people with the particular kinds of knowledge necessary to create an effective and self-sufficient team. With Wernher von Braun's invaluable assistance, Toftoy made his selections, and eventually over one hundred and twenty people accepted contracts. They were transported to the United States in groups, with von Braun and a handful of other top specialists arriving first. After making stops for debriefing in the eastern United States, the groups of specialists moved to Fort Bliss over the next several months. Their families were housed in Germany, and the Americans promised to keep them well-fed and comfortable.

These specialists had contracted to provide three services: to give information to Army, Navy, and Air Force contractors to save time in missile development; to assist with firing A-4/V-2s shipped from Germany; and to work on a new weapon, the Hermes II experimental missile. Concerned that the American people would not be sympathetic to hiring defeated enemies and providing them a home in the United States, the existence of the "Paperclip specialists" was kept secret, adding a layer of tension and intrigue to their situation. For many of them, an entirely new life was about to begin.

In August, a request was received from the USA for twenty-six civilians drawn from Garmisch Partenkirchen to be handed over to the US authorities, as they were urgently required for development work on weapons needed for use in the Japanese war. These twenty-six were all key personnel, and it was pointed out that their withdrawal would seriously prejudice the success of Operation Backfire. Eventually, the Japanese war having ended, fourteen were handed over, and the remaining twelve being handed over after the operation. Some replacements were necessary, and twenty-five technicians were obtained from Witzenhauseneschwege and incorporated into AVKO.

The status of the Germans employed varied at the start. Some were Prisoners of War, some were disarmed enemy personnel, and some were civilians. To put the matter on a proper footing and comply with international law, all the soldiers were converted into 'disarmed enemy personnel ', and all civilians were made into officials of the German Army.

In all, some six hundred Germans were employed, of whom not more than seventy were A-4 technicians from experimental establishments, and about one hundred and twenty-eight were troops of the A-4 Division. The remainder were troops and civilians who had had no previous connection with A-4.

Co-ordination of Effort

Even during the early stages, it was appreciated by Supreme Headquarters, Allied Expeditionary Force, that if such A-4 equipment as was available were allowed to be evacuated and shipped overseas haphazardly, the chance of obtaining sufficient material to carry through the operation would be indeed slender. Accordingly, on 4 May, orders were issued to all Allied formations, freezing the stocks of A-4 equipment in the European theatre until the question of allocation - with particular reference to Operation Backfire had been settled. This order was later confirmed by the Combined Chiefs of Staff.

Among the first enemy units to be withdrawn when threatened by the advancing Allied armies were the rocket-firing troops based in the Zwolle-Enschede area in northeast Holland and the Hachenburg Montabaur area northeast of Koblenz. These units made eastwards,

Original caption: 'German V-2 Rocket being shown by the US Navy in Washington, DC. This bomb measured 45 feet in length and was captured intact near Nordhausen, Germany. Rear Admiral Willard A. Kitts explains the details of the tail mechanism which controls the bomb while in flight. Photograph released July 10, 1945'.

evacuating their field equipment and most of their stores. As they retreated, they scattered, and as fuel supplies gave out and the chain of command broke down, their equipment was abandoned more or less where it stood at scattered points along the Western front. Destruction of the equipment by the rocket-firing troops had been carried out half-heartedly and haphazardly, but weather and looting combined to make up for the lack of thoroughness on the part of the troops. It soon became apparent that few complete and undamaged rockets were available, so arrangements were made to recover sufficient sub-assemblies and parts for all purposes.

Many technical reports, principally those published by the Royal Aircraft Establishment, Farnborough had appeared before May 1945, and the Air Defense Division was, so far as the actual rocket was concerned, in possession of accurate details regarding the electrical and mechanical components required, including the 'onboard' control equipment.

It was proposed that all types of control for range and line, which the Germans had employed, be used. On 20 May, a request was submitted to the G-2 Division (Technical Intelligence), Supreme Headquarters, Allied Expeditionary Force, to allocate parts for thirty complete rockets to represent all types of control. The matter did not rest with a formal demand having been submitted. Work was pushed ahead on collating all available information about the location of A-4 equipment and production centres.

Information for this purpose was obtained principally from reports by Allied armies, intelligence reports, and the interrogation of Prisoners of War.

From all the information thus

A-4/V-2 missiles were objects of curiosity to many soldiers. Here a partial rocket is discovered on a railway waggon is uncovered for inspection. *[Photos: NARA]*

Numerous specialist vehicles in various states of damage were taken to the Krupps site at Cuxhaven. Here a Feuerleitpanzer - fire control vehicle - awaits being pressed into service. *[Photo: NARA]*

available, it soon became clear that there were four main sources of supply:

1 The vast underground factory and assembly centre Mittelwerk at Niedersachswerfen near Nordhausen.
2 12th U.S. Army Group Area .
3 21 Army Group Area.
Both of these were dumps of A-4 and associated ground equipment.
4 The various factories throughout Germany had been engaged in A-4 production in one way or another.

About the middle of May, it was decided to exploit the first three sources as rapidly as possible because Nordhausen was destined to come under Russian control shortly, and the equipment abandoned in the Army Group areas was deteriorating daily and was constantly liable to be removed by other interested parties. The vast underground assembly plant at Nordhausen had been exploited initially by United States Ordnance Officers. They reported at the end of May that they had recovered sufficient A-4 parts and sub-assemblies to construct the one hundred rockets required for the United States and that sufficient equipment remained for the thirty rockets necessary for Operation Backfire and the one hundred and twenty rockets required by the Air Ministry. Air Defense Division, therefore, undertook the recovery of this equipment. The evacuation from Nordhausen began on 3 June, and was completed on the 20 June, despite very considerable difiiculties. The underground tunnels and bays at Nordhausen cover approximately eighteen miles, and the whole of this vast assembly plant was combed for the equipment required. Fortunately, electric power was still laid on to the factory, and the overhead cranes were working. Use was made of the detailed knowledge possessed by the German personnel who had worked in the factory and were still living in the district. It was discovered that there were few complete sub-assemblies available. Therefore, it was necessary to recover those component parts required for building the control

Sometimes the rockets had not been packed to manufacturers specification for shipment.*[Photo: NARA]*

compartment, the centre section, the steam unit, the thrust unit, and the tail unit of the rocket. In addition, specific jigs, tools, and other machinery required for assembling the various rocket sections were recovered, and some six hundred and forty tons of equipment were removed from the factory at Nordhausen and put on rail cars for delivery at Cuxhaven. In all five trainloads left Nordhausen, two were despatched from Kassel and two from Gottingen. The absence of complete sub-assemblies at Nordhausen meant that considerably more time would be required for the construction of rockets than had been planned. This was particularly true of the tail units, the assembly of which required special jigs and tools which it was impossible to recover from Nordhausen. Accordingly, six of the tail unit sub-assemblies, previously retrieved by the United States Army Ordnance Department, were requested for Operation Backfire. Before authority could be obtained for their release, they were loaded for rapid shipment to the United States. Fortunately, the authority arrived before the ship sailed, and unloading began. The units eventually arrived at Cuxhaven and were used.

On 25 May, it was arranged that a search party, consisting of British and United States officers, should begin the search in the US Army Group area. On arrival at Headquarters, 12th US Army Group, the party was told that the area had already been thoroughly combed. The matter was referred to Ordnance, Headquarters US Forces European Theatre, who agreed with the view expressed by 12th Army Group and stated that the equipment recovered in that area to date was not merely for US projects but would also be made available to other bidders. In the face of this it was decided to withdraw the party from this Army Group and to push forward the search elsewhere.

As soon as the search party returned from 12th U.S. Army Group, a second was organised and left for the 21st Army Group area on 31 May. The party covered a large part of Northern Germany. It returned to base on 10 June, having uncovered a considerable quantity of rocket equipment abandoned by German operational units, including eighteen incomplete rockets which were located on rail at Jerxheim and various bits and pieces such as valves, pipes, batteries, fuses and electrical components.

By the beginning of August, all the rocket equipment involved had been received at Cuxhaven. On 21 August, a further consignment of twelve rockets arrived from Leese and Duren; these had also been found by the above-mentioned search party and included the best specimen ever recovered. Their unloading was delayed by the fact that they were found to have the original demolition charges in position.

Rocket components in sufficient quantity were fairly readily available for the operation, with one crucial exception, control equipment. As far back as 27 May, all interested parties reported that there was an acute shortage of all types of control equipment. Not only were the control compartments of recovered rockets almost always completely gutted but few parts of the ground installations necessary for radio control were ever found. Nordhausen itself, home of the A-4/V-2 rocket, yielded little or nothing in this direction. A considerable amount of information had been obtained from Prisoners of War as to sources of supply of this equipment. Still, the Germans themselves stated that certain items of control gear had been in very short supply even when rocket operations were at their height. The information available was immediately converted into briefs for search parties. Since the operation began, all the search parties sent out had the location and recovery of control equipment as the whole or part of their task. Reports from these parties were disappointing. Many of the sources reported by the Germans, apparently in good faith, were unproductive for various reasons. Factories had suffered from bombing, shortage of materials before the final collapse, and so on; control equipment on the rocket itself had been the first target for destruction by the rocket troops.

By the beginning of July, it was realised

The collection of A-4/V-2 missiles at Cuxhaven meant that components were scattered everywhere, including what appears to be parts of at least one V-1 Flying Bomb. . *[Photos: NARA]*

that it would not be possible to use all the different methods of control that the Germans used and that efforts would have to be concentrated on obtaining sufficicnt equipment to ensure that the rocket was put on to its trajectory, and fuel cut-off obtained, by means of the Zeitschaltwerk or time switch, ordinarily used as an overriding control should the normal method Funkbrennschluss, or I-Gerat, fail.

There were three main difficulties even in this. Some one hundred and sixty rocket gyros had been recovered from Kiel by the search party operating there from the 1 to 7 July, but these were all Vertikant (vertical); only two or three Horizont (horizontal) had been discovered. The batteries required were of unusual construction, and the specimens left in abandoned rockets or buried in the ground had been ruined by exposure. Third, only twenty Control Amplifiers - Mischgerat - in various states of repair had been recovered in the course of the search for control equipment; all needed thorough tests and a large number of the necessary radio valves were missing. 'his situation gave rise

A British soldier inspects a pair of fuel tanks sitting in a half-casing, while an officer looks on. The other half of the casing, complete with insualation material is inverted to the right. Note the fin casings sitting vertically on the right of the picture. *[Photo: NARA]*

to a considerable amount of anxiety, and it was realised that herein lay a severely limiting factor. Eventually, it was decided to assemble only eight rockets, sufficient elementary control equipment being available to make this number fit for firing.

Before the task of recovering the necessary ground equipment could begin, detailed information was essential as to precisely what was required. This information was primarily obtained by interrogation of Prisoners of War. It will be appreciated that prior to the surrender, intelligence on this matter fell far short of what was known about the construction of the rocket itself. By 19 May, interrogation had been completed, and a list was drawn up of those items of ground equipment required. The amount of equipment to be recovered was formidable, including, as it did, control cars, oxygen, alcohol, and hydrogen-peroxide tankers, firing platforms, transport and erection vehicles, testing vehicles, generators, cranes, ladders, air compressors and other ancillary equipment such as cables, connecting plugs, hoses and igniters.

The search party, which operated in the 21 Army Group area from 31 May to 10 June, uncovered considerable quantities of ground equipment. Their targets were based on information provided by Prisoners of War. Often hundreds of miles were covered, only to find that the equipment had been effectively destroyed; on more than one occasion, targets proved to be just within the Russian area, and the party had to return empty-handed from such expeditions. Despite innumerable setbacks, most of the items were, in fact, uncovered but seldom in serviceable condition. The area most productive of equipment was that around Celle and Falling Bostel; it was to this locality that most of the equipment used by the units operating from The Hague and Enschede had been evacuated. As each item of equipment was located, it was tagged and complete lists were sent in to T-Force, 21 Army Group, who undertook the task of recovery and transportation to Cuxhaven.

The area around Nordhausen also produced many items of ground equipment. The Germans used this region as a

The fin assembly of an A-4/V-2 sitting on a transportation trolley, with the end of a rocket motor on a similar trolley of the the left. The light-coloured 'rectangles' on the fin unit are thought to be identification/ explanation tags. *[Photo: NARA]*

concentration area for A-4 equipment and, incidentally, for personnel withdrawn from Peenemünde and operational firing sites. The area was therefore thoroughly combed by search parties and, despite the fact that large quantities of the equipment had been thoroughly destroyed, a number of serviceable items were obtained before the area was handed over to the Russians.

It is, perhaps, worthy of note that, although many of the firing sites used by the Germans were visited by search parties, not one item of ground equipment had been recovered from these sites.

In July, many items of ground equipment were still outstanding. Accordingly, further interrogation of Prisoners of War was carried out with the object of establishing additional sources of supply. Prisoners of War who had buried equipment, or otherwise hidden it, accompanied search parties, whose operations at this stage ranged from Leiden, in Holland, to Uelzen in Germany, and from Heide, in Schleswig-Holstein to Hannau near Frankfurt en Main. Often excavation was carried out, and, in one instance, dredging proved to be necessary.

By the middle of September, all the ground equipment necessary for the operation had been assembled at Cuxhaven. Unfortunately, much of the equipment arrived in an unserviceable condition, but all essential items were repaired by the German staff or the Corps of Royal Electrical and Mechanical Engineers (REME), who were forced to cannibalise extensively.

Chapter Three

The Technical Challenges

The Allies were already well aware that with the A-4/V-2 it was not simply a matter of lighting the blue touch-paper and standing well clear. They already knew that the missile was both highly complex and highly dangerous. The Americans had already shown signs that they wanted all the technology for themselves with the attiude and actions of Major General Holger Nelson Toftoy in spiriting as many men and materiel as he could back to the good 'ole USA as soon as he possibly could.

The British on the other hand appeared to be interested in doing the same thing - gathering together as much documentation and equipment as they could, but with one major difference - they did it in Germany, close to the original manufacturing facilities, builders and development engineers. Not only did the British set about gathering together everything, they also set about translating all the original specifications and engineering drawings so as to understand exactly what had been designed and built. They then planned on launching a number of missiles learning from those previously directly involved.

It did not take the Backfire team long to realise that while the research and theorical work and processes were well recorded, the operational side - specifically the use of the mobile launchers - was not that well documented. They set out to rectify this.

We now need to consider in detail what had been located for use.

Engineer Tools and Stores

The rockets and the parts recovered varied enormously in their state of repair; the work of stripping, examination and reconditioning was an unexplored field, and one of the main drawbacks encountered was that it was never possible to say precisely what was required in the way of tools, plant and materials. Every day, some new difficulties and new requirements were produced for the materials to overcome. The German personnel also complicated the problem. The demand for every kind of tool and engineering store was enormous. It was only due to painstaking checking and investigation that a marked weakness of the German personnel was discovered. They were unwilling, in the extreme, to indulge in any form of improvisation. They were very often unaware of the destruction which had overtaken the German-producing centres as a result of the war. Consequently, each day made new and lengthy demands and glib references to sources of supply that no longer existed. Nevertheless, a great need did exist for machine and hand tools and practically every form of workshop requisite due to the incredible amount of repair and construction work that had to be undertaken. The problem was to meet these requirements in the shortest possible time so that vital work would not be held up.

Many of the tools and stores were standard British Ordnance supply, but the majority were, naturally, in metric sizes. Some of the tools were specially manufactured, and only one or two firms in Germany were known to have made them. Even for those requirements that could probably be met from British Army sources, another factor- time - was entered into the calculations, and the expected time lag involved in the provision of stores through Ordnance channels could not be accepted.

The answer was not far to seek but considerably more challenging to put into practice. Search parties could be organised to scour all the big German industrial and manufacturing towns, clumps of captured material, airfields, and the like, with the task of locating and recovering the tools so urgently wanted. Thus, a time lag of several weeks in the normal Ordnance channels could be reduced to days. First of all, the difficulty of requisitioning had to be overcome. The standard drill required approval of Corps Headquarters on each occasion - regardless of the time involved in that process. So far as Operation Backfire was concerned, that procedure involved too much delay, and therefore, on 30 July, permission was obtained to carry out requisitioning throughout the 21 Army Group area of technical equipment needed for Operation Backfire without prior reference to Corps Headquarters.

Once freedom of action had been obtained, no time was lost. During August, twelve search parties, with German guides, interpreters and transport, were sent out to Dannenberg, Celle/Hanover, Brunswick, Alfeld/Wennigsen, Blankenburg/Goslar, Gottingen, Hamburg, Kiel/Lubeck and Munster/Ruhr.

By the end of the second week in August, a very fair measure of success had been obtained, and about seventy per cent of the requirements were met in twelve days. It was found that electrical measuring instruments were the stores most diflicult to obtain, and comparatively few of these were ever found. However, suficient material was recovered to enable the work of repair and minor manufacture to continue unhindered.

Up to this time, the demand had been almost entirely for standard tools, electrical components, welding and soldering materials, glassware, insulation materials, cable, hot air blowers, technical books, mathematical tables and optical instruments,

An A-4/V-2 is seen partially erected on its launching table at the Krupps site at Cuxhaven. *[Photo: NARA]*

all of a standard nature, and therefore collection could be allocated to Search parties as described above. Towards the end of the month, however, demands were received for more basic materials such as steel, brass, and copper in sheet, bar, and strip form, as well as a wide variety of lubricating media. This introduced a further complication, as the materials were known to be in short supply in Germany, and the military Government were controlling their issue with certain essential services. Headquarters, 21 Army Group and the Ministry of Aircraft Production came to the rescue. The former gave a blanket authority to visit the concerned main Service Depots and obtain whatever was required. The latter permitted the taking of stores from the Hermann Goering Aeronautical Research Institute at Volkenrode, near Brunswick. This Institute provided a vast amount of the raw materials required.

Organising and running the Search parties was almost a major operation in itself and was in the hands of Colonel W S J Carter. Every machine and hand tool, from a power-driven lathe to an electrician's screwdriver, was supplied in six weeks. Officers had to be instructed in the technical and administrative details necessary for running a Search party; most of the personnel involved in the task of procuring the tools and materials required were untrained in the engineering sense, and the task for them was, therefore, much more complex than might be supposed. Transport had to be supplied, often at short notice, and all the necessary arrangements made for German personnel to accompany the parties, without, if possible, removing key men from work in hand. Since the beginning of June, up to the end of the operation, Special Projectile Operations Group Search parties have employed over two hundred men working for nearly 200,000 man-hours, using one hundred vehicles and over four hundred rail waggons. These search parties covered roughly half a million miles, operating throughout the length and breadth of Germany and many other European countries.

Fuel

The A-4 rocket was propelled by a bi-fuel propulsion unit using liquid oxygen, called A-Stoff and ethyl-alcohol, known as B-Stoff. The main fuel pumps were powered by a turbine driven by steam generated in an auxiliary power unit employing hydrogen peroxide termed T-Stoff and sodium permanganate, known as Z-Stoff. The supply, transportation, and handling of these fuels presented many problems.

When stored, liquid oxygen suffered heavy evaporation losses, and transportation facilities were limited. It was, therefore, necessary to find a production source not too distant from Cuxhaven. Unfortunately, no suitable plants were in operation, and eventually, it was decided to open up the plant at Fassburg, one hundred and thirty miles from Cuxhaven.

Allowing for evaporation losses, producing at least six tons of liquid oxygen for every rocket launched was necessary. The Fassburg plant had an estimated maximum production of two tons per day and a storage tank which would hold fifty-six tons; the plant had been idle since the spring but was put to work again on 7 August, solely for Operation Backfire. Unfortunately, production was far below the estimated maximum due to electricity supply failures. It became necessary to install a special generating plant and draw thirteen tons from another liquid oxygen plant at Brunswick to meet requirements.

The Germans transported liquid oxygen over long distances in thirty-ton rail tank cars and used the six-and-a-half-ton A-4 road tankers for distribution from railhead over short distances of not more than fifteen miles. It was not practicable to use rail tank cars in Operation Backfire; therefore, the A-4 road tankers drew directly from Fassburg. The jolting over bad roads on the long journey failed the brass bellows piece leading to the bottom outlet valve, and two fuel loads of thirteen tons were lost through leakage. Subsequent interrogation revealed that these bottom connections had been a constant source of trouble for the Germans.

The fact that this valve was always covered with ice indicates that it was added to the design without fully realising the handicap involved. Two five-ton commercial tankers, without bottom outlet valves, were then used For the journey from Fassburg to Krupps, where the oxygen was transferred to A-4 road tankers for transport to the firing site. Losses from evaporation were about one-third of a ton per tanker during the journey from Fassburg and about the same amount each day whilst just standing in road tankers. The time required for filling or emptying two five-ton tankers was slightly under one hour. On more than one occasion, the round trip to Fassburg and back, including filling, was completed in fourteen hours. Complete sets of asbestos clothing were provided for the Germans fuelling the rocket, but they only wore the gloves. Two liquid oxygen pumps were used and gave no trouble except during a preliminary fuelling trial when one of them froze up. The pump had been left exposed to rain the previous night, and moisture in the pump froze, locking the impeller against the rotation. The pump body was later discovered to include a drain plug to free water accumulations.

Five twenty-ton rail tank cars containing

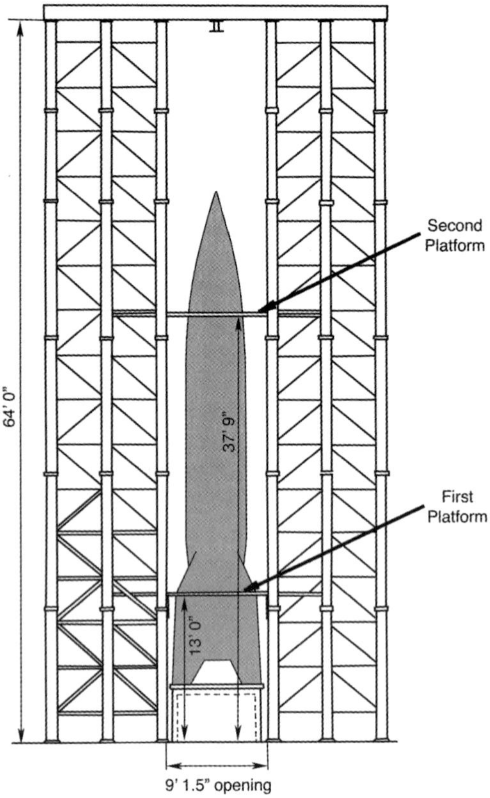

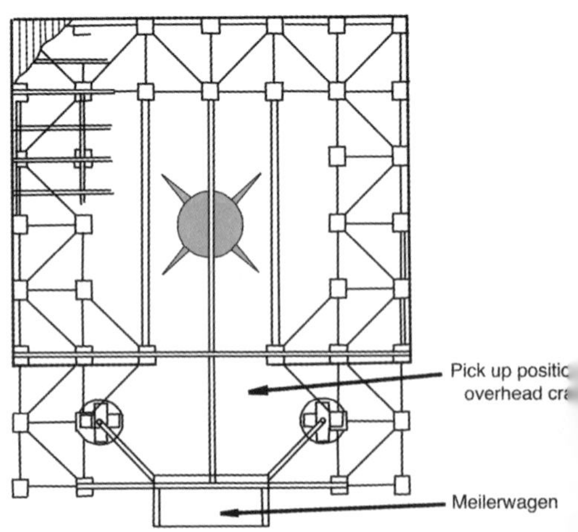

A newly-assembled A-4/V-2 sits on a Meilerwagen outside the vertical test tower at Cuxhaven. The propulsion unit assembly, including the fins are still shrouded by tarpaulins. *[Photo: NARA]*

An A-4V-2 inside the vertical test tower at Cuxhaven.

Allied personnel can be seen posing for the camera on the upper platform level that give the photograph scale.

An A-4/V-2 on a Meilerwagen is prepared to be erected inside the vertivcal test tower at Cuxhaven
[Photos: NARA]

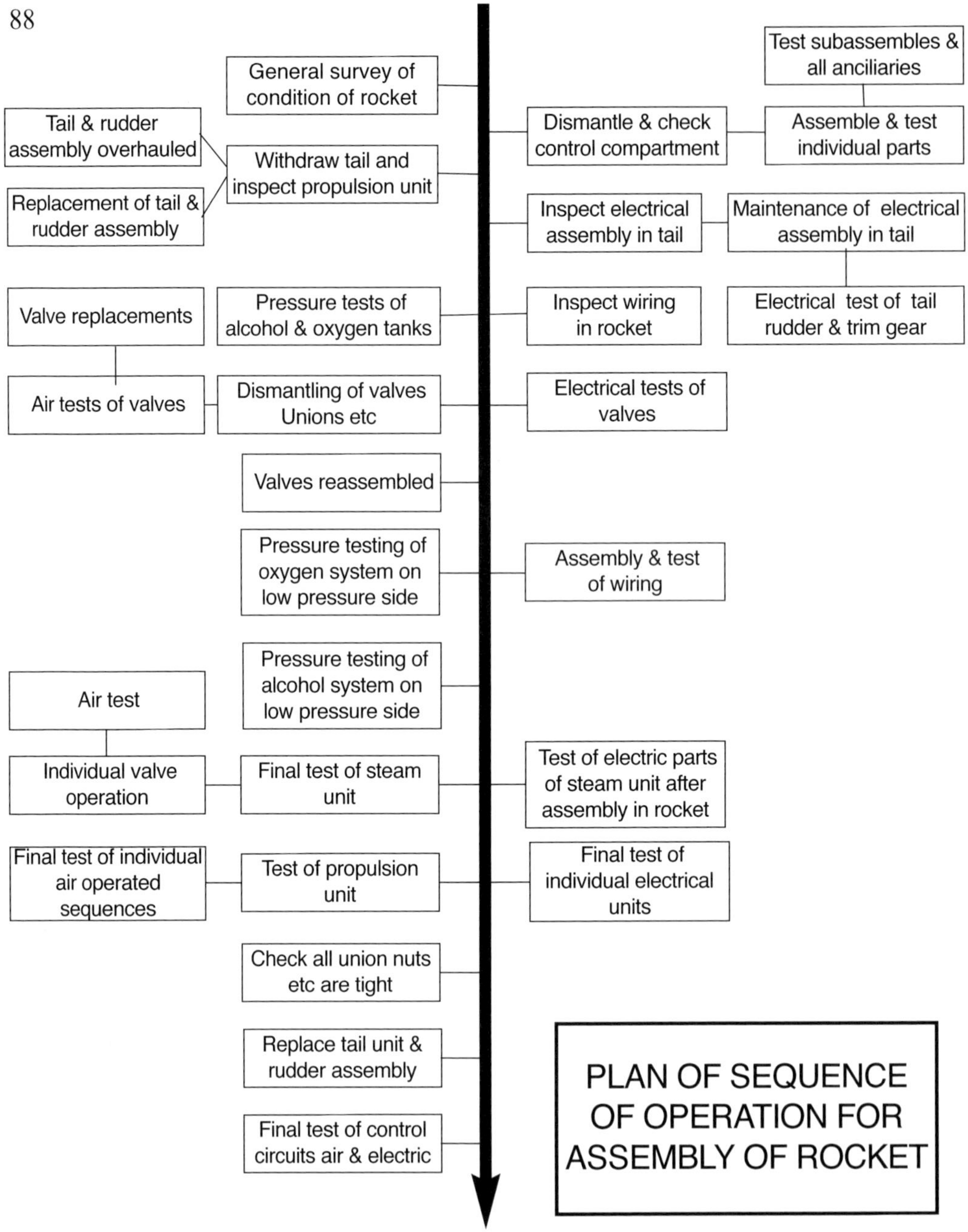

seventy tons of ethyl alcohol were found in the Nordhausen area and despatched to Cuxhaven, where the fuel was transferred to A-4 road tankers.

Analysis revealed that the alcohol was initially at ninety-three per cent concentration. It was diluted by adding about ten per cent distilled water, and the pump was used to stir the liquid by circulating it back to the top of the tank. One launching required four tons of alcohol.

Except against fire, no precautions were necessary when handling alcohol, but measures had to be taken to prevent stealing the fuel for purposes other than rocket propulsion.

At the firing site on 1 October, a considerable leak occurred on the delivery side of the alcohol pump, although the pump had previously given good service. The Germans found no objection to continuing to use the petrol engine of the pump with the surrounding concrete flooded with alcohol, nor later did they show any hesitation in starting up the second petrol engine of the liquid oxygen pump.

They did, however, delay handling the hydrogen peroxide, where spillage might have fallen on the alcohol. When alcohol pumping had been completed, the fire party washed over the concrete before the handling of the hydrogen peroxide began. At all times during fuelling, the Army Fire Service was in attendance.

Hydrogen peroxide was obtained from the Walterwerke at Kiel, which the Royal Navy had taken over. It was transported to Cuxhaven in an A-4 hydrogen-peroxide road tanker, also made available by the Royal Navy. The factory-grade material was diluted with distilled water. Stirring was affected by using the pump to circulate the liquid back to the top of the tank.

The men employed in hydrogen peroxide fuelling wore chemical rubberwear clothing comprising Wellington boots, aprons, and gloves. A hand pump is preferred to a motor pump when fuelling as there is then no splashing of the liquid. Liberal water supplies were always available for flushing the hoses, measuring the tank on the Meilerwagen, and diluting any liquid spill.

Sodium permanganate was only used in tiny quantities, and search parties recovered enough from the Nordhausen area. No special precautions were necessary for

A4/V-2 sub-assemblies are seen inside the Marston shed at the Krupps site at Cuxhaven. *[Photo: NARA]*

This, and the previous image shows how the Marston building was laid out with specific work areas. *[Photo: NARA]*

handling this fuel. Before pouring into the rocket, the permanganate was heated, and failure to have it at the correct temperature caused a delay in firing on one occasion.

On-Site Facilities

As already stated, the site chosen for the assembling and testing of the rockets was the Krupps Naval Gun Testing Ground at Altenwalde, Cuxhaven. Certain facilities already existed on the site, including good store buildings, a reasonable carpenter's shop, and a very inadequate and out-of-date machine shop. The first problem was the provision of the extra shops required.

A Marston shed was erected to serve as the leading assembly shop. It was fitted with a ten-ton overhead travelling crane to handle completed rockets and heavy -assemblies. Two sets of rails, six hundred millimetres apart, were installed to carry the assembly bogies, with a seven-inch plate pillar drill, lathe, bench drill and two tool post grinders.

Benches, Assembly Platforms and Steps, etc., were made in the woodworking shop. A small platform was erected on the end of the assembly line for the electrical test gear. To cater for the cleaning of pipes, etc., a water tank and a small acid tank were provided. Three sets of gas welding equipment were installed to repair tanks and other assemblies. Men engaged in the handling of glass wool were provided with gauntlet gloves, protective suits and respirators. A twenty-seven-volt supply and a four-stage 230-atmosphere air compressor were installed for test purposes.

A Vertical Testing Chamber was erected to conduct the necessary tests with the rocket in the vertical position. It was provided with a five-ton overhead travelling crane to lift the rocket off the Meilerwagen and carry it vertically into the Chamber. The design caused some trouble owing to the large area exposed to wind whilst resting on a relatively small base.

An existing building was allocated as a Sub-assembly Shop for control gear. It was fitted out with benches equipped with vices, a bench drill, a pillar drill, and a small fitters' lathe. Two main test benches were installed with reducing valves, three-way cocks, batteries and air reservoirs. Compressed air lines were run from the compressor house, and a small outside test shed, approximately six feet square, was built for steam unit tests, vision being obtained through an armoured glass slit in the Sub-assembly Shop. Reducing valves, air reservoir and the necessary copper piping were installed, and an electric control panel with steam units under test could be remotely controlled.

A shop was set up to repair towing vehicles, special vehicles used for rockets, firing platforms, pumps and trailers. The shop was equipped with a portable forge, power saw, one twelve-inch and one seven-inch screw-cutting lathe, pillar drill, a twenty-one-inch shaper, two gas welding plants and two 350 kw electric welding plants, three benches and a bench drill. One portable gantry-type crane was also available.

Concurrently with the preparation of shops, supplies of rocket parts and tools were continually arriving by road and rail. Much work was required to sort, clean, list, and store these.

A programme of work was drawn up which aimed at having the first rocket assembled and tested ready for firing by the middle of September. The first aim was to take one of the damaged rockets, overhaul it and replace as the missing or defective parts from stock. This missile was used as a museum specimen and teaching aid. To obtain a view of the rocket's interior, appropriate outer shell sections were cut away.

The Museum was also equipped with sub-assemblies, individual parts, and drawings to serve as exhibits for visitors and familiarise the British technical staff with the functioning and details of various rocket components. This work was carried out when the Assembly Sheds were completed.

The next rocket was assembled from new but untested parts from the store to satisfy British and German technicians that all the necessary parts were available on the site and

Four A-4/V-2s on their railcars at Cuxhaven, along with a lifting crane. Many of the rockets were damaged or incomplete. *[Photo: NARA]*

Building 15 at Cuxhaven, which contained the A-4/V-2 Museum. *[Photo: NARA]*

to practise the German personnel in the assembly technique.

Examination of the damaged rockets showed that few would provide anything to match the components that were fit for use. Some had come from railway trains that had been set on fire; automatic weapons or explosive charges had deliberately sabotaged some; others had been stripped of essential parts. All had suffered from corrosion and exposure to the weather. Nevertheless, the least damaged were picked out for rebuilding, and valuable parts were removed from others.

The Germans had made little or no attempt to cater for long-term storage. Where grease had been introduced for this purpose, it was of poor quality and useless. Even valves stamped by inspection authorities as serviceable and still in their cardboard cartons showed signs of deterioration and rust. All components had, therefore to be subjected to tests, and test rigs had to be designed. Building and equipping a suitable precision workshop at Krupp's was impracticable to manufacture this testing gear. Arrangements were made for an AVKO party to be attached to the Ministry of Aircraft Production establishment at Volkenroode, where excellent workshop facilities and adequate electrical laboratory accommodation were available.

A further difficulty in using miscellaneous assemblies and components gradually became apparent. It slowly became clear that the Germans had used a system of selective assembly, which allowed the matching of calibrated results, thereby reducing the number of rejects. In the main, this procedure rendered the substitution of one part for another impossible unless the characteristic performance of that part had been adjusted to suit its new working conditions. No technical data had been found, and no information was available regarding the tolerances of this selective assembly. It was, therefore, decided to arrive at mean values by interrogation and, so far as possible, to select combustion chambers and pumps to conform to these mean values.

The German technicians went out of their way to stress the dangers due to rust in the venturi. This component combines the nozzles, combustion space, and venturi tube and is a complete all-welded steel fabricated structure with two, and in some places, three skins. It was impossible to extract the small nozzles for cleaning, and eliminating rust from inside the various components appeared almost impossible. In the nozzles were over three thousand minute apertures, all liable to become blocked by rust. According to the Germans, this might result in an incorrect fuel mixture, and so cause the rocket to topple over when fired. To deal with this problem, various rust eliminators were obtained from the UK, and the Army Fire Service pumped water under high pressure through every venturi.

The Germans were also pessimistic about the state of the aluminium fuel tanks and pipes. Their manufacturers had made no efforts to protect their welds as the life of the parts was assumed to be short, and the Germans had experienced failures due to weld decay. Many welds in the available tanks showed distinct signs of weakening, and all parts had a much longer life than any previously used. The only solution was to select the aluminium parts that appeared serviceable, subject them to air pressure tests, and hope for the best. This solution worked.

These were some of the significant problems. By the second week in August, the prospects appeared excessively gloomy. Then, on 21 August, twelve rockets were consigned to Cuxhaven. Amongst them were an almost perfect specimen and several others in reasonable condition. From that date, the assembly never looked back. Using the mean values for tolerances, it was possible to find a sufficiency of matched components. Every part was examined, and those defective were replaced; every sub-assembly was tested, and a month later, the first rocket passed out of the Assembly Shop.

Electrical Assembly

The electrical system of the rockets built for Operation Backfire was designed to be as simple as possible. No radio control was fitted as no radio ground equipment was available. The electrical system's primary

Building 19 at Cuxhaven. This has no purpose or user identified, although one dual language sign states 'No Entry Unless On Duty'! *[Photo: NARA]*

function controlled the rocket in flight, and the subsidiary functions included managing fuel valves and initiating fuel cut-off. With the sole exception of a circuit diagram of the control amplifier, no circuit or wiring diagrams were available. These had to be reconstructed either from memory or examination of parts that were considered to be complete. Eventually, a full set were made, traced, checked and issued.

A complete control system working model was made and installed at Krupps for initial investigations and demonstration purposes. This model comprised a control compartment arranged on a special mounting permitting three degrees of freedom; a skeleton tail unit was equipped with servos, trim motors, vanes, etc., to demonstrate their operation; and a control desk to enable items of control apparatus to be operated and tested. The model could also be free of the control desk but under the control of the gyroscopes so that electrical signals could transmit any desired movement of the control compartment via the control amplifier to the vanes on the tail unit.

A good supply of miscellaneous rocket cables and cable forms was obtained and sorted as far as possible into complete sets. Where sets were incomplete, the missing cable forms were made using wire obtained by stripping surplus cable forms or wire obtained from the United Kingdom. Great importance was attached to the construction of these cable forms. They connected the electrical apparatus in the rocket's tail with the control apparatus mounted in the control compartment. Any failure or low insulation in these cable forms would have failed the rocket in flight; consequently, they were tested for sound construction, continuity and insulation resistance.

There are two types of distribution panels in each rocket, the larger carrying all the wires from the control compartment in the nose of the missile, including the leads which come to ground test equipment via special throw-off plugs and sockets, and some relays which are arranged to connect the control apparatus inside the rocket to the ground test

A-4 oxygen tanks in store at Mittelwerk, ready for final assembly. *[Photo: NARA]*

Building 13 at Cuxhaven under Operation Backfire. On the left are A-4/V-2 alcohol tanks, while in the foreground on the right are warhead containers. *[Photo: NARA]*

equipment. The smaller one is an intermediate distribution panel located approximately at the centre of the missile for convenience of manufacture and carried the connections to the steering mechanisms in the tail. These panels were received in fair condition and carefully examined for broken plugs, sockets, relays and bad connections. The faulty parts were replaced and all relays were readjusted. In some cases, the distribution panels had to be completely rewired.

Two gyroscopes were fitted to each rocket, one (vertical) to control the roll and yaw, and the other (horizontal) to control the rocket's pitch when in flight. A large number of vertical gyroscopes were obtained, but few horizontals. The vertical gyroscopes were examined mechanically and tested electrically, and the best were selected for use. The horizontal gyroscopes were made by dismantling the vertical types and rebuilding them. The control potentiometers were modified, and small programme motors were fitted to initiate the turning of the rocket in flight from the vertical onto a forty-seven-degree trajectory. The programme motors had been exposed to severe weather and badly corroded. They were completely dismantled, cleaned and re-assembled, and mounted on the gyro-plates. The horizontal gyroscopes thus produced were then thoroughly tested since the rocket's successful flight depends on this component's correct functioning.

A small number of control amplifiers - Mischgerat - were obtained but were practically all damaged. This amplifier, which comprises five independent panels mounted on a common base plate, accepts the signals given by the gyroscopes and translates them into signals recognised by the servo mechanisms controlling the steering vanes. It is a complicated apparatus with many small parts built into a compact assembly. A survey was made of all the amplifiers, and a programme was laid down to rebuild as many complete amplifiers as possible using damaged ones. By this means it was possible to make nine complete amplifiers. Without detailed testing information, it became necessary to investigate the performance of the best amplifiers and adjust the remade amplifiers to the mean values thus obtained. The supply of thermionic valves for these amplifiers was complex, mainly because they had to be matched in pairs, with two pairs to each amplifier. Reconstructing these units was highly skilled and required special test instruments. Later, a further supply of damaged control amplifiers was obtained from Paris.

Time - or sequence - switches were obtained in good condition. They consisted of a camshaft operating several electrical contacts driven through gears from a small electric motor. There was, in addition, a small vibrator unit mounted inside the case, which had nothing to do with the time switch but was used to generate an interrupted current that drove the programme motor in the horizontal gyro. The cam-operated contacts were used to time the sequence of operations during flight. The cams must, therefore, be accurately set, and the timing of the contacts must be carefully checked. The bakelite moulding on which the vibrator was mounted had warped and upset the small contact clearance on the vibrating reed. These were, therefore, dismantled and readjusted.

Servo-mechanisms were used to translate the steering signals from the control amplifier into movements of the control vanes in the rocket's tail. Many were received in good condition, but they were inspected and tested. The test consisted of connecting the servo-mechanisms to a testing jig and verifying that a given weight could be lifted to the required distance at the correct time with a predetermined current. This test revealed that a number were below standard, and only servos whose minimum performance could be guaranteed were selected. Associated with the servo motors are separate trimming motors which control the external tabs on two of the rocket fins.

Not the best set of images, but this sequence has been taken as stills from a 16mm film.

Above: a Hanomag towing an alcohol bowser.

Below: A Opel Blitz alcohol tanker towing a trailer pump.

Bottom: the liquid oxygen trailer being filled from a rainway tanker.

These were inspected and tested for correctness of operation and current consumption.

There were two batteries in each rocket. The main battery was a lead-acid accumulator of 32 volts and supplied the current for operating all the electrical apparatus in the missile. The second, a nickel-cadmium battery of 50 volts, a small capacity, provided the control current to the gyroscope's potentiometers. Efforts were made to obtain these batteries from German sources, and contact was also made with battery makers in the United Kingdom to provide the nearest equivalent batteries should the German supply fail. A suitable German source was located late, and the German batteries were used in all the rocket launches. The British batteries were also available by then for use if required. The initial charging of the lead-acid battery was carried out on-site.

It had been a practice of the Germans to build a desk type of test equipment that incorporated the switches, relays, lamps, etc., needed to test the rocket during manufacture and before launching. Some of these were found at Nordhausen, but panels,

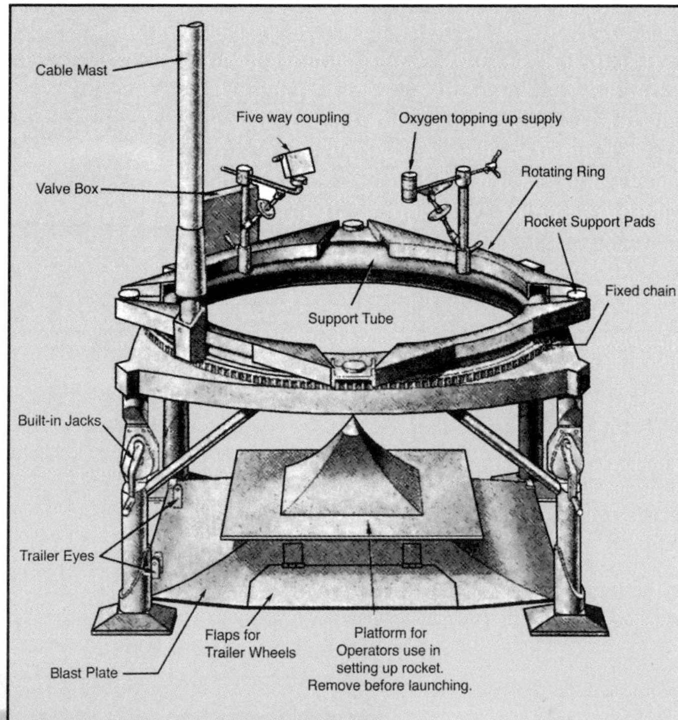

Above: Translated from German documentation, a diagram of the A-4/A-4/V-2 Launching Platform showing the components.

Left: the Launching Platform in actuality. *[Photo: NARA]*

instruments, and wiring were badly damaged and wholly stripped and remade. The circuit drawings for these desks had to be reconstructed and aligned with the circuits in the rocket. Every apparatus was examined for mechanical and electrical damage and repaired where necessary. Then, each desk was rewired according to the diagrams previously prepared. Three types of desks were required. The first was used to test the rocket when it was still in the main Assembly Shop in a horizontal position, and the second was when the missile reached the Vertical Testing Chamber and was in a vertical position. These two desks differed because it was impossible to install the gyroscopes in the horizontal position of the rocket. Hence, they were not fitted until the missile was in a vertical position. The third desk, which was normally built into the Feuerleitpanzer, is used for the final checking of the electrical control apparatus when the rocket is on the launching platform and to ensure that damage had not been caused in transit. This desk also included a panel that controlled the sequence of operations inside the rocket when it was about to be launched. The large multiple-pin sockets and cables required to connect the test desks to the rocket were carefully inspected for mechanical accuracy, electrical continuity, and insulation.

Time to Build

Within Operation Backfire there was an esoteric interest in discovering how long it took to build, and therefore the financial cost, of each A-4/V-2. The more questions the Allies asked of the Germans, the more it became clear that given the use of slave and forced labour - Zwangsarbeit - in Nazi Germany and throughout German-occupied Europe took place on an unprecedented scale. It was a vital part of the German economic exploitation of conquered territories. It also contributed to the mass extermination of populations in occupied Europe. The Germans abducted approximately twelve million people from almost twenty European countries; about two-thirds came from Central Europe and Eastern Europe.

Many workers died as a result of their living conditions – extreme mistreatment, severe malnutrition and abuse were the main

Building 18, the No.1 Sub Assembly Shop at Cuxhaven, with No.3 Liquid Oxygen Road Trailer parked alongside. Note the narrow-gauge light railway tracks in the foreground. *[Photo: NARA]*

TIME STUDY OF ASSEMBLY OF A-4/V-2 ROCKET

	Men	Hours	Total Man Hours
Tail Unit			
Assembly thrust ring			
Fit brackets	2	3	6
Install hydraulic servos	2	3	6
Fit potentiometers	2	1	2
Fit carbon rudder adjustment box	2	1	2
Connect cable forms	2	3	6
Connect hydraulic servos	2	2	4
Load test of hydraulic servos	2	6	12
Total			**38**
Tail Unit			
Measure tail unit	2	12	24
Overhaul outer cover	4	24	96
Overhaul chain case	4	8	32
Assemble torsion bars and simplex chains	2	4	8
Install thrust ring	4	2	8
Fit flanges to carbon rudder	4	16	64
Install coupling for supplementary fuelling and five branch pipe coupling	1	2	2
Final tapping of threads (approx. 500)	4	16	64
Install Trim motors	1	4	4
Fix chain cases, rudder flaps, cowlings and fuelling doors	4	8	32
Install cable form	1	4	4
Adjust fins of tail unit	4	2	8
Tests	6	8	48
Total			**394**
Propulsion Unit			
Clean, rinse and dry combustion chamber	3	3	9
Check joint seatings and renew if necessary	1	1	1
Fit blanking caps	1	1	1
Fit blind plugs	1	1	1
Test	2	8	16
Install on alignment rig	2	0.5	1
Mount and line up tubular framework	2	2	4
Remove to rotating assembly platform	2	0.5	1
Fit turbine unit	2	0.5	1
Fitting pipes	3	9	27
Fit air bottles	2	0.5	1
Install steam unit	2	1	2
Fit steam exhaust and heat exchanger	1	0.5	1
Pipe up air supply lines	1	6	6
Test	2	6	12
Fit restricting shorts or pump outlets	3	3	9

Stress relieve aluminium pipes	2	3	6
Wire nuts and adjust locking plates	2	2	4
Remove top ring	1	0.5	0.5
Total			**103.5**
Assembly of Centre Section			
Half Sections			
Survey, measure, adjust and prepare half sections	2	4	8
Install wooden chocks	1	1	1
Install cable form	1	1	1
Install air pipes	1	1	1
Put in glass wool and secure with wire netting	2	4	8
Total			**19**
Assembly of oxygen container			
Fit struts and fish plates for fixing of container	2	4	8
Clean container	1	1	1
Pressure test of container	2	2	4
Fit dummy flanges	1	1	1
Total			**14**
Assembly of alcohol container	4	1	4
Install supports and brackets	1	1	1
Fix pressurising valve, and fix regulator valves	1	2	2
Install alcohol tank valve	1	1	1
Clean container and close manhole oover	1	1.5	1.5
Pressure test of container	2	1.5	3
Total			**12.5**
Assembly of oxygen and alcohol container in the lower half sections	3	1	3
Fix suction pipe on to alcohol container	2	0.5	1
Insulate suction pipe with glass wool string	3	2	6
Total			**10**
Laying on of upper half sections	3	0.5	1.5
Connecting (screwing) of both half sections	4	1.5	6
Install frame work ring and screw in bracket appliance	2	1.5	3
Fit sealing strips along shell joint	4	2	8
Fill in oxygen front with glass wool and fit dividing wall..	2	2	4
Secure centre distribution box	1	0.5	0.5
Fix oxygen vent valve	1	0.5	0.5
Install oxygen filler pipe with valve and fix brackets	1	1	1
Install tank brackets alcohol side	1	4	4
Fill in alcohol tank end with glass wool and secure with wire netting	1	0.5	0.5
Total			**30**
Control Compartment			
Installing wooden sections	2	3	6
Fit electrical distribution box	2	1	2
Attach pressurising pipe	2	0.5	1
Install sequence switch	2	0.5	1
Install altemators and regulators	2	1.5	3

Install gyro mountings	2	1	2
Install control amplifier	2	2	4
Build in air bottles	2	1.5	3
Install cable forms	2	2	4
Fit emergency cut off hose	1	0.5	0.5
Fit doors and panels	1	2.5	2.5
Test	2	11	22
Total			**51**

Complete Assembly

Fitting of control compartment on to the centre section	2	4	8
Fitting of propulsion unit to the centre section	10	5	20
Pressure test	2	9	18
Electrical test	4	2	8
Joining of tail unit			
Adjust tail unit	4	1	4
Tighten junction screws	4	1	4
Screw exhaust pipes and oxygen drain valve	1	2	2
Fix supplementary fuelling pipes to coupling for supplementary fuelling	1	0.5	0.5
Joining of five branch way coupling	1	1	1
Install counter brackets, and fix asbestos-string	1	6	6
Test of steering	3	0.5	0.5
Final test	4	1	4
Close flaps and cowlings	2	3	6
Total			**82**

Joining of Warhead

Preparation of war-head including weighing	4	1	4
Joining of war-head	2	2	4
Joining of expansion flange to war-head	1	0.5	0.5
Total			**8.5**
Grand Total	**761 Man Hours**		

causes of death. Many more became civilian casualties from enemy (Allied) bombing and shelling of their workplaces throughout the war. At the peak of the programme, the forced labourers constituted twenty per cent of the German workforce. Counting deaths and turnover, about fifteen million men and women were forced labourers at one point during the war. Besides Jews, the harshest deportation and forced labour policies were applied to the populations of Belarus, Ukraine, and Russia.

It was impossible to calculate how many of these workers had been involved in the manufacturing process or how many man-hours went into the rocket's manufacture - at the very best it could only be a very rough 'guesstimate'. What was possible, however, was to chart out the process and man-hours required to assemble each missle.

Ground Vehicles

A number of dedicated-purpose ground vehicles and ancillary equipment were used to transport and/or launch a V-2 rocket. The Operation Backfire group reported on all in detailed submissions to the Big Ben Sub-Committee of the Crossbow Committee under references BBS/P (45) 21 to 25. These illustrated reports were made available to US

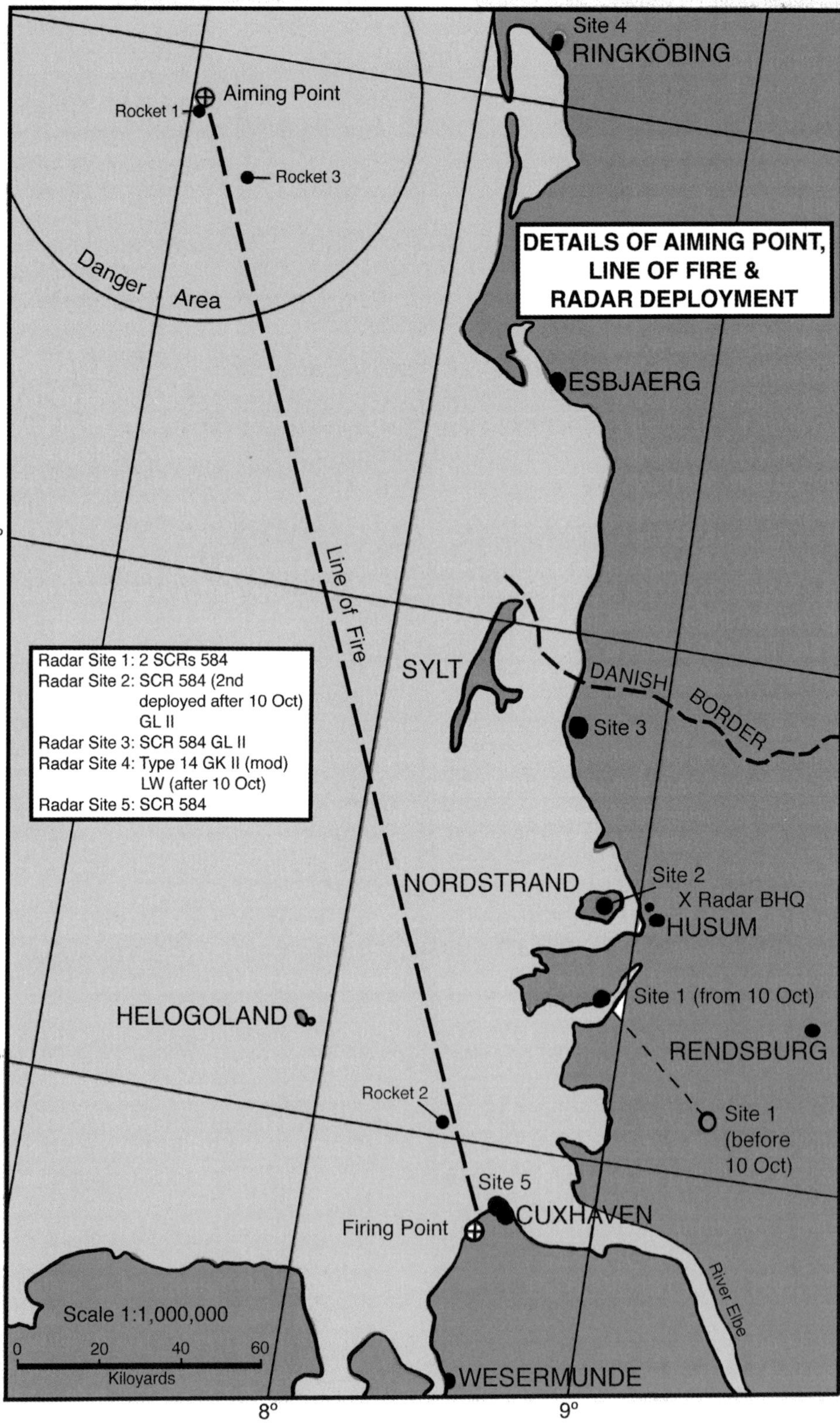
DETAILS OF AIMING POINT, LINE OF FIRE & RADAR DEPLOYMENT
Aiming Point
Rocket 1
Rocket 3
Danger Area
Site 4
RINGKÖBING
56°
ESBJAERG
55°
Line of Fire
SYLT
DANISH BORDER
Site 3
55°
Radar Site 1: 2 SCRs 584
Radar Site 2: SCR 584 (2nd deployed after 10 Oct) GL II
Radar Site 3: SCR 584 GL II
Radar Site 4: Type 14 GK II (mod) LW (after 10 Oct)
Radar Site 5: SCR 584
NORDSTRAND
Site 2
X Radar BHQ
HUSUM
Site 1 (from 10 Oct)
HELOGOLAND
RENDSBURG
54°
Rocket 2
Site 1 (before 10 Oct)
54°
Site 5
CUXHAVEN
Firing Point
River Elbe
Scale 1:1,000,000
0
20
40
60
Kiloyards
WESERMUNDE
8°
9°

The gloomy tunnels of Mittelwerk reveal A-4 combustion chambers in storage. *[Photo: NARA]*

Forces under ETO Ordinance Technical Intelligence Reports. These I have listed for those who wish to do further research on their own, but I go into no great detail here.

Alcohol fuel was transported in the Alcohol Tank Truck (ETO Ord.Tech. Int. Report 277, dated 13 May 1945). It was similar in construction to a normal petrol tanker and built on a standard three-ton chassis. It was accompanied by a towed Alcohol Pumping Set, driven by a four-horsepower electric motor.

Liquid Oxygen Tank Trailer (ETO Ord. Tech. Int. Report 280, dated 14 May 1945) was a specially insulated tank mounted on a four-wheeled trailer chassis. The tank consisted of an inner and outer container, and the interspace was filled with Iporka, which is said to be Urea Formaldehyde.

The inner tank, which contained six thousand litres of liquid oxygen, was fitted with a pair of vertical baffle plates to prevent 'sloshing' when moving.

Hydrogen Peroxide Tank Truck. (ETO Ord.Tech. Int. Report 284, dated 15 May 1945). It was built on the chassis of a three-ton truck and was comprised of three sections: the water tank - which held one hundred and sixty litres - and hose compartment behind the vehicle cab; central was the peroxide tank, which held two thousand one hundred litres, and finally there was the pump compartment. There could also be a Peroxide Pre-Heater that was used to prevent the hydrogen peroxide from freezing in weather below minus ten degrees Celsius.

Meilerwagen. (ETO Ord.Tech. Int. Report 252, dated 2 May 1945). It was a long wheelbase, three-axle trailer fitted with a hydraulically operated lift frame equipped with clamps for holding the rocket. Two of its axles were on the forward bogie, with a third at the rear. A pair of outrigger arms were fitted to the rear of the third axle. These were equipped with jacks so that before the rocket was raised to the firing position, the outriggers were swung out, and the jacks operated to raise the rear wheels from the ground.

In addition to carrying the rocket clamps, the lift frame was fitted with collapsable platforms and a scaling ladder to allow final tests and fuelling to be undertaken with the rocket in the vertical position. Air and fuel lines, along with electric cables, were run

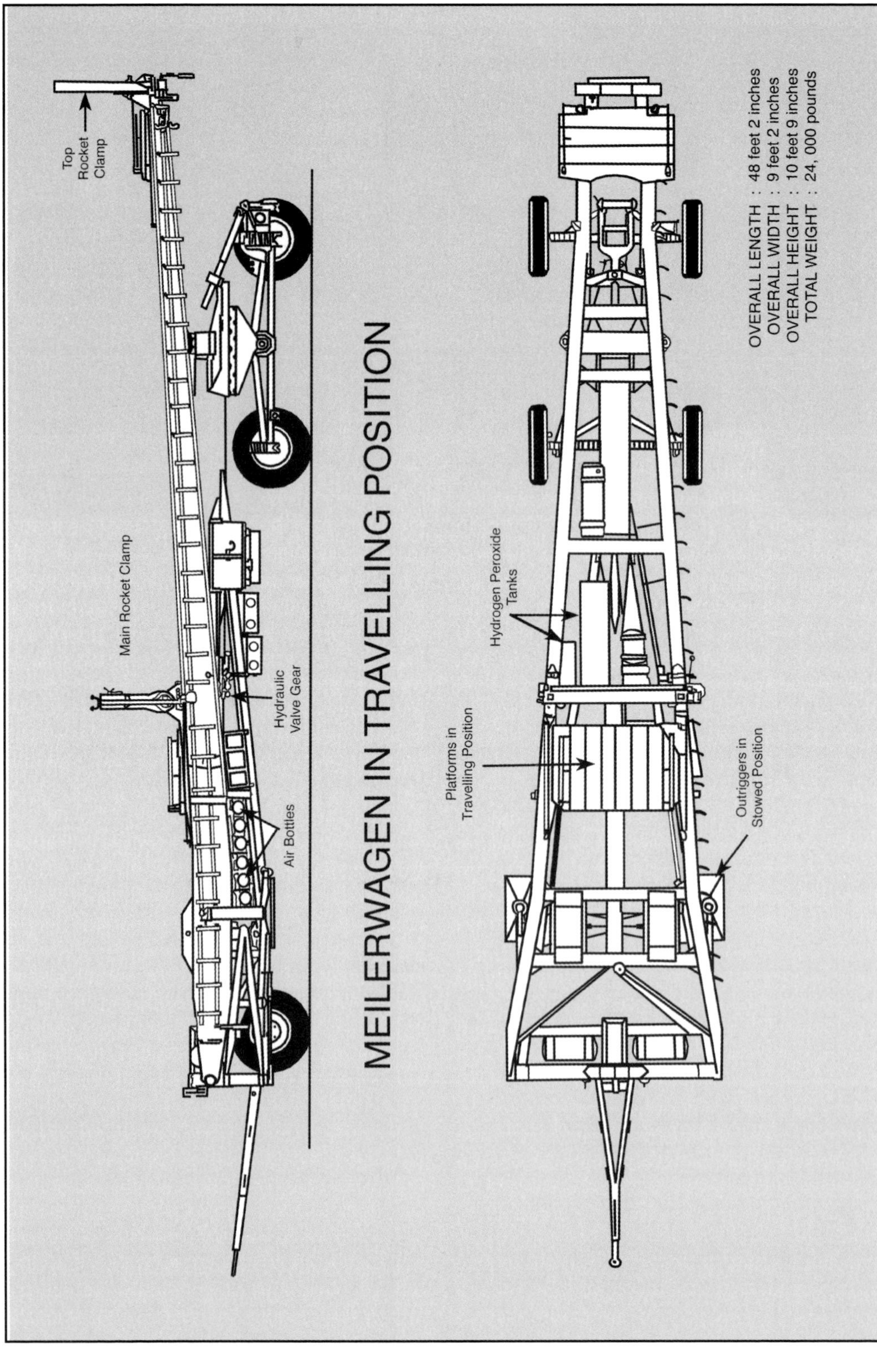
MEILERWAGEN IN TRAVELLING POSITION
Top Rocket Clamp
Main Rocket Clamp
Hydraulic Valve Gear
Air Bottles
Hydrogen Peroxide Tanks
Platforms in Travelling Position
Outriggers in Stowed Position
OVERALL LENGTH : 48 feet 2 inches
OVERALL WIDTH : 9 feet 2 inches
OVERALL HEIGHT : 10 feet 9 inches
TOTAL WEIGHT : 24, 000 pounds

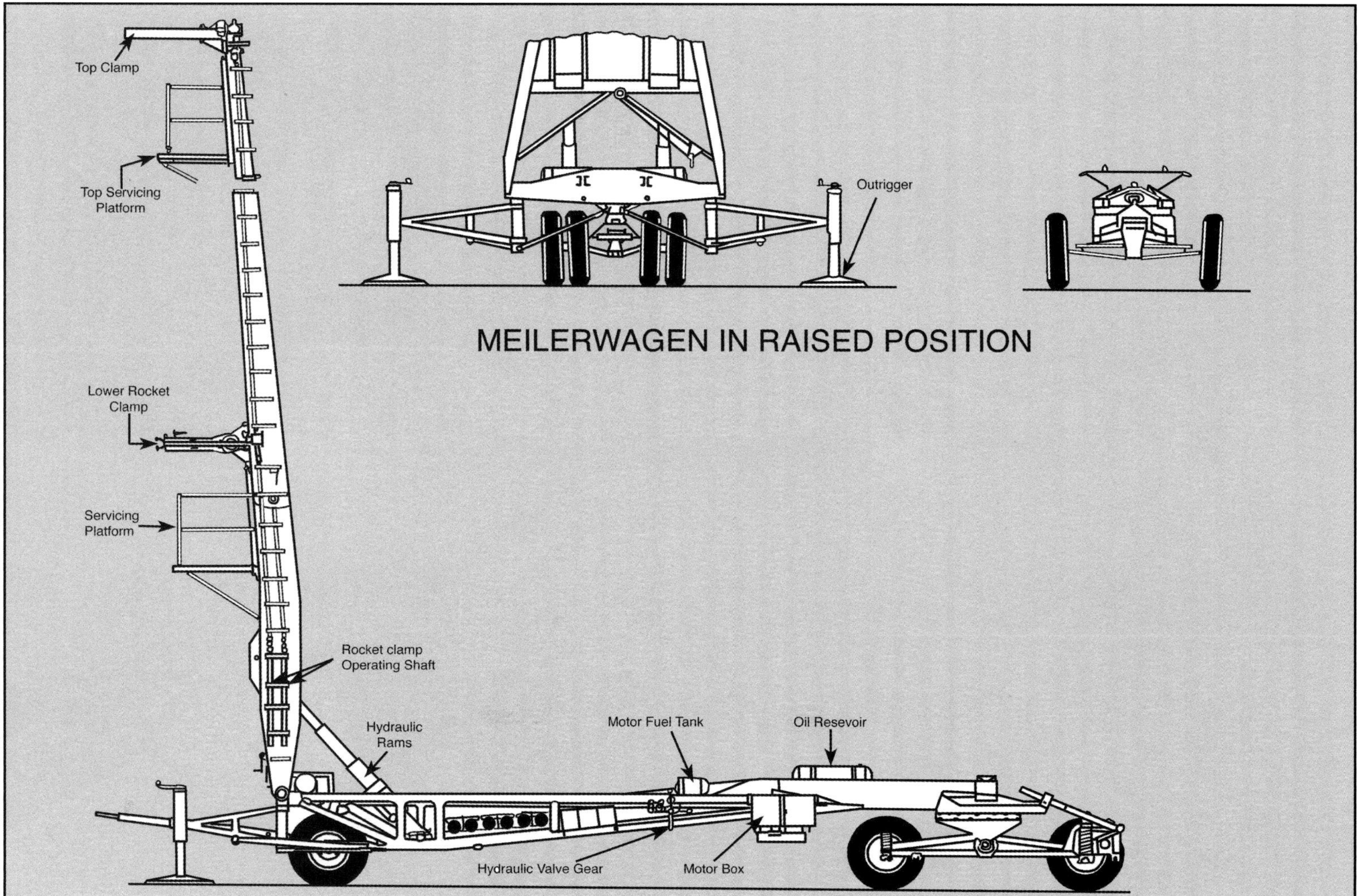
Top Clamp
Top Servicing Platform
Lower Rocket Clamp
Servicing Platform
Rocket clamp Operating Shaft
Hydraulic Rams
Motor Fuel Tank
Oil Resevoir
Hydraulic Valve Gear
Motor Box
Outrigger
MEILERWAGEN IN RAISED POSITION

within the framework.

Approximately half way up the lifting frame a hydrogen peroxide tank was fitted, the capacity of which corresponded to that of the tank in the rocket.

A pair of multi-stage extension cylinders telescoped down into the lowered position to raise or lower the lift frame. Oil for their use was stored in a tank on top of the chassis frame, and the pressure was obtained by a single-action, three-cylinder high-pressure pump.

Launching Platform. (ETO Ord.Tech. Int. Report 263, dated 4 May 1945). This served as a platform on which the rocket could be levelled and prepared for firing and orientated to it's target bearing. The trailer, such as it was, was of a two-wheel type, the chassis being fabricated out of steel tube. It consisted of a lower platform supported by four adjustable legs on which a turntable was mounted on a ball race. The turntable was rotated by a ratchet-driven chain pinion, engaging a static chain secured to the lower platform. The adjustable legs were raised and lowered by means of built-in jacks, the full plate of which was on ball and socket joints to facilitate levelling on even ground. Attached to the fixed portion of the legs was a pyramid-shaped blast deflector, two sides of which incorporate flaps to receive the trailer wheels. The turntable ring was fitted with four extensions at 90°, each carrying an adjustable plate on which the rocket's fins rested.

Various holders for the accommodation of the oxygen topping-up pipe connections, the oxygen topping-up connection, and the air supply valve box were located on the turntable electrical connections for the emergency, cut-off cables, and programme release switch fitted before firing. A tubular socket was fixed to the turntable to carry a mast that supported the ground connection cables to the rocket's control compartment.

In operation, after the meilerwagen had been manoeuvred into position and the rocket raised to the vertical position, the platform was raised until the four pads in the lowest position were about four inches below

PYROTECHNIC IGNITER

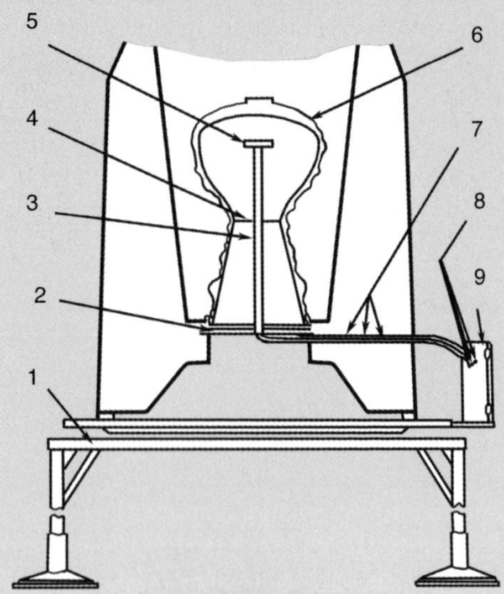

1	Firing platform.
2	Supporting Bar.
3	Supporting Tube.
4	Cross Support.
5	Igniter Body.
6	Venturi Chamber.
7	Cables.
8	Terminals.
9	Test Box.

The pyrotechnic igniter was supported by a pair of cardboard tubes inside the compustion chamber, the components of which are shown in the diagram above.

The photograph below, shows the supporting tube and supporting bar installed between the rudders. *[Photo: NARA]*

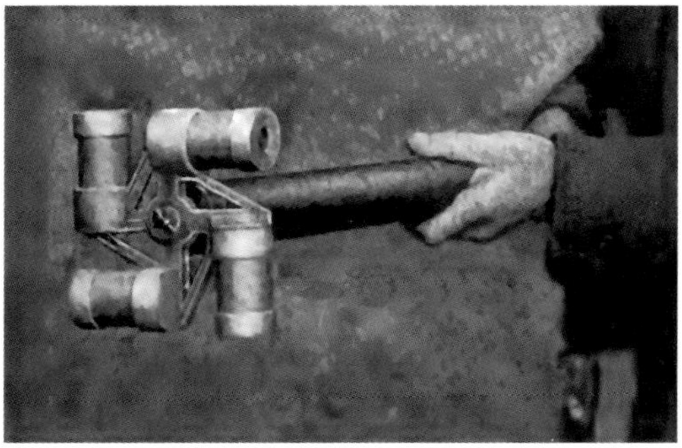

The Igniter body - looking very much like a Nazi swastika - sat on a pin atop the supporting tube deep inside the cumbustion chamber.

The drawing below shows the make-up of the igniter body.
[Photo: NARA]

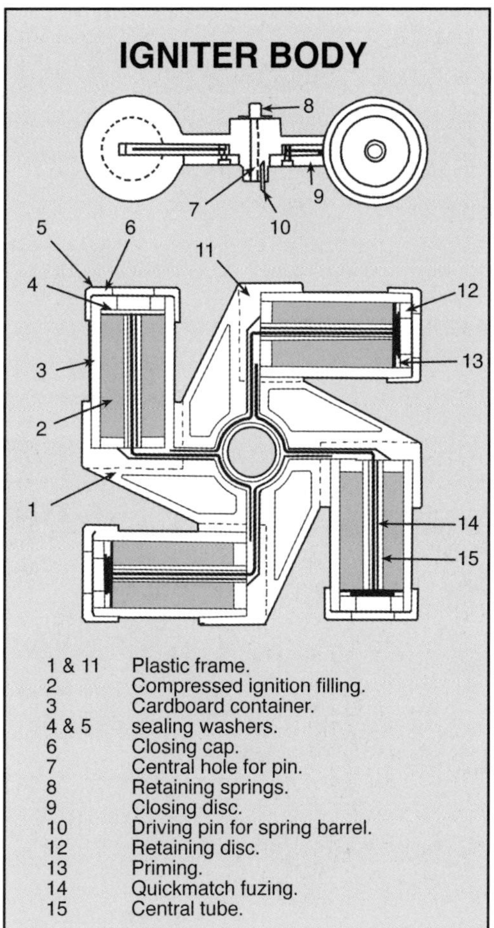

the supports on the rocket fins. The pads were now adjusted to make contact with the rocket fins and transfer the weight from the wagon to the platform.

The cannibalisation of damaged road and railway Meilerwagens built up three serviceable Meilerwagens. In two cases, the petrol-driven pump units were replaced by electric motors.

The Meilerwagen was a trailer used to transport a A4/V-2 rocket from the 'transloading point' of the Technical Troop Area to the 'launching point', to erect the missile on the Brennstand, or firing stand and to act as the service gantry for fuelling and launch preparation.

At Krupps, work had started on reconstructing several Vidalwagens, but it was not continued as three factory-fresh vehicles were found.

The Vidalwagen was used to transport the A4/V2 from the railhead to the field stores and then again to the firing troop transfer point, where the missile would be hoisted onto the Meilerwagen. It was lightweight but robust. The 46-foot long A-frame tubular design could easily support the 4,485 pounds/2040 kg weight of the empty V2. Otto Daus and the chief constructor in the Tempo-works at Vidal & Sohn Co designed the Vidalwagen.

Three firing platforms, complete with transporting trailers, were eventually built from a large number of scavenged and even damaged components. An armoured fire control vehicle was reconditioned to move under its own power. The control panels inside. were not rebuilt because fire control was carried out from a concrete command post, in which unique firing panels were built. A mobile telescopic Strabo-crane was also reconditioned. Two static and one transportable compressors were produced from a total of five that had been received damaged. An additional compressor booster was repaired and held as a standby set. Hot air blowers delivering air at 100°C. were reconditioned. Small air blowers, very similar to domestic hair-dryers, were obtained for drying the smaller mechanical

This page: tail fins in one of the Mittelwerk tunnels. Forced labour workers had to assemble them here.

Opposite page: a close up of one of the compartments in the control section of the rocket. *[both photos: NARA]*

assemblies and components. To dry electrical components, ovens were installed, and vacuum cleaners were provided to remove dust and other debris.

For liquid oxygen - A-Stoff - four tankers, each of seven tons capacity, were fully overhauled, parts of pipework and fittings repaired or renewed, and tanks were pressure-tested, cleaned and washed out. Two pumps, capable of handling approximately 1,200 pounds or 540 kilograms per minute, were rebuilt, and the petrol engines were overhauled. For alcohol - B-Stoff - one tanker, about three tons capacity, and one tanker trailer with around three tons capacity were repaired, cleaned and tested. Two pumping units, approximately fifty-five gallons per minute capacity, were rebuilt, one with an internal combustion engine drive and an electric motor drive.

For hydrogen-peroxide - T-Stoff -one tanker truck, three tons capacity, fitted with water tank, was received in good condition. A semi-rotary hand pump had to be adapted for use with this vehicle. One preheater was

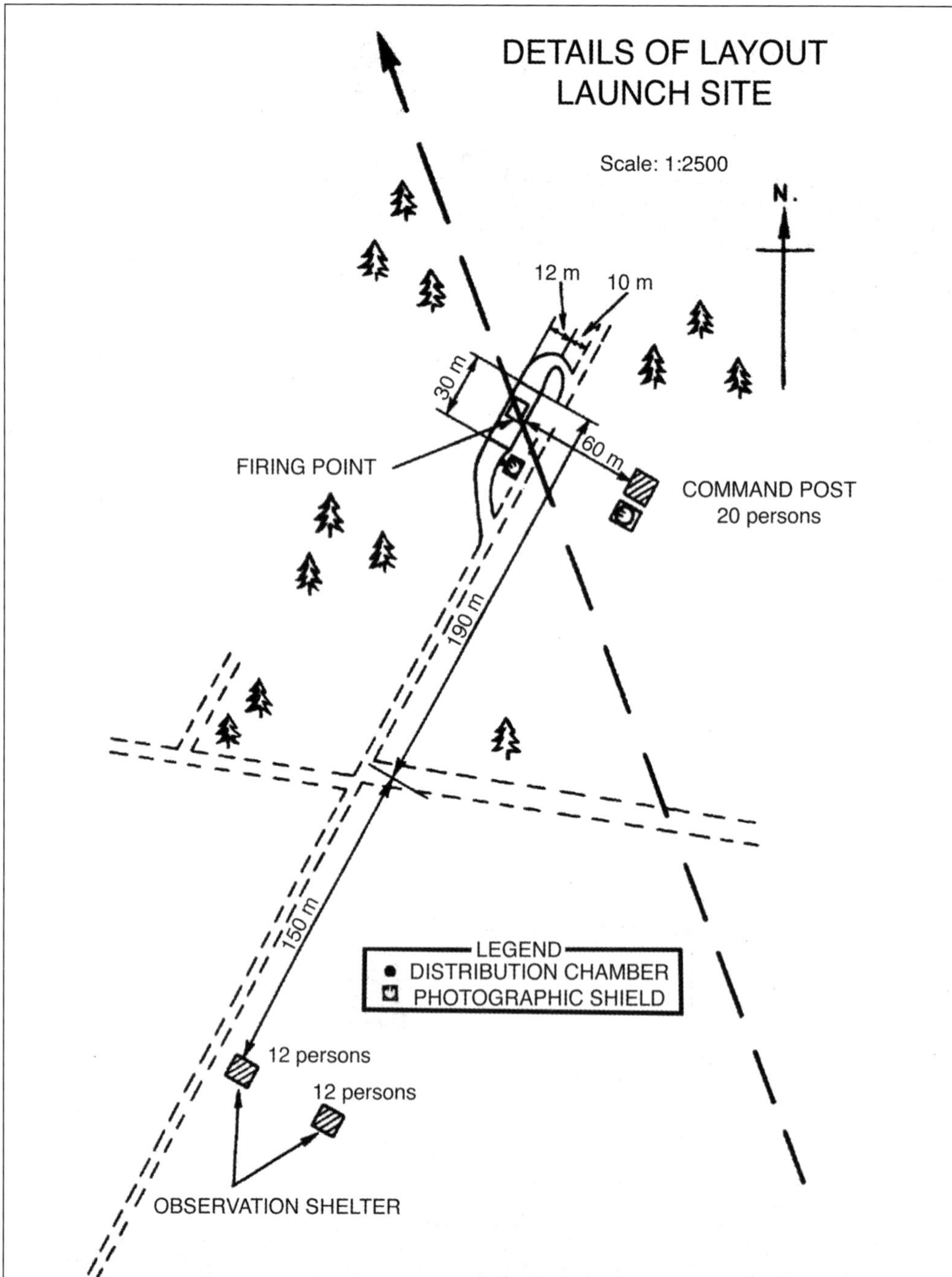

rebuilt from composite parts and had to be modified to carry a pump. This entailed manufacturing new parts and fittings to complete the assembly, including a fully rebuilt chassis. Six Hanomag towing vehicles and three Tatra lorries were also acquired and used for towing and general transport. Three of the towing vehicles and three lorries had to be completely overhauled.

Working in the Field

The British organisation set up to study the German field procedure operated independently of the technical staff responsible for the rebuilding and repairing of rockets and auxiliary equipment. The technical staff's responsibility regarding the rocket ceased when its final tests in the Vertical Testing Chamber had been completed. Regarding the ground equipment, the British Field Staff took over when it was repaired. This staff consisted of several Instructors in Gunnery and Assistant Instructors in Gunnery, working under the direct control of Col. W S J Carter.

The original one hundred and seven German operational personnel were organised into a firing troop under British supervision. While the complete establishment of a firing troop could not be filled, sufficient personnel were available to make each section capable of carrying out its functions in a satisfactory manner in the conditions of Operation Backfire The entire German establishment was, of course, designed for continuous operations in the field.

No attempt was made to use a technical troop, whose function in the field was to receive the rocket at the railhead, transport it to the field store, fit the warhead and specific control equipment, test the missile in the horizontal position and carry out any repairs or replacements necessary. Finally, to hand the rocket to the launching troop. A technical troop was not required for Operation Backfire because the distance between the factory and the firing point was only a few miles. The rocket was thoroughly tested and fitted when handed over to those responsible for the field operation. A careful study was, however made of the operation of the technical troop using interrogation and demonstration by the Germans of certain aspects of their work.

Many German operational personnel were rebuilding rockets and ground equipment; therefore, it was impossible to carry out

One of the test area for A-4/V-2 rocket components. *[Photo: NARA]*

Parts of A-4/V-2 rocket components were collected and stored at Cuxhaven. Some items were perfectly servicable, others were used for 'parts reclamation'. *[Photo: NARA]*

elaborate rehearsals of the field operations whilst assembly was still ongoing. However, detailed studies were made of the operation and use of all ground equipment as it became available, and a 'drill' rocket was also built for handling. It provided a basic knowledge of the general handling procedure, including fuelling.

It was planned to launch the first rocket on 1 October, and the last week of September was spent carrying out complete field rehearsals including the testing procedure on the firing site. The information obtained from these rehearsals supplemented the knowledge already received and completed during the launch.

Firing Arrangements

One small question that puzzled the Allies - and something they fully intended to investigate with Operation Backfire - was how the Germans' started' the missile.

Was something 'built-in' or some kind of external device used? It did not take them long to discover that it was an externally controlled pyrotechnic device consisting of three main parts: the body, the supporting head and a supporting tube that carried the igniter cables.

The device's body consisted of four cardboard tubes containing a suitable mixture of gunpowder, fine metal and filler, pressed together to form a single 'Roman candle'. Each tube was finished off with an orthodox primer. These four tubes were mounted in a frame of inflammable plastic so that the whole body rotated at a design speed of approximately 400 RPM on the ignition. Quickmatch fusing was led from a central annular recess to all four primed heads.

A hole in the centre pierced the frame, and on the upper surface was fixed two small

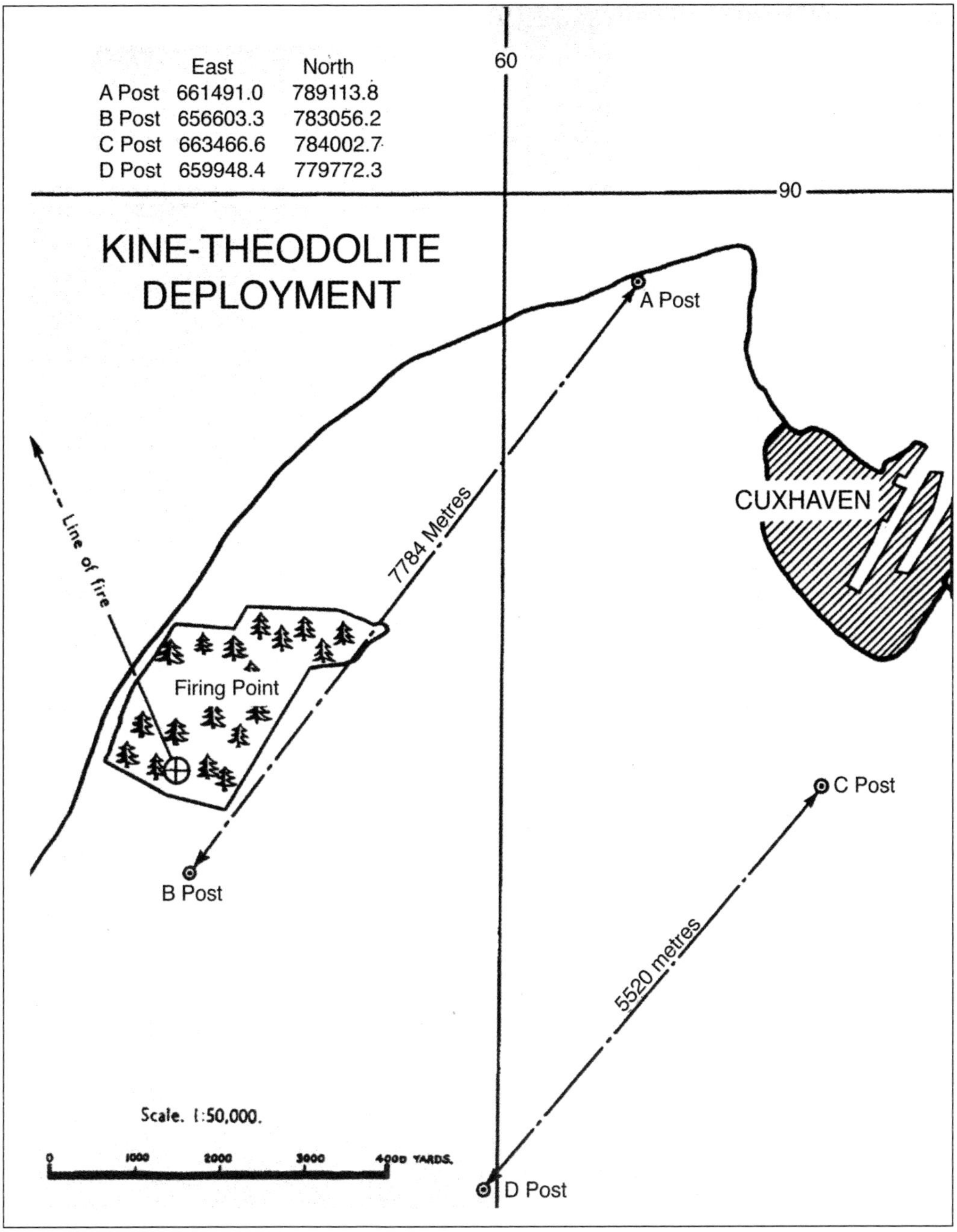

springs forming a jaw to engage in the cannelure at the top of the pin of the supporting head. A small pin that engaged the barrel on the supporting head was in the underside and slightly offset. Over the pin was a small barrel which had a light spring fitted to it, the length of which allowed ten revolutions to be made before breaking. All this was on a strong cardboard tube which supported the whole assembly in the venturi chamber

Lateral support was achieved by means of a small wooden stick pushed into holes in the tube and laid across the venturi throat when the whole assembly was positioned.

The device worked with the closing of the circuit so that the small electric igniters fired the quickmatch in the body, which in turn ignited the four 'candles'. As the rate increased, these started spinning and formed a perfect ring of flame. After ten revolutions, the copper bridge wire is broken, which released a reply, allowing the first stage of main ignition to commence.

When it came to the actual Backfire firing tests, the selected firing point was RR.564841 (Norde de Guerre Zone Grid). So that firing could be carried out in the best possible conditions, a site was constructed with a sixty by thirty-yard concrete strip and good approach roads. In addition, strips of coconut matting, held down by heavy mesh wire, were laid over the rough ground between the firing point, command post and armoured camera shelters so that visual observation would not be prevented by dirt and dust thrown up by the missile blast. Slit trenches were provided for the German launching troop personnel within one hundred yards of the firing platform. It is interesting to note that personnel feel no undue discomfort at the time of launch in the open within sixty yards of the firing platform. In contrast to this, an operational site consisted simply of a clearing twenty-three feet by twenty-three feet in wood, usually of coniferous trees, with fourteen feet wide approach roads, and only slit trench protection was provided for personnel, not in the Feuerleitpanzer.

The bearing of the line of fire was 336 degrees 51 minutes true, including a correction of minus 34 seconds of arc for the rotation of the earth. This line was selected so that the expected ninety-eight per cent zone would still be clear of the Danish coast. The other two per cent of rounds were so unpredictable that they were not considered. The point of aim was at VQ.960432 (North European Zone Grid), and arrangements were made to clear shipping outside a circle of thirty miles radius from this point. Aircraft were also warned off the course. This line of fire enabled radar stations to be deployed up the Schleswig Peninsula into Denmark, thus permitting radar observation of practically the complete trajectory as well as the target area. Nine radar stations and four kine theodolite stations were deployed to record the flight of the projectile.

It was decided not to use the maximum range of the A-4/V-2 because this would have put the fall of the shot at such a distance from the Danish coast that observation

An A-4/V-2 on a Meilerwgen parked near the rail yard at Cuxhaven. *[Photo: NARA]*

Part of the Operation Backfire project was the identification, recording and display of items at Cuxhaven. Here is seen what could be called an 'Exhibition Area' with specific items shown, along with sectioned drawings, many of which appeared in the final Operation Backfire report. *[Photo: NARA]*

would have been improbable. Therefore, the range was reduced from two hundred to one hundred and fifty-six miles.

Fire control was exercised from the concrete command post and not from a Feuerleitpanzcr (Fire Control tank) to allow several officers to study the actual firing procedure.

The average working time from when a rocket was set up to when it was fired was just under four hours. No attempt was made, however, to hurry. The various operations were tackled singly rather than collectively so that the British Gunnery Staff could study them.

It should also be noted that all the rockets used were 'fresh,' fired within a few days of leaving the Vertical Testing Chamber and after very short road journeys. In other circumstances, the main tests on the site might have brought to light dificulties, which would have taken some time to remedy.

Throughout the summer of 1945, work was undertaken at Cuxhaven to gather and record all knowledge and expertise on the V-2, and to prepare for the test-firings later in the year. By the end of August, SPOG was drawing on the services of over 600 German personnel - 79 technicians (49 of whom were working in the various workshops at the test site, while another 30 served as consultants), 120 military mechanics, and 414 unskilled PoWs. The military commander of the German A-4/V-2 programme, Lieutenant General Walter Dornberger, was also separately detained nearby for interrogation. The British would later plan to try him on a war crimes basis for his role in the indiscriminate rocket bombing of London, but this flimsy case unsurprisingly came to nothing, though Dornberger did spend almost two years in a Welsh PoW camp.

Despite a few obstacles along the way, not least the poor condition of many rocket components that had to be salvaged from ditches and railway sidings, Operation Backfire progressed well.

The team regularly reported to SHAEF as to the progress of their interrogations, the reports usually prefaced with the warning: 'All information in this report has been obtained from Prisoners of War and should therefore be read with the usual caution'.

One such document located in the archives provides insight into who the Operation Backfire team interrogated, and what information was obtained.

- Oberst Lt. Weber: Acting Commander Div. z.V. Had no specialised knowledge.
- Maj. Thomschke: Reserve Regimental Commander, 902 Regt. Provided no useful information.
- Maj. Schlesiger: OC 901 Regt, Provided information on targets and order of battle.
- Hptm. Schmoller: Adjutant z.V. Provided details of the staff picture.
- Hptm. Bauch: OC mFunk Horch Abt 1192. Provided general picture as to function of the unit.
- Hptm. Mueller: C/O Ver. U. Lehr Batt. 444. Provided details as to battery movements and the rocket setting up proceedure.
- Hptm. von Chlingsperg: Staff of 902 Abt. Questioned on site locations and supply.
- Oblt. Graetz: I.a.Tech. at Div z.V. Covered all questions of the rocket and its controls.
- Oblt. Ralle: OC Technical Battery. Provided details of employment in Gruppe Sued.
- Oblt. Bader: OC Technical Battery. Provided details of employment in Gruppe Sued.
- Lt. Lohmann: Responsible for optical measurement at Hachenburg. Provided knowledge of prrocedures used.
- Lt. Pills: Responsible for frequency monitoring. Provided details of Toscana and direction finding systems.
- Lt. Thies: Optical measurement. Added nothing to Lt. Lohmann's statement.
- Uffr. Dietreich: : Optical measurement. Added nothing to Lt. Lohmann's statement.

Two Germans are photographed transferring Liquid Oxygen (LOX) from an insulated railway wagon to road trailer No.4. The white areas on the trailer is hoar frost generated by the LOX.*[Photo: NARA]*

Four A-4/V-2s on their railcars at Cuxhaven. *[Photo: NARA]*

- Lt. Lucke: I/C Sendezug Lucke. Gave details of activity.
- Lt. Zimmerman: Leading engineer in The Hague. Provided details of rocket performance.
- O.Faehnr Wroost: Mobile L/S monitoring equipment. Gave details of activity.
- O. Fawhnr Priesner: B/S monitoring. Gave details of operation.
- Fhj.Wacht. Brink: Maintenance engineer for Tarnsender. Provided information on D/F methods and enemy coding principals.
- Wachtmstr. Belwe: Assistant maintenance engineer for Tarnsender. Provided no additional information.
- Wachtmstr Baas: Surveyor. Questioned on aiming points.
- Gefr. Blasche: Operator of L/S monitoring equipment at Companie. Gave details of equipment used.
- Gefr. Dankwerts: Operator of salerno monitoringm equipment. Provided details of equipment used.

From talking to these Prisoners of War, the Backfire team learned much about which Firing Unit had been targetting where during the last eighteen months.

Firing was opened by Lemr and Versuchsbatterie 44 on 6 September 1944, when two rounds were fired at Paris from Site 'Fracture' in the Ardennes.

While there, the battery was under the tactical control of 836 Abteilung and was supplied by road from Euskirchen in North Rhine-Westphalia, Germany. This battery then moved to Serooskerbe on Walcheren Island in the Dutch province of Zeeland, a position it occupied from 16 - 18 September. Six rockets were fired on London, one of which fell into the sea. The battery got rockets from Bergen Op Zoom and fuel from Goes in Zuid Beveland.

Following the airborne landings at Arnhem, the battery withdrew to Rijs in Friesland, the Netherlands, a position it is recorded as have occupied from 21 September until 20 October 1944. About eighty rounds were fired, ten or twelve at Antwerp, three or four at Great Yarmouth, and the remainder at Norwich.

There was no suggestion that any trials were undertaken during the Norwich firing. The first two rounds were fired at Antwerp and were aimed at the town; subsequent rounds were fired at the docks. Both rockets and fuel were supplied from Steinwijk and, later, from Sneek, both in the Netherlands.

The battery then moved to The Hague and occupied positions there from 31 October to 27 January 1945. From 1 November to 20 December, the battery was alone in The Hague. During this period, it was strengthened by the attachment of one firing troop. All rounds fired were aimed at single point in London. Great uncertainty exists as to the geographical position of the aiming point. While most Prisoners of War interrogated considered the 'Stadtmitte' - meaning the City of London to have been a point of aim. 'Stadtmitte', or City Centre, was a Berlin U-Bahn station on lines U2 and U6, located in the Mitte district of the city. However, another prisoner said the rockets were targetted on the London docks area.

At the end of January the battery withdrew to Karlshagen to undertake trial firings designed to remove minor faults from the equipment. No firings occurred, as General Kammler had ordered that all rockets produced be used operationally.

1/485 later became I/902, which deployed to The Hague at the beginning of the operation and fired at London. On 18 September, it withdrew to Legden and fired at Tournai, Hasselt, Charleroi and Antwerp until 17 December, when the unit returned to The Hague. It remained there until the general withdrawal at the end of March 1945.

2/485 later became II/902 and was originally deployed in the Ahaus, where it fired on Hasselt, Charleroi and Maastricht for ten days. At the beginning of October, it

British soldiers pose for the camera with an A-4 on its railway waggon. *[Photo: NARA]*

A-4/V-2 missiles were discovered abandoned over large areas of Germany, some marked with graffiti on their canvas covers. *[Photo: NARA]*

returned to The Hague, and it remained until the beginning of November. During this time, its only target was London. In early November, the battery withdrew to Burgsteinfurt and remained there until the end of active operations, when it fired a large number of rockets at Antwerp.

3/485, later III/902, deployed initially to the Ahaus area and moved to The Hague about the middle of January. It remained there until the end of operations.

SS Werfer Abt. 500 were deployed at Ommen in the eastern Netherlands in the middle of November 1944 and remained there until the conclusion of operations. All rounds fired were against Antwerp except for eleven fired against Remagen. All their supplies passed through Ommen, but towards the end, oxygen was being brought by road all the way by as bombing was seriously interfering with rail communications. The order to fire at Remagen came directly from Adolf Hitler, with one day's firings only being sanctioned. The target was the area of the Rhine Crossing and not necessarily the bridge itself. The exact aiming point was not known.

1/836, later, I/191 was conducting trials at Tuchel when the operations began. They had battery HQ at Reinsfeld with firing sites first deployed operationally around Technische on 23 October 1944. Rockets were unloaded at Poslerrt, with the only target being Antwerp.

About 1 December, the battery moved to Montebaur in Westerwald, Germany, occupying a firing position alongside a road there, the Technical Battery being some distance away. Rockets were unloaded initially at Goldhausen, and later, following an air attack on Hadamar, the process moved to Ransbach. Oxygen was unloaded at Wirges, and the Fuel Battery was located at Vielbalch first and then at Dernbach on 1 February.

2/836 and 3/836 became II/901 and III/901, respectively, and were first deployed near Rottgen, the firing sites and Technische

Battery being nearby. The rockets were unloaded at Heidgen. From this position, the battery fired at Antwerp, Lille, Tourcoing, Roubaix, Cambrai, Arras, Liege and Hasselt. After three weeks, the two batteries moved to Hachenburg and fired from platforms alongside a road there. The Technische Battery was located some distance away, and the rockets were unloaded at Selters. Antwerps was their only target from now on. After about five days, when thirty missiles were fired, both batteries moved to Greimerath.

As was standard at the time, the firing platforms and Technische Battery were located some distance away, and the rockets were unloaded at Neider Zerf. 2/386 left towards the end of this period for Karlshagen and 3/386 moved to Hermeskeil, the missiles being unloaded at Dhronechen in the Rhineland.

About 4 December the battery moved to Hachenburg, also in the Rhineland and operated from roadside firing platforms. Their rockets were unloaded at Korb and taken on vidalwagens to the technical battery by way of Alpenrod. The snow and poor local roads made travel difficult, and the smokescreens concealed daytime movements as protection from air attack. The unit stayed in this area until ceasing operations.

Monitoring the Launches

It was one thing to launch the missiles; it was another to see what was happening during the entire process. A way had to be used to record the rocket's launch, trajectory, altitude and position at every stage.

The SCR-584 - short for Set, Complete, Radio #584 - was an automatic-tracking microwave radar developed by the MIT

An interesting, if complicated photograph taken at Cuxhaven during Operation Backfire. A-4/V-2 - almost in the background sits on its launch platform, with the Meilerwagen tower supporting it. In the foreground, on the right is an American Fire Service truck, complete with star on its side. The main vehicle combination in the foreground is a Hanomag with a sodium permanganate carrier and pump unit on its rear deck, towing a liquid oxygen trailer.
[Photo: NARA]

A closeup photograph taken at Cuxhaven during Operation Backfire. The A-4/V-2 sits on the launch platform, with the Meilerwagen tower supporting it. The picture shows many details of the wagen including the air bottles, the hydraulic rams and parts of the ladder and platforms on the wagen's side. Behind are German staff monitoring the liquid oxygen tanker that was fuelling the rocket., shown by the hoar frost-coated pipes on the Meilerwagen tower.
[Photo: NARA]

Radiation Laboratory during World War II. It was one of the most advanced ground-based radars of its era. SCR-584s, GL5 II and a Type 14 Radar were deployed along the western coast of the Danish peninsula to track the rockets during flight and to determine their point of fall. To obtain more precise data of behaviour during the period of burning, kine theodolites were used to produce an accurate optical record of the initial part of the trajectory.

'X' Special Radar Battery and No. 2 AA (ATS) KT Detachment were made available to operate radars and kine theodolites, respectively, and a detachment of nine HAA Recording Vans to record the data obtained. By suitable tie-up between radar and optical results, it was hoped to gain experience of the accuracy and the general behaviour of radars used in tracking long-range rockets.

Two German Askania kine theodolites that used F300 lenses were obtained to supplement the two brought from the United Kingdom using F600 lenses by the KT Detachment. Four posts were established.

Five radar sites were deployed around the area. All SCRS 534 except that at R5 and all GL5 II were fitted with long range modifications.

It was desirable to avoid sites to the east of the river Elbe as they were in the German Army concentration area 'G.' Site R I was therefore deployed south of the Kiel Canal. Originally, the site was very similar to that at Steenburgen in Holland, which had been used to observe rocket launches from the Hague area to London, but at a later date, however, the proposed line of fire was swung four degrees to the west, thus making aspect angles from this site less favourable. The equipment was located on the highest ground in the area, with a clear view of the direction of the launching point. Two SCR-584s were deployed side-by-side. It was found that, so located, mutual interference due to unlock pulses made simultaneous operation of the sets impossible. When looking towards the launching sites, the dipoles of the radar were indivisible. Thus, only one radar was in service for the first two launches at this site.

The results from R5 on rockets one and two were unexpectedly good and had a

Previous page: This picture is something of a conundrum. Initially thought to be a launch erection, the more one looks at it, the more that does not seem to be a possibility. Although the rocket appears to be sitting on a launch table, it is more likely to be a test demonstration assembly. for it is surrounded by too many ladders, towers and equipment.

Below: A view of part of the Krupp site at Cuxhaven when under Operation Backfire use, with rockets scattered about.. *[Photos: NARA]*

longer duration than those from R1. R1 was, therefore, of little use in its first position as area 'G' had been reduced in size. It was decided to move R1 further north to a position where it could be expected to obtain trajectory data before the end of the prop plot produced by R5. Redeployment was completed in time for the third and final launch on 15 October. A site at Tonning, which was recommended by the Army Operational Research Group (AORG), was chosen so that the maximum length of follow would be achieved. However, it was realised that the head-on aspects likely to be encountered might make the following difficult. At first, the equipment was recorded on a Wessex recorder modified to receive data transmitted from two SCR-584s. An accurate 1/100-second stopwatch was used.

Two views of different sections of the control compartment unit with test equipment attached. *[Photos: NARA]*

Site R2 was also chosen to have a good field of view in the direction of the launching site. The SCR-584 was fitted with an eight-foot paraboloid transmitter and receiver, with the aid of which it was hoped that the rocket would be followed from launch. That did not prove to be so, and it was found that a longer aerial spinner was necessary, where an eight-foot paraboloid was used. This was not supplied with the paraboloid but was obtained in time for rocket three, for which a second SCR-584, with an N2 gate borrowed from the RAF, was deployed. This radar was modified for auto follow in range by means of the unit provided and fitted by 9th Air Defence Command, United States Forces European Theatre. A GL2 with a normal array was deployed with the intention of obtaining constant following to provide trajectory data and to assist the SCR-584 in picking up the target should it fail initially. The aerial heights were modified slightly to give optimum results, and provision was made for putting the SCR-584 on target by suitably marrying the magslip and selsyn transmissions. Recording was carried out in the usual manner, using a 1/10 of a second stopwatch.

At R3 both SCR-584 and GL2 were sited with the intention of picking up and tracking rockets as they near the peak of the trajectory As at R2 the GL2 was intended to do constant following and if necessary to put the SCR-584 on target. For this purpose, data transmission was modified in the same way, as at R2. On account of the high angle of search the location was not critical. Recording was carried out in the normal manner, using a 1/10 of a second stopwatch.

Equipment at R4 was deployed with the intention of determining the fall of shot. Then modified AMES type 14 radar was located on a suitable hillock, some twenty feet above the surrounding ground with a clear view of the direction of the target area. The GL2 fitted with the normal BB modifications was originally located on the assumption that rockets would be fired at a range of 200 miles. The shorter range of 156 miles made the expected aspect angle of rockets unfavourable. Still, it was nevertheless decided to retain the radar but with aerials set to lower the beam. By this means, air break-ups might be detected, which would be missed by the Type 14. The GL 2 was alocated normally on flat ground. An unmodified LW set (AA No. 4, Mk. III) was deployed to observe the fall of Rocket 3 in order to

An Opel Blitz T-Stoff truck, used for carrying hydrogen peroxide for the A-4/V-2s.

At the rear of the truck was the pump unit.
[Photos: NARA]

test its suitability in this role. It was located as for the Type 14. All recordings at R 4 were done manually.

At R5 an SCR 584 was located on the sea wall roughly 8,000 yards from the firing point. A long follow was not expected due to‘ aspect angle and range rate considerations, and the set was not modified for following beyond 32,000 yards. The selsyn data was recorded in Westex Recorder using a Filmo 70 DA Cine camera, running at twelve frames per second. A 1/100-second stopwatch provided time. An electric pulse counter was situated on the dial board of the recorder and this provided the means of tying up kine theodolite and radar records. The exact time of take-off of rockets was recorded using a light switched on automatically by the rocket as it lifted from the firing table (an external 'Abhehekontakt'). On the paraboloid of the SCR-584 was fitted a Kodak Cine camera with a telephoto lens that recorded at sixteen frames per second a picture of the accuracy of following the radar.

No special apparatus was installed to tie up in-time data recorded at the various sites. A special BBC broadcast of the Greenwich time signal at half-hourly intervals between 14:00 and 16:00 each day was arranged.

All recording vans received these signals. All stopwatches were started simultaneously at 14:00 or on a later time signal if launching was delayed. They were all stopped simultaneously on the time signal immediately following the recordings.

A recording control point was established at RR615891, the same place as Kine Control, Kine Theodolite Site A, and Radar Site R5. Thus, at RR615891, there was one SCR 584, one kine theodolite, and two HAA recording vans. One of these vans housed kine control with its speech and impulse lines to all Kine Theodolite sites, and the second van was the recording gear for the radar and the speech lines to all radar sites. Communication with the radar sites was done directly by linking to the HQ X Radar Battery at Husum and then by radiating pairs to sites R1, R2, and R3.

All recording vans and telepeaters used one at the end of each line: it proved possible to have all radar sites on the line simultaneously. The recording vans at the recording control point had a line to the command post at the firing point. The second line was available as a standby.

It was originally intended that R4 in Denmark should be served with lines communications in the same way as R1, R2 and R3, but a delay in installation forced this station to rely on the alternative wireless net. This was provided by a Wireless Section equipped with No.33 sets. One was deployed at each site R1, R2, R3 and R4, with two sets at the Recording Control Point R5. The sets. were netted R5 to R4 and R5 to R1, R2 and R3, two sets being necessary to cover all the sites. The net R5, R1, R2, R3 was able to work Radio Telephony (R/T); that to R4 only Wireless Telephony (W/T).

Chapter Four

Understanding the Process

Not only was Operation Backfire charged with discovering what went in to building and operating the A-4/V-2; they also desparately needed to know how the launch process worked.

Due to the complexity of the missile and the need for extensive testing before launch, the A-4/V-2's designers at the Peenemünde Army Research Centre favoured using heavily defended fixed sites where the missiles could be stored, armed and fuelled from an on-site liquid oxygen production plant before launching. However, the German Army and the V-2 project's head, Major General Walter Dornberger, were concerned that the sites would be vulnerable to aerial attack by the Allies. The Army's preferred option was to use mobile firing batteries, which presented a much smaller target for the Allied air forces.

The Army was overruled by Hitler, who had a long-standing preference for huge, grandiose constructions. He preferred fixed installations along the lines of the virtually impregnable U-boat pens built to protect Germany's submarine fleet. In March 1943, he ordered the construction of a massive bunker - now known as the Blockhaus d'Éperlecques - in the Forest of Éperlecques near Watten, north of Saint-Omer. The bunker was soon spotted by Allied reconnaissance, and on 27 August 1943, a raid by one hundred and eighty-seven Boeing B-17 bombers wrecked the construction site before it could be completed. The Germans reused a surviving portion as a liquid oxygen production facility.

The successful attack against the Watten bunker forced the German Army to find an alternative location for a launch site nearby. They had already taken possession of an old quarry between the villages of Helfaut and Wizernes, south-west of Saint-Omer and some seven and a half miles south of the Watten bunker, near the river Aa alongside the Boulogne–Saint-Omer railway line, about half a mile from Wizernes station. The quarry had been designated as a missile storage depot where A-4/V-2s would be housed in tunnels bored into the chalk hillside before being transported for launching. The Germans undertook major work in August 1943 to lay extensive railway sidings to connect the quarry to the main line.

On 30 September 1943, Hitler met with Albert Speer, the Minister of Armaments and War Production, and Franz Xaver Dorsch, the chief engineer of the Todt Organisation, to discuss plans for replacing the out-of-commission Watten facility. Dorsch proposed to transform the Wizernes depot into a vast bomb-proof underground complex requiring a million tons of concrete. It would be constructed within a network of tunnels to be dug inside the hillside at the quarry's edge. A concrete dome, sixteen feet thick, two hundred and thirty-three feet in diameter and weighing 55,000 tons, would be built over the top of the central part of the facility to protect it from Allied bombing. Beneath it, about four and a half miles of tunnels were to be dug into the chalk hillside to accommodate workshops, storerooms, fuel supplies, a liquid oxygen manufacturing plant, generators, barracks and a hospital.

A standard gauge railway tunnel, codenamed Ida, was to be built on a curving path connecting it with the east- and westbound mainline railway, allowing trains to run straight through the complex without reversing or being turned around. It would serve as the main unloading station, where missiles and supplies would be offloaded onto trolleys that would transport them into the connecting galleries Mathilde and Hugo. Hugo connected with Sophie, a dead-end railway tunnel branching from the main line into Ida. Each main tunnel had several unnamed side tunnels of the same dimensions as the main ones and up to three hundred feet long. The central feature of the complex was a huge octagonal rocket preparation chamber directly under the dome. It was never completed but would have been one hundred and thirty feet in diameter and up to one hundred and eight feet high. Several intermediate floors, possibly as many as ten, would have been built up the sides of the chamber.

The western side of the chamber opened onto two tall passageways, opening onto two tracks to the outdoor launchpads, with the tracked passages and launchpads named Gustav (the southerly-located pad) and Gretchen (the northerly-located pad), both on the western side of the domed complex. Each was to have been protected by bomb-proof doors made of steel and concrete. The passageways were to be thirteen feet wide and at least fifty-six feet high and were angled in a Y-shape, both exiting westwards into the quarry. The outdoor launchpads for the V-2 rockets would have been at the end of each passageway. The two passageways were angled at 64 degrees 50 minutes and 99 degrees 50 minutes west of north, respectively - not aligned with any probable target but merely permitting the rockets to be transported to either one or the other of their pair of sufficiently separated launch pads.

Like its predecessor at Watten, the facility was designed to receive, process and launch A-4/V-2 rockets at a high rate. Trains carrying A-4/V-2s would enter the heart of the complex through the Ida rail tunnel, where they would be unloaded. Many A-4/V-2s could be stored in the side tunnels; liquid oxygen would also be produced on-site ready for use. When the time came, the rockets would be moved into the octagonal preparation chamber, which would be lifted to a vertical position for fuelling and arming. From there they would be transported on motorised launch carriages, still vertical, through the Gustav and Gretchen passageways. The launch pads were located at the end of the track on the quarry floor, from where the missiles would be fired.

The priority target for the A-4/V-2s was one hundred and seventeen miles away: London, which Hitler wanted to see pulverised by the end of 1943. The Allies were alarmed when an analyst found that part of the complex was aligned within half a degree of the Great Circle bearing on New York, and its equipment was large enough to accommodate a rocket twice the size of the A-4/V-2: the 'America Rocket', the proposed A10 intercontinental ballistic missile.

Although physically separate, another facility built nearby, Roquetoire, was thought to be an integral part of the Wizernes complex. It was suspected by the Allies that Umspannwerk C was built to house a Leitstrahl radio command guidance system which was intended to be used to send course corrections to missiles launched from Wizernes to fine-tune their trajectory during the launch phase.

The Allies became aware of the Wizernes site in August 1943 when the Germans began laying extensive new rail sidings, which were spotted by RAF reconnaissance flights. In late 1943, a Belgian, Jacques de Duve, supported by German opponents, informed MI5 about a rocket production site in Saint-Omer. MI5 did not believe de Duve, who was interned for the rest of the war in Latchmere House. In November 1943, the Allied Central Interpretation Unit reported that the Germans had begun constructing the concrete dome and were undertaking tunnelling works in the east face of the quarry. However, it was not until the following March that the Allies added the site to the list of targets for the bombing campaign against V-weapon sites that had already wrecked the Watten bunker and numerous V-1 flying bomb launching sites. Over the next few months, the USAAF and RAF carried out sixteen air raids involving 811 bombers that dropped 4,260 tons of bombs. The bombing caused destruction across a wide area, killing fifty-five residents of the nearby village of Helfault.

Conventional bombing raids only achieved a single bomb hit on the dome itself, causing negligible damage. However, in June and July 1944, the RAF began attacking the site with 12,000-pound ground-penetrating Tallboy bombs. The external construction works were completely wrecked by the bombing and one Tallboy landed just beside the dome, blowing out the entire quarry cliff face and burying the entrances to the Gustav and Gretchen tunnels. The entrance to Sophie was also buried, leaving Ida as the only entrance to the facility. The dome was unscathed but the buttresses supporting the protective Zerschellerplatte were dislodged and slid into the quarry. Serious damage was also caused to the tunnels beneath the dome. The damage made it impossible to continue work on the site. Dornberger complained: 'Persistent air attack with heavy and super-heavy bombs so battered the rock all around that in the spring of 1944 landslides made further work impossible.' His staff reported on 28 July 1944 that, although the Tallboys had not hit the dome, 'the whole area around has been so churned up that it is unapproachable, and the bunker is jeopardised from underneath.'

Although the Germans formed three launch battalions in late 1943, they never got the chance to deploy to the V-weapons launch sites at Watten and Wizernes. On 3 July 1944, the Oberkommando West authorised the cessation of construction at the heavily damaged sites. On 18 July 1944, Hitler abandoned plans for launching A-4/V-2s from bunkers and authorised the downgrading of the Wizernes bunker to make it a liquid oxygen production facility. However, these plans were overtaken by the Allied liberation of Northern France following the Normandy landings. The site was finally abandoned a few days before the Allies reached it at the start of September during the rapid liberation of the area by British, American, Canadian and Polish

A photograph taken by a British Mosquito aircraft flying low above the dome at Wizernes that is still basically intact, sitting at the centre of the wrecked construction site on 6 July 1944, shortly before its abandonment. *[Photo:NARA]*

troops. British engineers inspected it on 5 September 1944.

Shortly after the Wizernes site had been captured Duncan Sandys, the head of the British 'Crossbow Committee' investigating the V-weapons programme, ordered the constitution of a Technical Inter-Services Mission under Colonel T R B Sanders. It was given the task of investigating the sites at Mimoyecques, Siracourt, Watten, and Wizernes, collectively known to the Allies as the 'Heavy Crossbow' sites. Sanders' report was submitted to the War Cabinet on 19 March 1945.

The purpose of the Wizernes site had been unclear before its capture. Still, Sanders deduced its connection with the A-4/V-2 from the dimensions of the complex and some intelligence information that his team had been able to retrieve. Sanders' report concluded that it was *'...an assembly site for long projectiles most conveniently handled and prepared in a vertical position'*. He conjectured the approximate length of the projectiles from the height of the Gustav and Gretchen tunnels, though he noted some doubt about the height of the doors at the tunnel entrances. Segments of the doors had been recovered from a storage dump near Watten railway station but were incomplete. Judging from the size of the tunnel entrance, the maximum size of the projectile could have been between fifty-six and seventy-none feet in length and thirteen feet in breadth. Sanders noted that 'the dimensions of the site make it suitable for the A.-4/V-2 rocket, but the possibility of a new rocket up to half as long again as the A-4 and twice the

The Magirus Ladder, or Handlicher Feuerwehrleiter, was specially designed and used when the rocket was vertical. This ladder was used to access parts that could not be reached from the Meilerwagen lift arm. It could be towed short distances on the launching position but is not sufficiently mobile to be towed any distance along roads. It was, therefore, usually carried in a truck. *[Photo: NARA]*

Two views of a Strabo Crane in (above) the travelling and (below) the erected position.
[Photos: NARA]

weight cannot be ruled out.' He concluded that much of the site was becoming unsafe due to the progressive collapse of timbering and recommended that the tunnels and workings under the dome should be destroyed to prevent subsequent accidents or misuse.

Now the allies had an idea as to how Wizernes would have operated, they wanted to discover how the mobile sites worked.

They discovered that in selecting or laying out a railway station for unloading rockets, it was important that they would be a circular road so that the heavy lorries and rocket trailers could drive in, pick up their loads and drive out again without having to turn round. It would be convenient if rocket trailers could drive in alternatively from different directions, and when selecting a position for the Strabo crane, this should be born in mind.

One Strabo crane was kept at the station and was set up by the technical troop over the railway line in such a position that when the rocket train drove under, it was there would be a clearance of about six inches from the railway trucks on the far side. This would allow room for a heavy lorry or vidalwagen to drive in under the Strabo crane alongside the wagon.

When the Strabo crane was first set up at the beginning of an operation, a report of completion would be given to the headquarters of the technical troop. No subsequent report needed to be given, unless anything went wrong with the crane.

At the railhead, a transloading section, consisting of two NCOs, and thirteen men of the technical crew remained at the railway station while rockets were being unloaded, Besides setting up the Strabo crane and assisting in unloading, they were mainly responsible for inspecting rockets as they arrived and reporting to the officer in charge, Launching Troop, any damage which the rockets may have sustained during transit. This procedure prevented badly damaged rockets being sent to the technical troop, and having a major need to be sent back again. In other words, the Technical Troop Commander had his own representatives on the spot.

The rocket train itself was made up of sections, each section, consisting of three wagons. Two wagons carried rockets, lying on pillow supporting blocks. The rockets were without warheads. Another wagon carried two warheads, and in addition two sodium permanganate containers and two boxes, each box containing four carbon rudders.

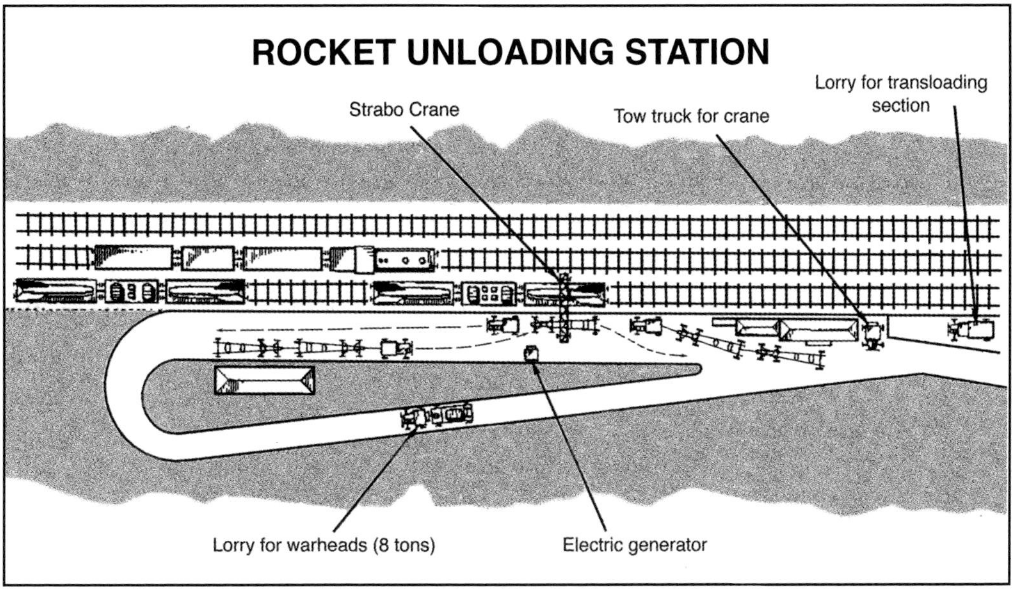

A rocket train, with covers removed is pulled under the Strabo crane about to have the canned warheads removed. *[Photo: NARA]*

The warhead wagon travelled between the two rocket wagons, and the rockets were loaded nose to nose with the control compartment overhanging, the warhead wagon. Camouflage covers were in position over the top of the railway wagons.

The arriving rocket train was met by the Railway Transport Officer, the Regimental Quartermaster, the Battery Quartermaster and representatives from the Technical Troop and the Fuel and Rocket Troop. As soon as the train arrived, they checked the contents with the transport vouchers and allotted the rockets to the technical troops, and they informed the headquarters of the fuel and rocket troop the numbers of vidalwagens required and times for unloading. The technical troop then commenced removing the camouflage covers from the wagons.

For unloading, the train was moved into position, so that the Strabo crane was over the first warhead wagon. The first heavy lorry moved into position beside the warhead wagon and unloading commenced. The warheads were carried in special containers that had three eyes for the attachment of a three point lifting sling. The railway wagon doors were opened, and the crane block was lowered until the ceiling could be hooked onto the warhead container. The warhead was lifted, and when it was clear of the wagon, it was moved out and moved over by the Strabo, crane through the wagon doors in a position where it could be lowered onto the waiting lorry.

The sodium permanganate containers and the boxes containing the carbon rudders, were removed by hand, and placed on the heavy lorry, which drove off to the technical troop unloaded, and returned to the railhead.

The train was then moved until the Strabo crane was over the first rocket wagon. Number one rocket trailer was moved into position alongside the railway wagon, then the block of the Strabo crane was lowered. The special lifting bracket was hooked on, the block was raised, moved into position over the rocket and again lowered.

The procedure of unloading first the warhead wagon, and then the two rocket wagons was repeated until the train was clear. The Germans insisted that a wide siding was required for the smooth and rapid unloading of the alcohol train. One railway tank within this train contained 22,000 litres of alcohol. One battery launching six to nine rockets today would require four rail tankers daily. A train normally consisted of fifteen tankers and trains arrived every third day.

As with the rocket train, the alcohol train was met by the Railway Transport Officer, the Regimental Quartermaster the Battery Quartermaster and representatives from the Technical Troop and the Fuel and Rocket Troop. They checked the contents of the train with the transport vouchers and allotted

wagon numbers. No.2 Platoon of the Fuel and Rocket Troop, with their fourteen alcohol wagons were sent for, and their time of arrival reported to the Headquarters Fuel and Rocket Troop.

The rail tankers were unloaded in pairs. When there was sufficient fule in a road tanker, the pump was stopped and hoses disconnected. Water was added and stirring of the contents achieved by connecting the fuel outlet via the pump to the fuel inlet. The specific gravity of the mixture was tested and should be 0.866, depending on the temperature, giving 7seventy-five per cent concentration of alcohol by volume. Each filled road tanker was despatched to No.2 Platoon parking area ready for sending to the lauch site.

It was No.1 Platoon's responsibility for Liquid Oxygen trains. Each rail tanker held 27,000 kilogrammes of liquid oxygen. One battery launching six rockets to nine rockets a day and required two rail tanker trains of oxygen per day - one train normally consisting of four rail tankers and trains came every other day.

For oxygen unloading, the Germans insisted on a 'roundabout' system, meaning that road taknkers could be towed up, filled and then towed straight away without having to turn around.

As with the supplies arriving by rail, the Oxygen train was met by the Railway Transport Officer, the Regimental

Four views of the unloading of a rocket train at the railhead.

Top left: An A-4/V-2 rocket, minus warhead is seen suspended on its lifting from from the Strabo crane.

Middle left: Two views of the rocket being lowered down on to the vidalwagen for onward road transport.

Left: A pair of warheads inside their cynindrical shipping containers, along with boxes of carbon rudders and containers of sodium permanganate. *[All photos: NARA]*

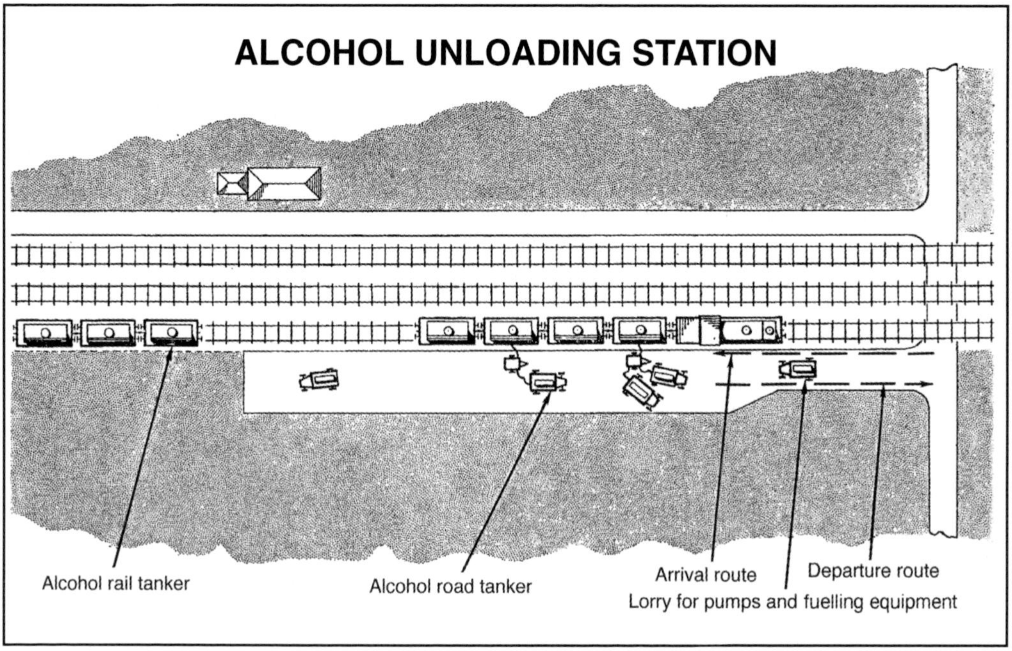

Quartermaster the Battery Quartermaster and representatives from the Technical Troop and the Fuel and Rocket Troop. They checked the contents of the train with the transport vouchers and allotted wagon numbers.

After the rail tanker was connected to the road wagon via the pipes, the valves were opened to cool the system for five minutes or so. Once the system was throughly cooled, the pumps were started and the liquid was transferred at a flow pressure of 1.5 kilogramme per square centimetre.

Speed was now impetrative, for once the inlet valve on the road tanker was closed, the pipework had to be quickly disconnected to prevent them from bursting through the oxygen contained within warming up.

The process was repeated until each of the four rail tankers were empty. The road trailers were then parked up until required at the launch site.

There was normally only one hydrogen peroxide tank in a train, but there are two kinds of railway tank. One held twenty tons of liquid, the other had four special tanks, each holding two and a half tons.

All that was required for unloading was a siding large enough for one hydrogen peroxide road tanker to turn around. It was only possible to load one road tanker at a time. The pump used was usually the ordinary hand pump in the rear of the tanker.

As with the other trains, the Transport Officer, Regimental Quartermaster, Battery Quartermaster, and a representative from the Fuel and Rocket Troop met the train and

Unloading at the railhead. Left: Sixty millemetre pipework connects the alcohol tanker via a pump to the road trailer. Right: unloading the liquid oxygen from rail tanker to road trailer. *[Photos: NARA]*

Above: two views of the the oxygen road trailer connected to the rail tanker.

Above right: oxygen and alcohol trucks staged in a area away from the launching site, ready to move in when needed.
[All photos: NARA]

headquarters for further information of the headquarters of the Launching Troop.

The driver and assistant driver put on their protective clothing. They connected the outlet on the top of the rail tanker to the pump inlet and the pump outlet to the inlet at the top of the road tanker. The three-way cock was set to 'Pump Back,' and hydrogen peroxide was pumped into the road tanker.

The required specific gravity was 1.34. Taking into account the atmospheric temperature of the day and using provided charts, water was added to the hydrogen peroxide until the specific gravity was closel to the required specific gravity. Stirring was obtained by using the pump to circulate from the outlet to the inlet connections.

When the road tanker was full at this concentration, the hoses were connected to the water pump and water was pumped through to clean them.

The full tanker drove to No. 2 Platoon

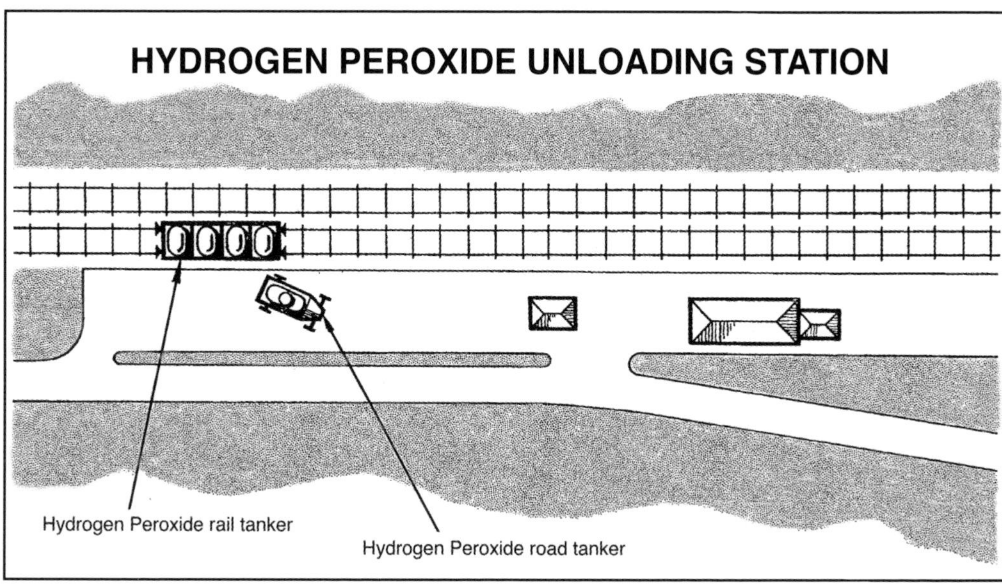

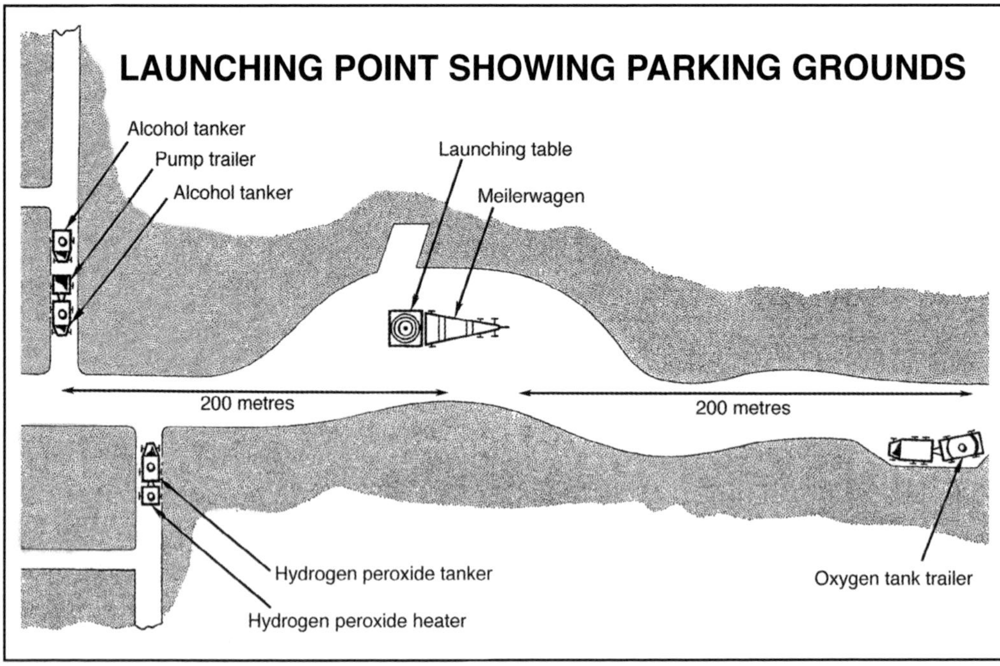

parking ground, refilled its water tank and remained there until called for by the launching platoons. The second road tanker took its place, followed by the third. When all three road tankers were full, a report was made to the headquarters of the Fuel and Rocket Troop. The rail tanker remained at the railhead until empty.

Within No.2 Platoon, there was a warhead mounting section or Spitzenmontage Trupp. A Warhead Mounting crane (Montage Bock) was set up in a tent on a by-pass road so that the rocket on the Vidalwagen could be driven into the tent, have the warhead mounted and drive straight through and out the other side.

The crane had two pulley blocks attached to two slings that fitted around the warhead container against its ribs. The pulley blocks were raised and lowered by hand. After the warhead was installed, its transport

Left: The warhead, still inside its transport 'can' is lifted into position and then bolted on to the rest of the rocket.

Below and opposite page: three views as the completed rocket is transferred by crane from the Vidalwagen to the Meilerwagen.*[Photos: NARA]*

'container' was removed.

The transloading point was on a road close by the railhead under cover, somewhere between the Technical Troop position and the launching position.

The Strabo crane was halted on the road, the towing vehicle disconnected and driven into a suitable position for winching. The winch cable was run out and attached to the rear axle of the Strabo crane. A drag rope was attached to the engine draught connector (EDC) and was used to bring the crane into position across the road. The crane was then brought into action and remained as long as the trans-loading point was used.

The Vidalwagen was driven under the Strabo crane. The Meilerwagen was reversed from the opposite direction and brought alongside the Vidalwagen. Each trailer's centre clamping bolt brackets had to be in line as no forward movement of the crane was possible. The lifting bracket was attached to the rocket. The clamps on the Vidalwagen were undone, the clamps on the Meilerwagen were opened and two guide ropes were attached to the carbon rudder brackets.

Once the transfer was complete, the Meilerwagen, with all its cargo, was handed over by the NCO i/c Technical Section to the NCO i/c Rocket Supply and Accessories Column of the Launching Platoon along with the factory data papers, the test report and the following accessories:

- one igniter and stand,
- one box containing four carbon rudders,
- one 50-volt nickel-iron battery.
- two 16-volt lead acid batteries,
- one sodium permanganate container.

The rocket and accessories are then taken by the Rocket Supply and Accessories Column of the Launching Platoon to the launching position, where they wait under cover until called for by the Officer i/c Launching Platoon.

Finding a Suitable Location

The Germans had a specific procedure for selecting a launch site - Operation Backfire had a different method, simply because they had different requirements.

In general, in wartime operations, the Germans knew that the position selected had to be prepared and surveyed before the rocket was brought up. The following vehicles and equipment had to be brought up and positioned:

- The Feuerleitpanzer, or fire control vehicle.
- The generator vehicle.
- The compressor
- The Magirus ladder, an additional ladder used when the Meilerwagen had the rocket erected, but there were areas of the build-in support structure that technicians could not reach.
- The Kabeltrommelanhaenger, or cable trailer. Cables were then laid out and connected up.

A survey had previously been conducted by a survey detachment, which was attached to the Regimental Headquarters. This was not primarily to find the best location for the launch, but to accurately lay out the bearings for the line of fire.

Like so many things, it was not simple. It

Above and below: The Feuerleitpanzer, or Fire Control Vehicle.

Within the Feuerleitpanzer was a telephonist's compartment that had a seat, a desk, a cupboard, various fittings for holding papers and a concentrator with ten or twenty lines. *[All photos: NARA]*

was soon realised by the 'Backfire' team that there was a huge problem with the incompatibility - or perhaps 'mismatch' was a better phrase to use - of whichever survey grids were used. The requirements were:

(a) Orientation and fixation in the strict geodetic relationship of several points in the launching area.
(b) Orientation and fixation of radar stations along the Danish Peninsula.
(c) The setting of a grid that would agree as nearly as possible with the map grid (Nord de Guerre) in the launching area and on which both (a) and (b) could be combined with a reasonably true relationship.

A regular triangulation, which included several trigonometric points, was carried out, and a mean azimuth and scale-corrected distance for a baseline were obtained. Nord de Guerre coordinates using true distance values were computed for Station 'Wood' (the launch site), and coordinates were then computed for the remaining points.

Nord de Guerre or European Zone III coordinates were obtained from 1/25,000 maps or trigonometric data and orientation from metro and/or trigonometric data. These values were then converted to fit into the Backfire grid.

The Nord de Guerre projection was unsuitable for the area to be covered due to excessive scale factors involved, and the North European Zone III projection was used. The values obtained on this projection were then given a simple change of grid based on the Nord de Guerre and European Zone III values obtained for Station 'Wood' thus creating the unique Backfire grid through an eyewatering technical set of conversion formulas.

Basically, this meant using a set of Lambert Projection Tables to:

- Convert Nord de Guerre to French Geographicals.
- Convert these to Danish Geographicals.
- Convert Danish Geographicals to Euro Zone III.
- Convert to Backfire.

Above: The cover is removed from the end of the rocket, before the Meilerwagen and it's cargo are slowly winched to the firing site.

Below: The protective cases are removed from the base of the fins - note the Roman numeral 'I' on the fin denoting which way round, the rocket was.

Bottom: The upper platform on the Meilerwagen is positioned before the rocket in moved to vertical.
[All photos: NARA]

The Nord de Guerre grid was based on French values. Euro Zone III and Danish grids were based on Danish values. 1/25,000 maps of the G.S.G.S.4414 Germany series gave German values, so correction factors had to be considered.

It also should be noted that the Lambert Projection Table for the Nord de Guerre and North Euro Zone III issued by the Office of the Chief Engineer, Washington, D.C., 1943, and the German scale factors chart issued in the SHAEF Survey Tech. Instr. No. I38, dated 10 March 1945, were used.

A bearing picket consisting of a peg with a nail on it was driven into the ground about twelve yards from the proposed position of the launching table. This bearing picket was used for the collimator during the final laying of the rocket on the line of fire. An aiming point and two or three reference objects (ROs) were selected. The ROs were marked on trees using a cross with a nail in the centre or on the ground using a peg and a nail.

To simplify the procedure for laying the rocket on the line of fire, a special bearing picket card was prepared. On this card, bearings to the aiming point and the ROs were calculated on the assumption that the line of fire was on a bearing of 3,200 miles from the bearing picket. The collimator was orientated with the aid of this card when it was laid on a bearing of 3,200 miles. It was automatically laid on the line of fire.

The launching table was towed behind the fire control vehicle onto the launching position and halted at the required point.

The launching trailer was disconnected from the Feuerleitpanzer and erected.

The Feuerleitpanzer - the fire control vehicle - meanwhile, was driven to a position about one hundred yards from the launching table behind the line of fire and with its rear facing the launching table.

The the fire control vehicle was armoured as a protection against rocket blast. It was powered by a six-cylinder petrol driven engine developing one hundred and twenty horsepower driving through two fourteen-inch wide tracks carried on eight-wheel bogies at each side.

The Mierlerwagen is positioned by the launch table for the rocket to be placed in the upright position. *[Photos: NARA]*

It was driven into position with the rear towards the launching table and was normally dug in to the depth of its tracks. On the left-hand side at the forward end of the control compartment there is a box with five sockets for telephone lines. On the same side at the rear there were two sockets for cable plugs, one for the power supply from the generator (27 and 220 volts), the other a 14-pin socket leading to the relay box in the generator vehicle.

On the right-hand side there was an entrance door and a tool box. On both sides there were catches and fittings for accessories. On top of the vehicle there was an observation manhole in the armour which was closed before firing. In the front there was the driver's compartment which was not armoured.

The generator vehicle was placed on one side of the fire control vehicle as far away as cables would allow and again about one hundred yards from the launching table.

Cables between the fire control vehicle, the relay box on the generator and the launching table were laid out and connected up. The cables were usually elevated off the ground - usually by hanging on trees or, if not possible, suspended on posts driven into the ground, in order to protect them from damp, spilled fuel and fire.

The compressor was towed to any suitable position about thirty yards from the launching table. The Magirus ladder was unloaded from its truck. A slit trench was dug next to the fire control vehicle for use by the steering and rocket motor engineers. Further slit trenches for the whole platoon, each to hold two men, were dug between one hundred and fifty and two hundred yards from the launching table behind the line of fire.

Remote parking grounds had been prepared. An ideal layout would have four parking grounds, one each for the oxygen tank trailer, the hydrogen peroxide tanker, the two alcohol tankers and the three Meilerwagens. In addition to the rocket being launched, two further rockets usually waited on Meilerwagens. These parking

Above: a pair of views of a Collimator being used by a technician to ensure that the rocket is set up 'true' and vertical.
Below: A Collimator and it's components.
[Photos: NARA]

grounds are about two hundred yards from the launching table.

A comprehensive array of telephone lines was laid from the concentrator in the fire control vehicle to the following points:—

- Troop Headquarters.
- The launching table (two lines).
- A general purpose telephone placed somewhere on the launching position.
- The generator vehicle.
- Two lines to the fire control vehicles of adjacent launching platoons.

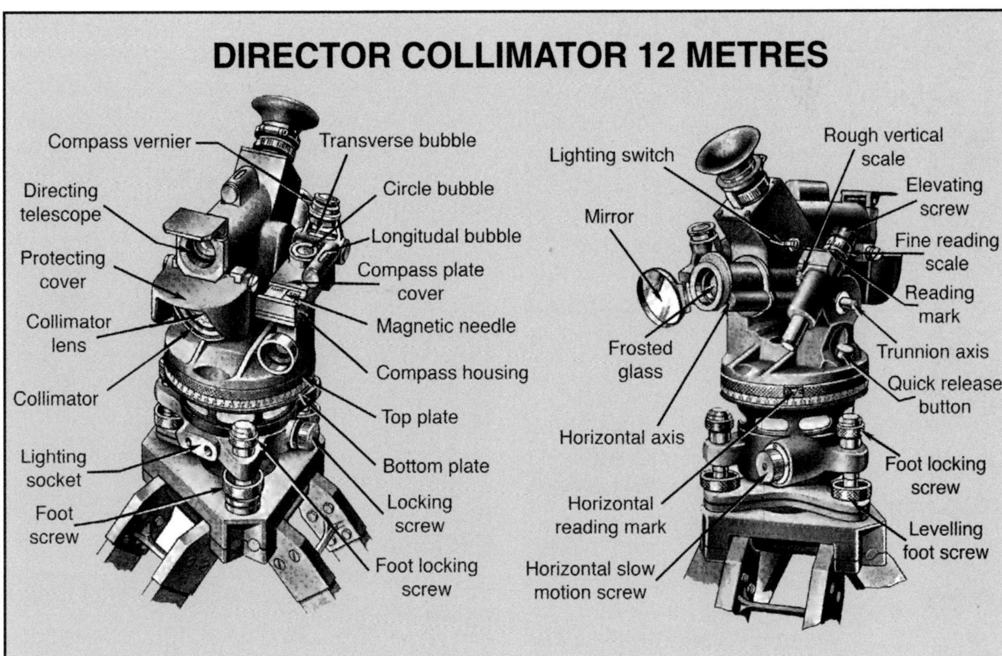

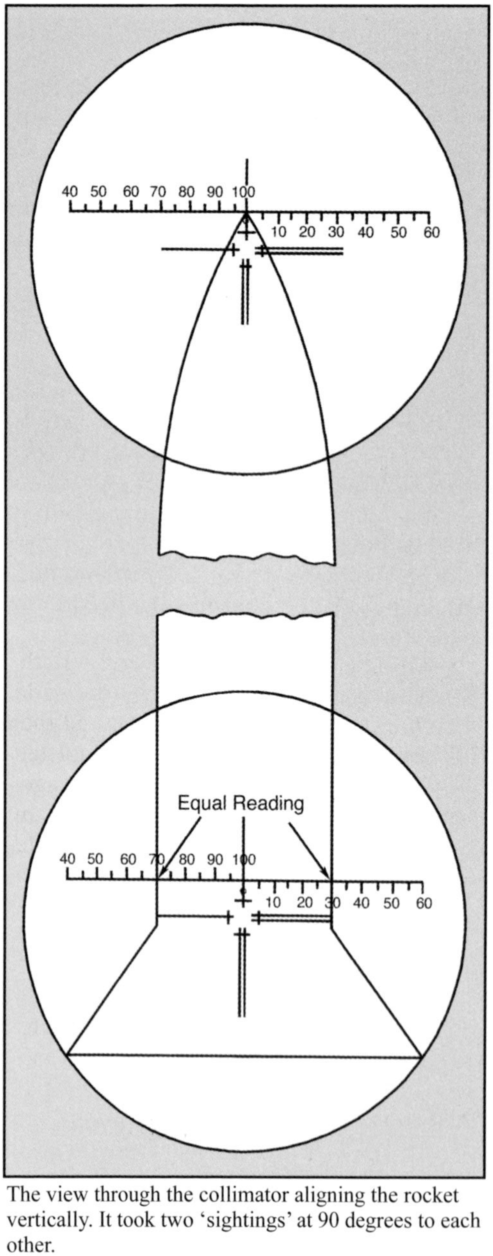

The view through the collimator aligning the rocket vertically. It took two 'sightings' at 90 degrees to each other.

- Battery HQ could be reached via Troop HQ, and Fuel and Rocket and Technical Troop HQ could have been reached via Battery HQ.

With the launch site prepared, the missile on its Meilerwagen was brought up to the site. The tail cover and the cases protecting the ends of the fins were removed, the Mielerwagen working platforms pre-assembled, and the wagen slowly winched into position for erection.

The lifting frame was then raised to the vertical position and the launching table was raised until it came into contact with the rocket fins. The clamps holding the rocket to the Meilerwagen are then released, and the missile stood free on the launch table.

However, it was not just a question of standing clear, pressing 'fire' and watch things move rapidly skywards. The rocket needed to be perfectly vertical when launched, and for this purpose, two optical collimators are used. Nos. 2 and 3 of the Laying Section set up their collimators facing two sides of the launching table. The collimators should be about ninety yards from the launching table, at right angles to each other and accurately levelled. The NCO i/c Laying Section stood by the launching table and directed the NCO i/c Truck Section. Four men of the Truck Section man

5. 4. 3. 2.1.We Have Ignition!
[Photo: NARA]

Blast Off!

The vehicle has cleared the tower [Photo: NARA]

the jacks of the launching table.

No. 2 laid his collimator on the rocket so that the horizontal graticule was on a level with the top of the fins. He traverses until, left and right of the vertical graticule, an even number of divisions of the interval scale cover the rocket. He then elevated until the horizontal graticule was laid on the nose of the rocket and then made signals to the NCO to bring the nose of the rocket on to the vertical graticule.

The NCO i/c Laying Section gave the necessary instructions to the NCO i/c Truck Section, who ordered the jack numbers to elevate or depress until the rocket was vertical, as seen by No. 2.

The same procedure was carried out by No. 3 of the Laying Section. Then a further adjustment might be necessary from No. 2 until the rocket was vertical from both directions.

Once the missile was upright, all the hatches were opened, connections made, everything was thoroughly tested, and then fuelling began. After fuelling was completed, all hatches were closed up, the Meilerwagen lifting frame was lowered, all tools and accessories were stowed away, and the trailer was removed from the launch site.

Using the collimator, the rocket was turned to 'lay' on the line of fire. The igniter was put into position, then the final tests were made.

The NCO i/c Electrical Section connected the igniter leads to the terminals on the side of the valve box. The valve of the first air bottle was closed, and the second one was opened. The NCO i/c Rocket Motor Section checked the air pressure on the gauge in the valve box, and the reading was of ninety atmospheres. He then closed the oxygen tank vent valve and opened the air release valve in the valve box.

The NCO i/c Rocket Motor Section and NCO i/c Electrical Section reported to Officer i/c Launching Platoon: *'Rocket motor and electrical assembly are in order'*.

The Officer i/c Launching Platoon ordered: *Raumen!* (clear launching position!).

With all the German uniforms around, this could be mistaken for a wartime launch, but in fact, it's one of the missiles positioned on the launch table for the rocket to be placed in the upright position for one of the Backfire tests. *[Photo: NARA]*

Two men from the Rocket Motor Section remove the extending ladder clear of the position. All personnel other than the two panel operators and the telephonist in the fire control vehicle took cover in the slit trenches.

The Officer i/c Launching Platoon remained at the launching position and took a last look around to see that everything is in order. He then walked to the fire control vehicle.

Time to Light the Candle.

Officer i/c Launching Platoon reported to Battery Operations Room : *Rocket is ready for launch. Launching Position cleared.*

The Operations Room reported the air situation every twenty seconds. When the Battery Commander was satisfied there were no enemy aircraft in the vicinity, he ordered: *Launch!*

The Oflicer i/c Launching Platoon: *Steuerung Klar?* (is Steering panel ready?)

Steering Panel Operator reported : *Ist klar.* (is clear)

Oficer i/c Launching Platoon: *Triebwerk klar?* (is rocket motor panel clear?)

Rocket Motor Panel Operator reported: *Ist klar.* (is clear)

He was also on the telephone to the Battery Operations Room and reported: *Luftlage klar (*no enemy aircraft in the vicinity).

Oflicer i/c Launching Platoon ordered: *Schluessel auf schiessen.* (turn the main key to fire).

Rocket Motor Panel Operator turned key to fire and reports: *Schluessel steht auf schiessen.* (key turned to fire).

Officer i/c Launching Platoon ordered: *Durchschalten* (switch through as far as main stage).

Steering Panel Operator again reported: *Luftlage klar.* (no enemy aircraft in vicinity).

The Rocket Motor Panel Operator pressed 'Vorstufe (preliminary stage button). The switch through as far as main stage follows automatically. Oxygen tank pressurising took about fifteen seconds.

He reported: *Ist durchgeschalet. Beluftung klar. Zunding klar. Vorstufe klar. (Switched through as far as main stage. Tank pressurising lamp lights. Igniter lamp lights. Preliminary stage on.*

The Rocket Motor Panel Operator also noted the changeover from ground to rocket-borne power supply when the Bordspeisung (rocket-borne power supply indicating lamp) lights and the Bodenspeisung (ground power supply indicating lamp) went out. It took place just before the igniter lamp lights.

The Officer i/c Launching Platoon allowed the preliminary stage to go on. He watched the flame develop, and based on experience, he decided when the moment was right to switch on the main stage. This was usually after about four seconds. He ordered: *'Hauptstufe! (Press main stage button!)'*.

Taken from a fim that recorded the launch of this A-4/V-2, the camera recorded timng and launch data optically set in to the film via a split screen. *[Photo: NARA]*

The Rocket Motor Panel Operator pressed the main stage button and reported: *Hauptstufe ist gegeben,* (Main stage button pressed).

When he saw the indicating lamps Stotz plugs 1 and 2 go out he reports *'Stecker 1 und 2 gefallen'* (Stotz plugs have been thrown)'.

The Officer i/c Launching Platoon also visually observed that the Stotz plugs were thrown off. He watched the development of the main stage. The rocket remained on the launching table for a moment. The turbine could be heard roaring. The flame grew rapidly as full thrust developed. The missile rose slowly and steadily from the launching table. It gradually gathered speed. After four seconds, it turned over in the direction of the target and accelerated rapidly.

The officer i/c Launching Platoon looked through the top of the fire control vehicle. With a stopwatch, he timed the beginning of precession (that is, when the rocket turned over in the direction of the target) and the Brennschluss (the time to fuel cut-off point). This could be seen if the rocket was visible because the smoke trail would cease abruptly. If the missile was invisible, time could be taken to the point where the noise stopped, and an allowance could be made for the speed of sound.

It was one thing to understand who was doing what during a launch - the Operation

As the camera tracked upwards following the trajectory of the A-4/V-2 the timer with its rapidly spinning hands became clearer in the split screen. *[Photo: NARA]*

Backfire team knew that it was essential to understand what was going in sequentially during the launch sequence.

The following table is intended primarily to indicate the sequence of events of what was happening in the rocket during an actual launch - shown in the right hand column. The purpose of the middle column is to assist in tying up the sequence of events given in Column 3 with the drill at the rocket motor panel during launching.

STAGE	ACTION AT ROCKET MOTOR PANEL	SEQUENCE OF EVENTS ON ROCKET AND VALVE BOX
1	Primary Stage Button pressed.	Electrical circuits tested.
2	Lamp indicating all circuits clear (Klar) comes on.	-
3	-	Valve Olh on valve box operated. Air escapes down pipe, closing oxygen tank vent valve.
4	-	Valve Nlh on valve box opened. Air passes via pipe to oxygen tank, thus pressurising it to 1.5 atmospheres.
5	Lamp indicating oxygen tank pressurised (Belufrung) comes on.	-
6	-	Simultaniously with Stage 3 valve Olh operates Dlh in auxilliary motor unit. Compressed air passes to hydrogen peroxide and sodium permanganate vent vales and closes them.
7	-	Igniter is started and begins to spin when burning correctly. Spin of igniter breaks a contact thus causing Stage 8.
8	Lamp indicating all igniter started (Zundung) comes on.	-
9	-	Alcohol outlet valve control valve Slh opened. Compressed air passes to alcohol outlet valve and opens it. Alcohol flows to walls of venturi.
10	-	Oxygen main valve control valve (O3h) opened thus releasing air pressure on oxygen preliminary stage valve which opens under pressure of oxygen. Oxygen flows to the roses in the venturi.
11	-	Contact 03r operated. This in turn causes alcohol main valve control valve (S2h) to open and release air pressure on alcohol main valve which opens 5 mm. under pressure of alcohol which flows to jets.
12	Rocket-borne ground power lights up, ground power extinguished	Changeover from ground to rocket-borne power.
13	-	Ignition of alcohol and oxygen. Preliminary stage flame develops.
14	Lamp indicating preliminary stage completed (Vorstufe) comes on.	-
15	Main stage button pressed (Hauptstufe).	-
16		Ground connector (Stotz) plugs thrown off.
17		Valve Dh opened electrically by rocket-borne power allowing compressed air at 32 atmospheres to pass to hydrogen peroxide and sodium permanganate tanks.
18		Sodium permanganate forced under air pressure to auxiliary combustion chamber. Passage of sodium permanganate operates rubid contact (D2r).
19		Rubid contact operates valve D8h (8-ton valve). Hydrogen peroxide flows to combustion chamber via 8-ton valve.
20		Rubid contact also operates 25-ton valve control valve (D25l1) which opens to allow air pressure to pass to 25-ton valve and open it. Hydrogen peroxide passes to auxiliary combustion chamber via 25-ton valve.

21	-	Steam generated in auxiliary combustion chamber drives the turbine which drives the pumps. Alcohol and oxygen apumped via their main valves now fully opened by increased pressure of fuel to the combustion chamber.
22	-	Development of full thrust.
23	-	The rocket leaves the launching table. The take-off switch (Abhebekontakt) operates automatically and switches on the time switch (Zeitechaltwerk). The plug on the emergency fuel cut-off line (not Brennschluss) pulls away from its socket in the base of fin No. 4. The oxygen tank pressuring pipe non-return valve closes. The non-return valve on the air bottle charging pipe closes. The non-return valve on the oxygen tank pressure regulating pipe closes.
24	-	Pressurisation of oxygen tank by gaseous oxygen from heat exchanger begins. Tank is pressurised to 2.2 atmospheres, the oxygen vent valve safety valve acting as a pressure regulator. Pressurisation of alcohol tank by inrush of air through pipe in war-head.
25	-	Commencement of precession 4 seconds after take-off.
26	-	40 seconds after take-off the alcohol tank atmosphere pressurising valve control valve (S3I1) is opened electrically by the time switch. Compressed air closes the alcohol tank atmosphere pressurising valve.
27		End of precession 47 to 51 seconds after take-off. Carbon rudders 2 and 4 move back back to zero position.
28		Fuel cut-off (Brennschluss) effected by integrating accelerometer or radio equipment. The stages in fuel cut-off are : (i) 25-ton valve control valve closed electrically causing 25-ton valve to close on resultant loss of air pressure. Flow of hydrogen peroxide to auxiliary combustion chamber reduced. Turbine speed reduced. Flow of alcohol and oxygen reduced. Thrust reduced from 25 tons to 8 tons. (ii) 8-ton valve closed, when correct velocity has been attained, through electrical operation of D8h. (iii) Dh closed electrically through the operation of a double relay in the distribution box (Hauptverteiler). Pressurisation of hydrogen peroxide and sodium permanganate tanks ceases. (iv) Oxygen and alcohol main valves closed by operation of their control valves O3h and S2h. (v) Alcohol outlet valve control valve (Sih) closed electrically by a double relay in the main distribution box. (vi) Alcohol compressed air pressurising valve (S4h) opens and allows compressed air to pass to the alcohol tank. (vii) Outer rudders return to zero position.

Chapter Five

Politics and Rivalry

By the time the war had ended, the USA had emerged as one of only two global superpowers while the UK was a shattered, near-bankrupt empire, retaining some of its pre-war influence and international reach, but was in decline. They were no longer equal partners, and the nature of the 'special relationship' had to be re-negotiated. It manifested itself in a variety of ways, including the abrupt termination of the wartime Lend-Lease economic aid programme in August 1945, to be replaced with a much less generous loan and Britain's increasing post-war dependence on international alliances, especially with the US, to defend its global interests, as seen with the creation of NATO in 1949. Another indication was the end of scientific collaboration, as shown in the US Joint Chiefs of Staff Memorandum No.5, issued in May 1945, which stated that *'technical information involving research and development projects, the application of which are incapable of being introduced in the present war, shall not be released to foreign governments.*

This attitude was reinforced even more firmly in the field of atomic physics, despite the earlier collaboration of the Manhattan Project - in August 1946, the US Congress passed the McMahon Act which prohibited the sharing of American atomic secrets with any foreign power, including the UK.

General George Catlett Marshall Jr. GCB
(*b.* 31 December 1880, *d.*16 October 1959)

The ramifications of this split were felt in Germany too. On 13 July 1945, SHAEF was liquidated, and from that point on, practically all British and American activities in occupied Germany, including the exploitation of German science and technology, were conducted on a unilateral basis.

In terms of Backfire, this new relationship manifested itself first in the seemingly growing American disinterest in the operation, not least because it was seen as inferior to longer-term rocket research projects, also utilising German equipment and expertise, which had by then been initiated in the United States. Even as early as 4 June, the Chief of Staff of the US Army, General George C. Marshall, wrote to Eisenhower to make it clear that *these firings must not interfere with* [the] *important US program.*

The process of US withdrawal began gradually. A week after SHAEF had been disbanded, responsibility for Backfire was passed over to the British War Office but Cameron was informed that the *United States representative will participate on an equal basis at these firings and concurrence of US authorities concerning the programme for such firings will be obtained. The United States and the United Kingdom will each have full access to the*

An A-4/V-2 missile is seen on its launching table, and the Meilerwagen has been retracted but not yet removed.

This picture shows much of the structure of the Meilerwagen, with the supporting outrigger jacks in place and what appears to be snow chains in the front set of wheels.

The image is typical of many taken by the Germans and used in the Operation Backfire report . The image's background has been carefully removed at source to emphasise the subject clearly. *[Photo: NARA]*

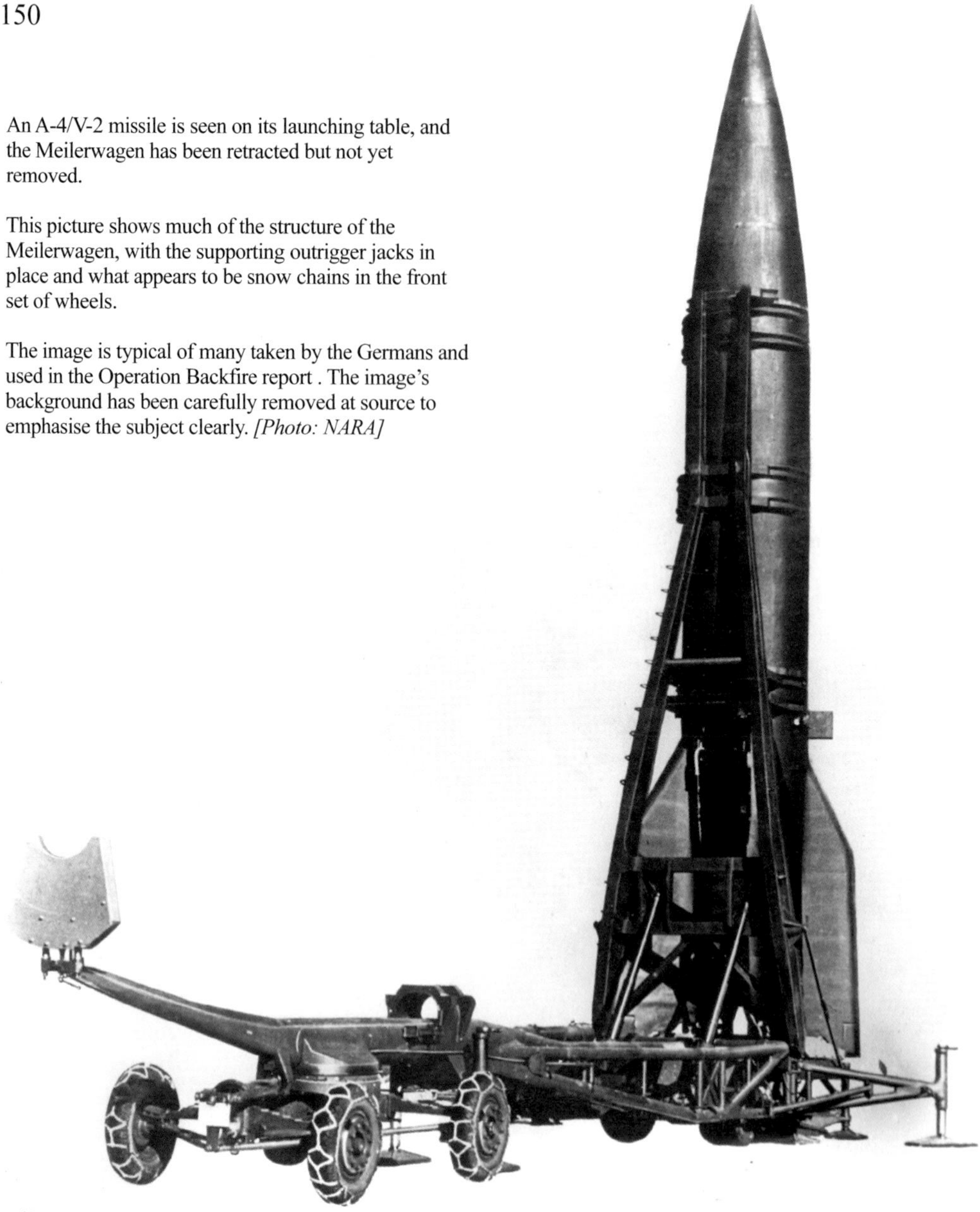

results obtained from such trial firings.

Despite the stated intention to continue working in close collaboration, the US immediately began to treat Backfire as something that was little more than a nuisance and an obstacle, rather than an integral part of broader Anglo-American strategy.

In early August, Cameron wrote to his superior, the Director of Royal Artillery, Lieutenant General Otto Marling Lund, with this ominous message: *I think I should warn you that a crisis is boiling up in the affairs of Backfire. I had a visit today from Colonel Toftoy of the US Ordnance Dept., who is now in charge of all the rocket development in the States. He says that he needs twenty-seven of the German civilians I am using here.*

Cameron was quite correct - the tug-of-war that developed over these German specialists resembled a full-blown crisis and highlighted how quickly a bitter and petty battle of wills had replaced Anglo-American cooperation.

Most of Germany's rocketry experts had ended up in American hands - especially Wernher Von Braun in May 1945 - and were detained at a US facility in Garmisch-Partenkirchen, in southern Bavaria. Eighty-five specialists had been grudgingly 'loaned' by the US authorities to SPOG for Backfire. Still, when the US launched Operation Overcast - a scheme to bring German rocket engineers to the United States for work on the American missile programme - these men were recalled as a matter of urgency. In something of a pancea to ruffled British feathers, the Americans only pushed for the return of twenty-seven of these specialists, those considered to have the highest scientific qualifications. The British agreed to return fifteen but insisted that they be allowed to retain the remaining twelve as they were considered critical to the execution of Backfire.

There seems to be something of contradiction in the American view. On one hand they were trying to state that there was little of value in the British Operation Backfire when considered against their own efforts to get their hands on as many German specialists as possible - including the 'jewel in the crown' Wernher von Braun and as much captured equipment and technical documentation as they could.

Diplomatic irritations

The diplomatic wrangling over these twelve individuals continued for some time, with messages regularly crossing the Atlantic in an increasingly heated exchange, each side insisting that they were more cooperative than the other while also fervently stating their case. The US argued that Backfire was *'limited to the assembly and launching of A-4/V-2 rockets rather than to their research and development aspects' and that alternates could easily be found for the twelve men in question.'* The British, on the other hand, made their case differently: *'If the Japanese war had still been in progress, and if it had been shown that the presence of these twelve scientists in the USA was vital for the defeat of Japan, no difficulties would have been raised as regards their despatch to the USA but it must be assumed that their employment in America can only be in connection with a long-term research project. Under these circumstances, we cannot believe that their retention at Cuxhaven for what would probably be a maximum of two months could seriously inconvenience the United States Chiefs of Staff. In contrast, their withdrawal at this juncture would prejudice the success of Backfire into which much hard work and valuable effort has been put.'*

The British authorities attributed much of the friction to what they termed *'...the mysterious and rather parochial way in which it pleased US Ordnance to work'*. Eventually, a solution was worked out between the British Director of Guided Projectiles, Alwyn Crow, and Lieutenant-Colonel R L Williams of US Ordnance - the British would return fifteen of the twenty-seven specialists immediately, and the remaining twelve as soon as Backfire was concluded. Despite this being precisely what the British had wanted in the first place, they also managed to secure a sweetener to the deal - the Americans would lend them four of the most prominent German rocket engineers who were not at Cuxhaven, including their de facto leader, Wernher von Braun, for one week for detailed interrogation in London. So it was that a crisis had been averted, but the whole affair left a bitter taste in the mouths of all those involved and rumbled on in the background.

Ironically, this dispute between the two largest Western Allies is that their conflicting demands were motivated by the same fear - that of another war, almost certainly involving long-range missiles, against the Soviet Union. Backfire was used as a reason to evacuate German rocket specialists from the region around Nordhausen - where rocket production had been moved after Peenemiinde was bombed in August 1943 - which was due to fall under Soviet occupation to the relative safety of Cuxhaven, deep in the British zone. Britain and the US even considered demolishing the massive underground factory there and destroying all its contents to preclude them falling into Soviet hands, but decided that so doing might have 'unfortunate repercussions'.

For the time being, they even maintained a facade of friendly relations with the Soviets, who were invited to send representatives to the final Backfire test-firing on 15 October. However, at his own discretion, Cameron was requested to *...refrain from showing foreign or Press visitors any part of the equipment or records that you consider it advisable to conceal.* The Soviets, for their part, did little to foster a relationship of trust either - despite only being invited to send three observers to the test-firing, they sent six, meaning the three who were denied access by the British had to try and catch a glimpse of the launch from beyond the site perimeter.

The Soviets' behaviour suggested that they viewed Backfire as an important exercise and wanted to learn as much as possible.

Discovering the exact value of the operation is one of the biggest challenges in studying Backfire, particularly as much of the literature on Britain's missile development dismisses it as, for instance, 'of little practical value'.

However, at the time, the War Office and Ministry of Supply allotted it *overriding priority over other guided missile projects to facilitate its early completion.* In pushing for this priority level, the Deputy Chiefs of Staff made their case as follows: *It may be that the demands in respect of Backfire may cause some delay in work now being done in connection with guided projectiles generally. On the other hand, the value to be obtained from Backfire may well lead to a shortening of the eventual time to be spent on Guided Projectile research. In any case, the duration of Backfire will be comparatively short.*

Despite this priority, not everyone in the UK was in support of Operation Backfire - Colonel Terence Sanders was sent to examine launch sites in northern France in early 1945. Sanders joined the Ministry of Supply in 1941, and in 1946, he was appointed Principal Director of Technical Development (Defence). Maintaining his army role, he was active in Operation Crossbow, hence his connection with the A-4/V-2. In November 1944, the 'Sanders mission' led by Sanders inspected the site at La Coupole, in the Pas de Calais area. He believed *that to assemble rockets from the components and then to launch them would be of doubtful value,* and the technical advisor sent by Alwyn Crow to act as Cameron's right-hand man had *no enthusiasm for the project at all.*

Terence Robert Beaumont Sanders (*b.*2 June 1901 – *d.* 6 April 1985). He is seen here as a member of the British Coxless four rowing crew in the 1924 Olympic Games held in Paris.

After the launches, the immediate response to the operation was largely positive. In the conclusion to his official Backfire report, Cameron summarised thus: *It is believed that all is known and that it now remains for others to make use of that knowledge!*

The British media responded enthusiastically, with *The Times, Daily Worker, Daily Express,* and *The Sphere* all publishing reports on the test-firing, each article accompanied by a number of photographs of the A-4/V-2 taking off. The special correspondent for the *Daily Telegraph,* Edmund Townshend, attended the launch on 15 October and described the rocket as '...like a pencil on a spear of flame as long as itself'. The *Daily Mail* reporter emphasised how much had been learnt from the operation, saying, *British scientists and army technicians have reached a point where, within three weeks, we could dispense with German help if we wished.'*

While it was true that Operation Backfire had allowed the British authorities to amass a substantial wealth of knowledge about the design, assembly, preparation and launch of the A-4/V-2, this did not mean that the services of German specialists were no longer needed.

British physicist Sir Edward Victor Appleton (*b.* 6 September 1892, *d.* 21 April 1965).

Looking ahead, German expertise was to be integrated into the post-war British missile programme. In terms of a final verdict on Operation Backfire, while its long-term implications may have been relatively minor, its importance at the time was considered to be very high - a fact demonstrated clearly by the willingness of British officials to risk souring their relationship with the Americans to ensure the retention of a few German experts for the duration of the operation. Ultimately, it met the terms of its limited mandate and laid the foundations for the guided missile research and development programme which emerged in Britain in the immediate aftermath of the war.

After the launches, the immediate response to the operation was largely positive. Those involved also celebrated the completion of a successful operation. Major P A Chittenden, who had served as Superintendent of Electrical and Electronic Assembly for SPOG, recorded details of a commemorative dinner held one week after the final launch and where dessert was the mysterious' A.4 Special'. He was also invited to attend lectures on the long-range rocket and screenings of the Backfire film, produced by a War Office film unit, and even received a 'Backfire trophy' in the form of a metal A-4/V-2 on a wooden plinth. The German participants had a similarly positive experience, though many saw Backfire as merely a bothersome delay to their real future in the United States. Dieter Huzel described the British treatment of him and his colleagues as 'generous', and commented that the extensive Backfire reports were all *more comprehensive than anything that existed in German files.*

British physicist and Nobel Prize winner Sir James Chadwick.
(*b.*20 October 1891, *d.*24 July 1974)

When asked to prepare a report on the future developments in weapons and methods of war, Henry Tizard and his Committee spent six months examining over three hundred documents and interviewing over one hundred witnesses. The resulting report was wide-ranging, comprehensive and bold in its predictions. These included the belief that long-range missiles would have an important role to play in future conflicts. In one area, however, information was not forthcoming - atomic warfare. Published in June 1945, before the use of the nuclear bomb against Japan and while the Manhattan Project remained a closely guarded secret, the Tizard Committee were denied access to any atomic information. *As a result, the best the Tizard Report could say in its section entitled 'The Atomic Bomb',* was that *'there is a possibility that some practical method may be found to release atomic energy explosively,* and that, if so, *a single bomber could do an amount of damage equal to that of a thousand bombers using normal bombs.*

Once the power of the atomic bomb had been revealed in August, it was decided that this predictive report was now distinctly out of date, so a new edition was deemed necessary. Tizard rejected the offer to make revisions, and the task was handed over to the Joint Technical Warfare Committee (JTWC) instead.

Could it be made Nuclear?

One must consider another reason why the British were interested in working out the mechanics of the A-4/V2 - this was the possibility of using it as an Intermediate Range Ballistic Missile with an atomic bomb on the top!

The British may have been sidelined by much of the Manhatten Project but there were British military and civilian personnel involved.

In the course of preparing the revised report, the JTWC received new information

As part of Operation Backfire the team set up demonstration areas, showing how parts of the rocket worked, including this sub-assembly demonstrating how the air and venturi rudders worked. *[Photo: NARA]*

on the atomic bomb from Sir James Chadwick, the senior British officer on the Manhattan Project, and from Wallace Akers, the head of the parallel British development programme, codenamed 'Tube Alloys'. The information presented had a direct bearing on the activities and importance of Operation Backfire.

Chadwick was an English physicist who received the Nobel Prize in Physics in 1935 for discovering the neutron. In 1941, he wrote the final draft of the MAUD Report, which inspired the US government to begin serious atom bomb research efforts. He was the head of the British team that worked on the Manhattan Project.

In October 1939, Chadwick received a letter from Sir Edward Appleton, the Secretary of the Department of Scientific and Industrial Research, asking for his opinion on the feasibility of an atom bomb. Chadwick responded cautiously. He did not dismiss the possibility, but carefully went over the many theoretical and practical difficulties involved. Chadwick decided to investigate the properties of uranium oxide further with Joseph Rotblat, a Polish post-doctoral fellow who had come to the UK to work with the cyclotron but was now destitute, as he was cut off from funds from Poland. Chadwick promptly hired Rotblat as a lecturer despite his poor grasp of English.

A special subcommittee of the Committee for the Scientific Survey of Air Warfare (CSSAW), known as the MAUD Committee, was created to investigate the matter further. It was chaired by Sir George Thomson and its original membership included Chadwick, along with Mark Oliphant, John Cockcroft and Philip Moon. While other teams investigated uranium enrichment techniques, Chadwick's team at Liverpool concentrated on determining the nuclear cross-section of uranium-235. By April 1941, it had been experimentally confirmed that the critical mass of uranium-235 might be eight kilograms - - eighteen pounds - or less. His research into such matters was complicated by all-but-incessant Luftwaffe bombings of the environs of his Liverpool laboratory; the windows were blown out so often that they were replaced by cardboard.

In July 1941, Chadwick was chosen to write the final draft of the MAUD Report, which, when presented by Vannevar Bush to President Franklin D. Roosevelt in October 1941, inspired the US government to pour millions of dollars into the pursuit of an atom bomb. When George B Pegram and Harold Urey visited Britain to see how the project, now known as Tube Alloys, was going, Chadwick was able to tell them: *I wish I could tell you that the bomb is not going to work, but I am ninety per cent sure that it will.* Some said that *Chadwick did more than any other scientist to give Churchill the Bomb. ... but he was tested almost to the breaking point.'*

So worried that he could not sleep, Chadwick resorted to sleeping pills, which he continued to take for most of his remaining years. Chadwick later said that he realised that *a nuclear bomb was not only possible - it was inevitable. Sooner or later, these ideas could not be peculiar to us. Everybody would think about them before long, and some country would put them into action.*

Sir Hermann Bondi suggested that it was fortunate that Chadwick, not Rutherford, was the doyen of UK physics at the time, as the latter's prestige might otherwise have overpowered Chadwick's interest in looking forward to the bomb's prospects.

The enormous scope of the effort became more apparent in 1942: even a

Leslie Richard Groves Jr. (b. 17 August 1896 d.13 July 1970) a United States Army Corps of Engineers officer who oversaw the construction of the Pentagon and directed the Manhattan Project.

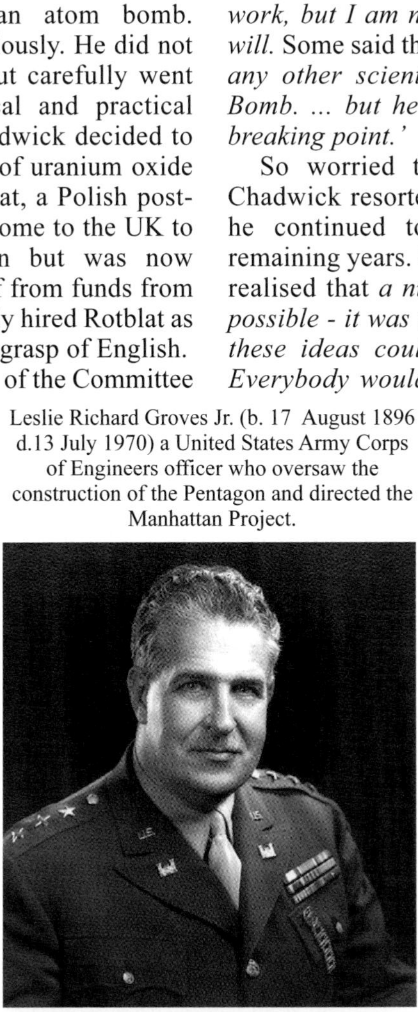

pilot separation plant would cost over £1 million and strain Britain's resources, to say nothing of a full-scale plant, which was estimated to cost around £25 million. It would have to be built in America. At the same time that the British became convinced that a joint project was necessary, the progress of the American Manhattan Project was such that British cooperation seemed not so important, although the Americans were still eager to use Chadwick's talents.

Sir Wallace Alan Akers CBE FRS (*b.*9 September 1888, *d.*1 November 1954) head of the Tube Alloys project.

The matter of cooperation had to be taken up at the highest level. In September 1943, Prime Minister Churchill and President Roosevelt negotiated the Quebec Agreement, which reinstated collaboration between Britain, the United States and Canada. Chadwick, Oliphant, Rudolf Peierls and Simon were summoned to the United States by the director of Tube Alloys, Sir Wallace Akers, to work with the Manhattan Project. The Quebec Agreement established a new Combined Policy Committee to direct the joint project. The Americans disliked Akers, so Chadwick was appointed technical advisor to the Combined Policy Committee, and the head of the British Mission.

Sir Wallace Alan Akers CBE FRS was a British chemist and industrialist who began his academic career at Oxford, specialising in physical chemistry. He was the director of the Tube Alloys project during the war, the clandestine programme aiming to research and develop British atomic weapons capabilities, from 1941 to 1945. After the war, he was director of research at Imperial Chemical Industries. He also served as a member of the Advisory Council of the Department of Scientific and Industrial Research and the committee that drew up the organisation of the United Kingdom Atomic Energy Authority.

Leaving Rotblat in charge in Liverpool, Chadwick began a tour of the Manhattan Project facilities in November 1943, except for the Hanford site where plutonium was produced, which he was not allowed to see. Apart from Groves and his second in command, he became the only man to have access to all the American research and production facilities for the uranium bomb. Observing the work on the K-25 gaseous diffusion facility at Oak Ridge, Tennessee, Chadwick realised how wrong he had been about even considering building the plant in wartime Britain. The enormous structure could never have been concealed from the Luftwaffe. In early 1944, he moved to Los Alamos, New Mexico, with his wife and their twins, who now spoke with Canadian accents. For security reasons, he was given the cover name of James Chaffee.

Chadwick accepted that the Americans did not need British help, but it could still be useful in bringing the project to an early and successful conclusion. Working closely with the director of the Manhattan Project, Major General Leslie R. Groves, Jr., he attempted to do everything he could to support the effort. He also endeavoured to place British scientists in as many parts of the project as possible to facilitate a post-war British nuclear weapons project to which Chadwick was committed. Requests from Groves via Chadwick for particular scientists tended to be met with an immediate rejection by the company, ministry or university currently employing them, only to be overcome by the overriding priority accorded to Tube Alloys. As a result, the British team was critical to the project's success.

Although he had more knowledge of the project than anyone else from Britain, Chadwick had no access to the Hanford site. Lord Portal was offered a tour of Hanford in 1946. *This was the only plant to which Chadwick had been denied access in wartime, and now he asked Groves if he could accompany Portal. Groves replied that he could, but if he did then 'Portal will not see very much'.* Chadwick received a knighthood in the New Year Honours on 1 January 1945 for his efforts. He considered this to be a recognition of the work of the whole Tube Alloys project.

By early 1945, Chadwick had spent most of his time in Washington, DC, and his family had relocated from Los Alamos to a house on Washington's Dupont Circle in April 1945. He was present at the meeting of the Combined Policy Committee on 4 July when Field Marshal Sir Henry Maitland Wilson gave Britain's agreement to use the atom bomb against Japan and at the Trinity nuclear test on 16 July, when the first atom bomb was detonated. Inside its pit was a polonium-beryllium modulated neutron initiator, a development of the technique that Chadwick had used to discover the neutron over a decade before. William L. Laurence, the *New York Times* reporter attached to the Manhattan Project, wrote that *never before in history had any man lived to see his own discovery materialise itself with such telling effect on the destiny of man.*

Chadwick informed the Tizard Committee that the current method of delivering the atomic bomb by aircraft had limited longevity, given advances in anti-aircraft

Some of the British Backfire Team. Back row, L to R: unidentified. Major Charles Black, Superintendant of Assembly. Unidentified. Unidentified. Front row, L to R: Unidentified. Colonel W G Raby, Chief Technical Superintendent. Wing Commander Joe Newman, Ballistics expert.
Although it is not known 'which is which', the unidentified are Lt Col J S Brown, Fuel Officer. Major P A Whittenden, Superintendant of Electronics. Major L R Targett, Technical Equipment Officer. Mr J Wortley, Assistant Fuel Officer.
[Photo: NARA]

Observers of the A-bomb drop - left: Group Captain Geoffrey Leonard Cheshire, Baron Cheshire, VC, OM, DSO & Two Bars, DFC (*b.* 7 September 1917, d. 31 July 1992)

Right: William George Penney, Baron Penney, OM, KBE, FRS, FRSE (*b.* 24 June 1909, *d* 3 March 1991)

defence and the ability to destroy enemy airfields. However, he described a rocket, or 'space projectile', as the 'ideal method of delivery for the atomic bomb', because of its greater range, the difficulty of shooting it down, and the reduced vulnerability of its small, perhaps mobile, launch sites.

Akers, meanwhile, warned that *...the only protection against an atomic weapon is to prevent it arriving or to live and carry on all industry in bomb-proof shelters burrowed some hundreds - or perhaps thousands - of feet in the earth.*

This echoed similar sentiments offered by others who were intimately aware of rocket development.

As early as November 1944, nine months before the bombing of Hiroshima, Professor R V Jones had written that a very long-range rocket, by virtue of its relative immunity from interception, might be a feasible weapon for delivering a uranium bomb, should such a bomb become practicable! Germany's Wernher von Braun, also saw possibilities in *the harnessing of atomic energy together with the development of rockets, the consequence of which cannot yet be fully predicted, though he may well have been referring to the possibility of nuclear engines rather than payloads.* In the conclusion of his official Backfire report, Cameron agreed: *if an atomic bomb can replace the high explosive content of the warhead, its destructive ability will be colossal.*

There were others who saw the benefits of using the A-4/V-2 to carry the atomic bomb. Group Captain Leonard Cheshire, VC, OM, DSO & Two Bars, DFC of the Royal Air Force and William George Penney, Baron Penney, OM, KBE, FRS, FRSE an English mathematician and professor of mathematical physics at the Imperial College London were seconded to the Americans as official British observers to the atomic attacks. The American authorities stopped them from observing the bombing of Hiroshima, but after an appeal to Chadwick, they were permitted to accompany the second mission. On 9 August 1945 they witnessed the bombing of Nagasaki. The vantage point was in the support B-29 *Big Stink.* They did not witness the event as close up as anticipated due to aircraft commander James Hopkins' failure to link up with the other B-29s. Hopkins was meant to join with the others over Yakushima but he circled at 39,000 feet instead of the agreed height of 30,000 feet. He tried to justify this by the need to keep the VIP passengers out of danger, but Cheshire thought that Hopkins was 'overwrought'.

Cheshire must have been aware of the dangers of the atomic blast and the procedure that Colonel Paul Tibbets and the other pilots of the 509th Composite Group had developed to get their aircraft as far away from the blasts as possible. The device reached its detonation altitude of 1,890 feet above ground level in 83 seconds. In that brief time, Tibbets had to get the B-29 *Enola Gay* to a slant range of at least eight miles from the blast. Using an escape manoeuvre he had practised over Utah, he muscled the aeroplane into a 60-degree-bank, 155-degree right turn. It was a risky endeavour, but they managed to succeed. Clearly, though, using an unmanned missile to deliver the bomb was a far better alternative, and, although this is speculation, it is by no means beyond the realms of possibility that Cheshire reported back as such. After all, Cheshire was a renowned bombing leader and target marker who knew what he was talking about, and by this time, the A-4/V-2 was no secret.

It should be noted, though, that one of the main findings of Backfire was that at that time, an A-4/V-2 could not carry an atomic warhead, as the maximum A-4/V-2 payload was 2,150 pounds, while the atomic bombs then available (that is, of a size and weight to those dropped on Japan weighed at least 9,000 pounds. As a result, the new JTWC report confirmed that rockets were likely to be the most effective method of atomic bombardment in the future but would not be ready for use for perhaps another ten years. Nevertheless, the principle remained sound.

It is well known that all military planning is based on a set of assumptions about which nation is likely to be the future enemy - for Britain, in the latter half of the 1940s, it was clearly the Soviet Union.

A few days after the war in Europe ended, and while the Grand Alliance was still in effect, Churchill asked his planning staff to devise a strategy for defeating the Soviet Union in open conflict, codenamed 'Operation Unthinkable'. The plan involved making use of 100,000 rearmed German soldiers, reinforced by British and American manpower and air support, to launch a pre-emptive strike on the war-weary Soviet Union. Later assessments suggested that the Soviet Union's overwhelming superiority in conventional manpower could only be counteracted by the use of weapons of mass destruction, such as the atomic bomb.

There was a profound fear among British strategists about what would happen if the Soviets developed atomic weaponry of their own. In the JTWC report of July 1946, it was estimated that *some 30-120 atomic bombs accurately delivered by the USSR might cause the collapse of the United Kingdom.*

Unsurprisingly, this thinking directly influenced British missile development - the range requirements for a long-range rocket were given as 800, 1,500 and 1,850 miles, based on calculations of the distance of major cities in the Soviet Union from 'Norwich, Nicosia in Cyprus, and Peshawar in India', that is, the places in British territory 'from which the best minimum range coverage is obtainable'.

The potential of rocketry discussed during this period was not limited solely to military applications. Cameron thought rockets might provide *...a mail service which could bridge the Atlantic in forty minutes [and which] might be of more value than a weapon of war.* This optimistic view of rocketry's potential for civilian use is a testament to the bright future of technology as seen at the time.

A *Daily Mail* article written in the wake of the Backfire launches speculated even more ambitiously. In a new form, the rocket 'could supplant aircraft and carry mail, goods and perhaps passengers across the Atlantic in fifteen minutes' - a topic that must have appeared very attractive, since it appeared alongside another article noting that Pan-American Airways' had just re-established New York-London service would take 15 hours! The A-4/V-2 article said, *German experts have ideas which seem to go into the realm of fantasy. They say that if the crews can make their own oxygen, there is no reason why the men in rockets should not travel beyond the power of gravitational attraction and anchor in the space between planets, or even 'reach the moon'.*

It is true that individuals like von Braun, whose work in rocketry had initially been inspired by the notion of travelling beyond

Earth's atmosphere, had bold visions of what this new technology could achieve. In the report he prepared for CIOS after the war, he was sure that, *when the art of rockets is developed further, it will be possible to go to other planets, first of all the moon.* He summarised his views (and those of many of his contemporaries, both German and British) in the following way: *We are convinced that a complete mastery of the art of rockets will change conditions in the world in much the same way as did the mastery of aeronautics and that this change will apply both to the civilian and the military aspects of their use.*

As a result, rocketry remained a high-priority field in the British scientific and technological exploitation programme, which continued to grow and expand in the early post-war period. The most important development in this respect is that Britain moved from merely removing equipment and investigating facilities to detaining, interrogating and even recruiting German scientists and technicians themselves. In July 1945, the Deputy Chiefs of Staff committee, which took the lead on this initiative, described German progress in a range of fields, including rocketry, and noted that *...the related equipment will be transferred to this country but it needs, for its full exploitation, the presence of the scientists responsible for its development.*

The Elephant in the Room - the German 'Brain Drain'

In August, the government Service departments were asked for subjects in which they would be keen to recruit German experts. Both the Ministry of Aircraft Production and the Ministry of Supply included missiles and guided projectiles on their lists in all cases, the individuals brought in would be vetted as to their political pasts,

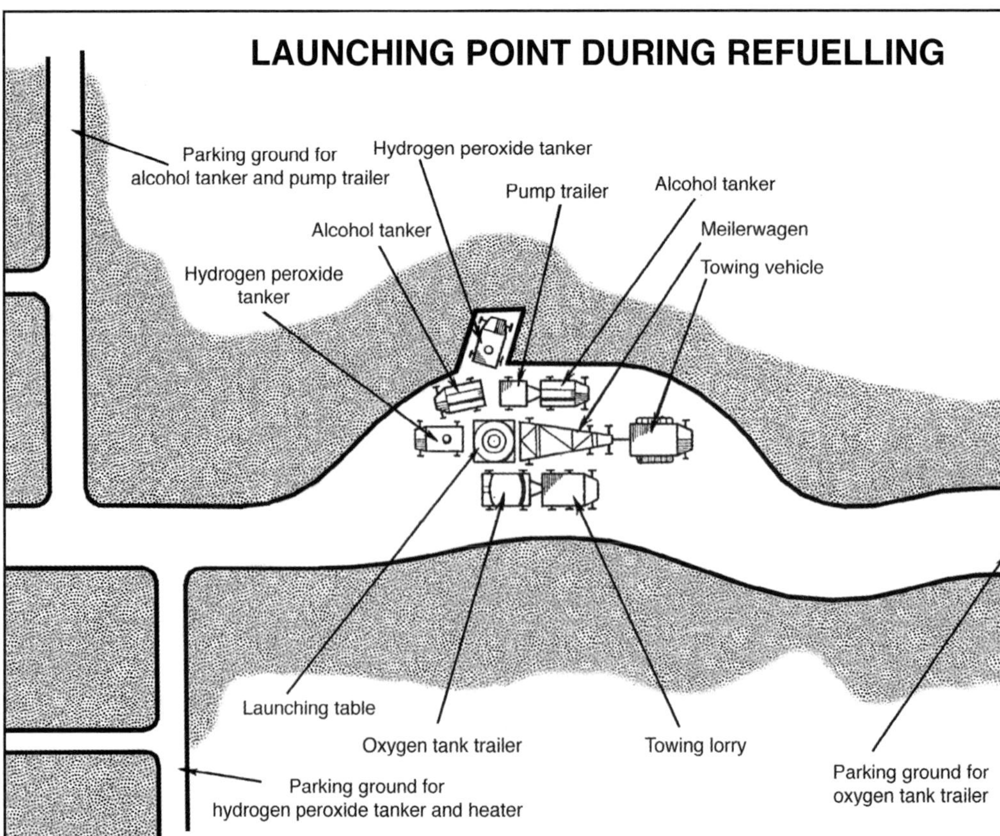

Plans and reality! The diagram of how the launching site was to be laid out and how it worked out in actuality.
[Photo: NARA]

subject to various security measures, and only employed on a limited basis, by way of renewable six-month contracts.

Operation Backfire offered the ideal platform for the British to recruit German rocketry experts. Once the test-firings were completed and SPOG was disbanded, the Ministry of Supply took complete control of the facilities at Cuxhaven, which became known as Ministry of Supply Establishment, Cuxhaven, or MOSEC. Here, the German personnel were tasked with documenting their work to date on guided projectiles, but a report on MOSEC filed in December 1945 noted that *'the purpose for this establishment, apart from general research, is to determine which German scientists it is considered could be taken for similar work in experimental stations in UK and to give practical experience to British scientists on German methods of guided projectiles.'*

One such specialist was a Walter J H 'Papa' Riedel a German-British engineer and rocket scientist who was the head of the Design Office of the Army Research Centre at Peenemünde and the chief designer of the A4 ballistic rocket. He was also known as 'Riedel I' for he was one of three - Klaus Riedel ('Riedel II') and Walther Johannes Riedel ('Riedel III') were also Peenemünde engineers.

Beginning on 27 February 1928, in December 1929, he was employed by the Heylandt Company and assigned responsibility for the development of rocket motors using liquid propellants, initially in collaboration with Max Valier, who had joined the company at that date. Riedel took over full responsibility for the rocket motor development in 1930 after Valier's death following a rocket motor explosion during a test using paraffin oil (kerosene) as fuel instead of ethyl alcohol.

In 1934, research and development of the Heylandt Company was taken over by the Army and amalgamated with the Wernher von Braun Group at the Army Proving Grounds at Kummersdorf, near Berlin, to carry out research and development of long-range rocket missiles. In March 1936, von Braun and Walter Riedel began consideration of much larger rockets than the A-3, then under development, which was merely a test vehicle and could not carry any payload. Along with Walter Dornberger, plans were drawn up for a more suitable and better-equipped test site for large rockets at Peememünde, to take the place of the rather confined Kummersdorf. From 17 May 1937, following the transfer of the rocket activities from Kummersdorf to the Army's new rocket establishment at Peenemünde, Riedel headed the Technical Design Office as chief designer of the A-4.

After the Operation Hydra air raid by the RAF on Peenemünde in August 1943, the development facility was transferred to a location that provided better protection from air attacks. The air raid had killed Dr Walter Thiel, the propulsion chief, and Erich Walther, the chief of maintenance for the workshops, two leading men at the Peenemünde Army facilities. In mid-September 1943, Riedel and two others scoured the Austrian Alps for a new site for rocket development to replace that at Peenemünde. The chosen location was at Ebensee, on the southern end of the Traunsee, one hundred kilometres east of Salzburg. The site consisted of a system of galleries driven into the mountains and received the code name Zement (Cement). Work on the site started at the beginning of 1944 and was intended to be completed in October 1945. From 1 October 1943, Riedel was responsible for supervising the transfer to Ebensee of the Peenemünde development facility.

Walter J H 'Papa' Riedel ('Riedel I')
(*b.* 5December 5, 1902, *d.* 15 May 1968)

From 29 May 1945 to 20 September 1945, following the end of the war, Riedel was held in protective custody (Sicherheitshaft) at the US Third Army's internment camp at Deggendorf, a significant location situated between Regensburg and Passau. From 1 November 1945 to

10 March 1946, he was employed by the MOSEC at Altenwalde, a location near Cuxhaven with historical significance, and from 11 March to 31 July 1946, at the MoS establishment at Trauen, a location near Braunschweig with its own historical context. After the Trauen establishment was disbanded, Riedel emigrated to England to work initially (from 1947) at the Royal Aircraft Establishment, Farnborough, a renowned institution in the aerospace industry, and later, from 1948 until he died in 1968, at the MoS Rocket Propulsion Establishment in Westcott, near Aylesbury, Buckinghamshire, another significant location in the history of aerospace development.

The 'recruitment' process was handled disastrously. No information was provided to the German experts about future employment until March 1946, when MOSEC was winding down. In addition, the British officials felt it was improper *'to enter into a contract with a beaten enemy'*.

As a result, the contracts which were eventually offered were ungenerous and were judged by the German personnel to be utterly inadequate on two grounds: there was no clarity as to the nature of the work they would be doing in Britain, and there were no assurances about the fates of their families who would be left behind in Germany.

With the contracts rejected, the British informed the German specialists that they were forbidden to work anywhere in Germany due to demilitarisation restrictions. They cut them adrift when MOSEC was shut down in May 1946. Most of the German experts then immediately approached the French, who quickly offered them all contracts they were willing to accept. Panicked that, as a result of their miserly tactics, they were going to lose out on all these German experts, the British authorities tried to hold the engineers at another facility at Trauen while they tried to arrange a better offer. On 23 May, new contracts arrived from London, only for the German experts to discover the terms had not changed at all from the originals. Eventually, a solution was devised, and ten German rocket engineers were brought to Britain in November 1946. Among their number were Walter 'Papa' Riedel and Johannes Schmidt, the de facto group leader, who had spent the war working on submarines but had reinvented himself as a rocket expert to secure post-war employment.

Some of these made important contributions to several British aircraft programmes. German weapons were on-site for study. These included the V-1 flying bomb, V-2, Feuerlilie F-55 subsonic missile, Messerschmitt Me-163B rocket-propelled interceptor, Rheintochter-1 anti-aircraft missile, Ruhrstahl X-4 air-to-air wire-controlled missile; Enzian E-1 3,150-lb missile; Henschel Hs 298 anti-aircraft missile; Hs 293 anti-shipping weapon; and Schmetterling and Wasserfall anti-aircraft missiles. The migration of this relatively small number of highly skilled scientists at the Royal Aircraft Establishment was out of all proportion to its influence on postwar history.

As a direct result of Operation Backfire, on 23 December 1946, a study group of the British Interplanetary Society headed by Ralph A Smith and Harry E Ross submitted a redesign of the A-4/V-2 rocket to the British Ministry of Supply. The adaptation consisted mainly of a small pressurised cabin in the nose of the rocket in place of the warhead and control compartment, which would enable a man to be launched as a passenger on the flight. The cabin was designed to detach, allowing the astronaut to experience several minutes of weightlessness before parachuting back to Earth. The proposal was not adopted, but the concept was very similar to the one eventually used by NASA with its Project Mercury.

A huge problem that the British faced was competition with their allies, the Americans and the French. Throughout the summer of 1945, relations became strained once the friendly but ultimately pragmatic wartime alliance broke down. One example was the wrangling over the fate of the twenty-seven rocket experts who were supposedly ‘loaned’ to Backfire by the US authorities. At the same time, concerned that the greater financial, political and logistical power of the United States would give them a blank cheque regarding exploiting Germany, the Chiefs of Staff pushed for a fair allocation policy between the two nations on all secret weapons and technological equipment. Driven by the fact that they were taking the lead in the ongoing war against Japan, the US proposal was ‘to give preference to the Americans in all cases where there are insufficient samples, personnel or equipment available to provide for development to be continued simultaneously both in Britain and the United States. The British felt that it would be better to have in place administrative machinery to decide which country was best placed to exploit each specific field but acknowledged that this would be time-consuming and would give *further grounds to US Army Chief of Staff General Marshall in his complaint that we are not being cooperative in this matter.*

As a result, the British signalled their assent on 4 July, but they still held clear reservations: *We agree in principle, but consider it most important that the Americans should not be given carte blanche to remove equipment, scientific personnel and documents without consultation, and we must insist that records of anything removed to either country must be exchanged.' As for the French, they were only to receive an allocation when US and British demands had been met, and even then only if a direct request was received.*

Without doubt, the elephant in the room in all of this was Wernher Magnus Maximilian Freiherr von Braun. Over the years there has been a myriad of investigations into whether or not he was a Nazi, including many FBI ones. Von Braun was an opportunist who joined the Nazi Party to continue his work on rockets for Nazi Germany. He applied for membership in the Party on 12 November 1937 and was issued membership number 5,738,692.

American historians have always played down Von Braun’s involvement with German National Socialism, even through the FBI files always have been riddled with evidence that he regularly inspected Mittlebrau and Camp Dora. Historians have written that ten years after von Braun obtained his Nazi Party membership, he signed an affidavit for the US Army. However, he stated the incorrect year: *In 1939, I was officially demanded to join the National Socialist Party. At this time, I was already Technical Director at the Army Rocket Centre at Peenemünde (Baltic Sea). The technical work carried out there had, in the meantime, attracted increasing attention at higher levels. Thus, my refusal to join the Party would have meant abandoning the work of my life. Therefore, I decided to join. My membership in the Party did not involve any political activity.*

It has not been determined whether Von Braun's error regarding the year was deliberate or not. That said, Von Braun, like other Peenemünders, was assigned to the local group in Karlshagen; there appears to be little evidence that he did more than send in his monthly dues. But he is seen in some photographs with the Party's swastika pin in his lapel – it was politically useful to demonstrate his membership.

Von Braun's later attitude toward the Nazi regime of the late 1930s and early 1940s was complex if it was to be believed - and dependant on which historian you reference. He said that he had been so influenced by the early Nazi promise of release from the post–World War I economic effects that his patriotic feelings had increased. In a 1952 memoir article, he admitted that, at that time, he most certainly had *...fared relatively well under totalitarianism.* Yet, he also wrote that *...to us, Hitler was still only a pompous fool with a Charlie Chaplin moustache and that he perceived him as ‘another Napoleon’ who was 'wholly without scruples, a godless man who thought himself the only god’.*

Later examination of von Braun's background, conducted by the United States Federal Bureau of Investigation, suggests that his background check file contained no derogatory information about his involvement in the Party. Still, it was found that he had numerous letters of commendation for outstanding performance of duties during his time working under the Nazi Party.

The FBI archives have a large amount of documentation - at least three hundred pages - on von Braun, a lot of which is still redacted. There is much documentation

Operation Backfire went to extraordinary lengths to record every details of the German missile programme, including things like this - photographing the ends of the fuel tanks. *[Photo: NARA]*

between J Edgar Hoover and a number of Special Agents in Charge (SAC) at regional offices holding various investigations. American historians report that overall, FBI conclusions point to von Braun's involvement in the Nazi Party to be purely for the advancement of his academic career, or out of fear of imprisonment or execution.

What is known is that Von Braun joined the SS horseback riding school on 1 November 1933 as an SS-Anwärter. He left the following year. In 1940, von Braun joined the SS and was given the rank of Untersturmführer in the Allgemeine-SS and issued membership number 185,068. In 1947, he gave the U.S. War Department this explanation:

'In spring 1940, one SS-Standartenführer (SS-Colonel) Müller from Greifswald, a bigger town in the vicinity of Peenemünde, looked me up in my office...and told me that Reichsführer-SS Himmler had sent him with the order to urge me to join the SS. I told him I was so busy with my rocket work that I had no time to spare for any political activity. He then told me, that...the SS would cost me no time at all. I would be awarded the rank of a 'Untersturmfuehrer' (lieutenant) and it were a very definite desire of Himmler that I attend his invitation to join. I asked Müller to give me some time for reflection. He agreed.

Realizing that the matter was of highly political significance for the relation between the SS and the Army, I called immediately on my military superior, Dr. Dornberger. He informed me that the SS had for a long time been trying to get their 'finger in the pie' of the rocket work. I asked him what to do. He replied on the spot that if I wanted to continue our mutual work, I had no alternative but to join'.

When shown a picture of himself standing behind Himmler, von Braun said that he had only worn the SS uniform that one time but in 2002 a former SS officer at Peenemünde told the BBC that von Braun had regularly worn the SS uniform to official meetings. He began as an Untersturmführer (second lieutenant) and was promoted three times by Himmler, the last time in June 1943 to SS-Sturmbannführer (Major). Von Braun later claimed that these were simply technical promotions received each year regularly by mail.

American efforts

Meanwhile, across the pond in the good ole US of A, at 2:47 on Tuesday, 16 April 1946, a captured A-4/V-2 missile ascended from the US Army's new White Sands Proving Ground in south-central New Mexico. It didn't get very far. The guidance system failed, a fin came off, and the rocket - after reaching an altitude of only three and a half miles - crashed in the desert.

Assisting in the first American launch were some of the very German rocket engineers who had designed the rocket used to kill people in Paris, London and Antwerp. A group of about one hundred and twenty-five scientists and technicians, led by Wernher von Braun, had been imported under Project Paperclip, which aimed to transfer German technological knowledge to the US military and industry.

The von Braun group was housed at Fort Bliss outside El Paso, across the Texas line. But they weren't put in charge of the V-2 launches. The General Electric Company was responsible for preparing rockets at White Sands under the Army's Project Hermes programme, which, following the discovery of the German rocket programme in 1943, was initiated to develop surface-to-surface guided missiles. Over time, as American personnel gained more experience, the German role in assisting GE at White Sands diminished. The von Braun team's primary job would be to develop Hermes II, an experimental ramjet cruise missile launched on top of a V-2.

Three-and-a-half weeks after the first launch attempt on 16 April, GE personnel tried again, assisted this time by the Army, the Germans, and two research groups tied to the Navy. On 10 May, the second V-2 ascended to an altitude of seventy miles - or one hundred and thirteen kilometres - well over the one hundred kilometre line now

Above: The original caption reads 'General Electric employees getting ready for the big bang'. Clearly it's White Sands Proving Grounds and it is thought that this A-4/V-2 was a training round painted to show the various sections.

Below: The storage area at White Sands Proving Grounds for captured A-4/V-2 rockets and associated equipment, as seen in 1946. *[Photos: NARA]*

widely accepted as the definition of where space begins. It was the first launch into space from the United States, and by anyone except the Germans, whose V-2 had routinely crossed that line during wartime testing and operations of the ballistic missile in Europe.

Inside the nosecone of the 16 April and 10 May rockets, as well as other early White Sands V-2s, were not warheads, but steel cylinders containing experimental equipment. Colonel Holger Toftoy, the Army Ordnance officer in charge of the rocket programme, had seen from the outset that A-4/V-2 flights provided an opportunity to do science in the upper atmosphere and near space. Such research would not only provide new knowledge, it would help the military understand the environment through which missiles would pass.

On studying the 212-page 1952 published *'Final report, Project Hermes V-2 Missile Program'* by L D White, of the General Electric Guided Missiles Department Aeronautic and Ordnance Systems Divisions Defense Products Group Schenectady, New York it is blindingly obvious that the Americans were, in fact going over what the British had already done at Cuxhaven, years earlier. There are even references to the five volume Operation Backfire report scattered throughout it! The only difference in the two reports is that Project Hermes contained far more data than Backfire, simply becuase of the length of time and number of launches made.

The primary experiment on the first flights was Dr. James Van Allen's cosmic ray detector. Van Allen worked for the John Hopkins University's Applied Physics

Below: White Sands Proving Grounds, New Mexico. It is thought that this was the preparations for the 16 April 1946 launch. Clearly, the Americans were using captured German ground equipment as well.

Opposite page: Getting the missile ready for the successful 10 May 1946 launch.*[Photos: NARA]*

III
I

Laboratory in Silver Spring, Maryland, which had developed the proximity fuse for artillery shells.. Based on his experience designing a miniature radar set that could withstand drastic acceleration, Van Allen believed he knew how to create equipment that could survive the forces of launch and impact.

Ernst Krause's Naval Research Laboratory team from Washington, DC, also placed inside these first V-2s armoured cylinders containing test film for future experiments. At the time, radio telemetry was primitive and unreliable, and scientists wanted to recover the recording devices. Unfortunately, there was no money or time to develop a separable nosecone that would descend on a parachute. So Van Allen, Krause and others hoped that the heavy steel containers would survive impact in a salvageable form. But after the first successful launch on 10 May, when they finally found the crater sixty-one miles away in the desert there was only a huge crater surrounded by metallic shards. Even following the 16 April failure, which impacted at a lower velocity, nothing usable was recovered. Four more successful V-2 launches into space from late May to early July produced similar results.

The solution to the problem came unexpectedly. The scientists' first idea was to separate the warhead section, which the Army might want anyway for missile development. However, on the first flight on which the separation system worked properly - incidentally, also the first flight to ascend over 100 miles - the missile's main body, not the nosecone, survived in recognisable form after impact. No longer streamlined, the 30 July rocket tumbled down, shedding velocity. Here was the place to put an armoured instrument—in a tail fin. Finally, on the 10 October flight, the Naval Research Laboratory team recovered its ultraviolet spectrograph in a usable form. The returned film revealed the first evidence of what the Sun's spectrum looked like beyond the blocking effects of the Earth's atmosphere. Two weeks after that, a 35-millimetre camera on a V-2 captured the first grainy, black-and-white images of Earth from space.

Contrary to Toftoy's expectations that the White Sands V-2 campaign would be brief, launches continued until 1952 for military and scientific purposes. More than seventy refurbished and modified German rockets were fired from White Sands.

On 22 May 1947, Operation Sandy was established, and the USS *Midway* (CVB-41) was designated as the aircraft carrier to conduct the V-2's test launch. Rear Admiral Daniel Gallery, the assistant chief of naval operations for guided missiles, oversaw the project.

'The primary purpose of Operation Sandy was to discover some of the answers to the problem of launching a larger bombardment-type rocket from a ship at sea. Lessons from this operation will be applied to the future design of guided missiles for naval use and a new type of warship, the guided missile ship, which may eventually be as important to the fleet as the present-day aircraft carrier.'

Within a few weeks, a select group of officers and enlisted personnel from *Midway* headed to White Sands for intensive training in preparing, handling and launching a V-2 rocket. Ultimately, the Army's ordnance department was directed to provide two live rockets for the test launch and a dummy V-2 for continued training on the ship.

The date for the launch on *Midway* was set – 6 September 1947. The vessel's crew training was complete by August, and preparations had begun to ship the rockets and support equipment to the East Coast. *Midway* was berthed at the Norfolk Naval Shipyard adjacent to the railroad tracks and cranes needed to transport the V-2s to and on board the ship.

On 2 September, with all the gear aboard and preparations finalised, *Midway,* along with four Navy destroyers, set sail and headed to the launch area approximately 250 miles south of Bermuda.

At 3:53 p.m. on 6 September, the rocket was ignited. Two seconds after launch, the V-

Above: the 'dummy round' V-2 is loaded on the deck of USS *Midway*. It is almost certain that this is the same dummy missile as seen on page 167

This picture shows the moment of launch of a V-2 from USS *Midway* while at sea on 6 September 1947. *[Photos: NARA]*

As I recorded in my book *Operation Lusty: The Race For Hitler's Secret Technology* (Pen & Sword 2016) much of the German equipment went to the USA, first arriving at Freeman Field, Maryland. Here one of the A-4/V-2s is displayed held up by guy ropes, with the tanks and combustion chamber alongside. *[Photo: NARA]*

2 unexpectedly tilted starboard 45 degrees, continuing its liftoff toward*s* the flight deck island of *Midway*.

Within a few seconds, the V-2 rose normally and returned to a vertical attitude. Shortly thereafter, however, the rocket's flight profile became erratic and it went out of control and broke up at approximately 12,000 feet. The rocket broke into three main sections and fell into the ocean a little more than three miles from *Midway*.

While the V-2 did not obtain the desired trajectory, it satisfied the major objectives of the test and was considered a success.

'This experiment marked the beginning of a new era in naval weapons," said Gallery in the operation's after-action report. *'Operation Sandy demonstrated the practicability of launching the war-proven German V-2 missile from a modern aircraft carrier without interfering with the primary purpose of that vessel. The rocket was launched from a ship underway at sea for the first time. It was the opening phase in an extensive program leading to the adaptation of naval vessels and the logistics of naval operations to use this new weapon.'*

Even before the V-2s ran out, the Army and Navy developed other rockets to replace it, such as the Aerobee and Viking.

It is worth noting, however, that this inter-Allied rivalry was only genuinely fierce in the first year or so after the end of the war, when all the occupying powers were adjusting to new positions in the global order. In any case, British officials and policymakers remained all too aware that the real future enemy was the Soviet Union, and that a Soviet missile capability was of far greater significance to British interests than any small-scale competition with the US or France. As such, Britain took active measures to prevent German rocket equipment or expertise from falling into Soviet hands. This need was sharpened by Operation Osoaviakhim, the Soviets' mass deportation of German scientific and technical workers from occupied Germany to the USSR, which they carried out in late October 1946.

Operation Osoaviakhim was a secret Soviet operation in which more than 2,500 German specialists (scientists, engineers and technicians who worked in several areas) from companies and institutions relevant to military and economic policy in the Soviet occupation zone of Germany (SBZ) and Berlin, as well as around 4,000 more family members, totalling more than 6,000 people, were taken from former Nazi Germany as war reparations to the Soviet Union. It took place in the early morning hours of 22 October 1946 when MVD (previously NKVD) and Soviet Army units under the direction of the Soviet Military Administration in Germany (SMAD), headed by Ivan Serov, rounded up German scientists and transported them by rail to the USSR.

A race between the Allies developed to acquire as many scientists and engineers as possible, particularly nuclear physicists, needed to develop nuclear weapons, followed by rocket technology, such as the A-3/V-2 missile and the Messerschmitt Me 163 Komet. Expertise in gyroscopic instrumentation for inertial guidance and modern advances in aeroplane construction, such as turbojet engines or swept wings, were also sought. Other fields of remarkable interest included but were not limited to miscellaneous electronic devices, colour film products, chemical weapons, and optics. Hiring or abduction of these skilled workers was one of the objectives of the so-called 'Trophy commissions'.

Immediately following the German

The infamous 'Paperclip' photograph showing over one hundred German scientists and technicians in the USA. Former SS Major Wernher von Braun can be seen front row, seventh from the right with his left hand in his pocket. *[Photo: NARA]*

Instrument of Surrender, skilled workers, documents, laboratories and materials were shipped abroad to the Western occupation zones. Among these, the 'abduction of German nuclear physicists to Farm Hall' as a part of Operation Epsilon became particularly well known. The Soviet atomic bomb project secured a group of nearly one hundred German specialists including Gustav Hertz, Nikolaus Riehl, Peter Adolf Thiessen, and Manfred von Ardenne. It brought them to the Soviet Union *not entirely voluntarily, but without physical pressure.*

In the Soviet occupation zone of Germany, the Soviet Union initially set up many design offices, e.g. the Institut Nordhausen near Bleicherode and the Institut Berlin to reconstruct German guided missiles. By May 1946, the Soviets founded the Zentralwerke, which included both institutes and manufacturing and test sites from the earlier Mittelwerk underground factory in the Nordhausen, Thuringia area, with more than 6,000 German employees. It was directed by Helmut Gröttrup, who had profound knowledge of the V2 intricacies from his work on V2 development at the Peenemünde Army Research Centre.

The operation, formally known as Operation Osoaviakhim, was decreed on 13 May 1946 under resolution No. 1017-419 by the Council of Ministers of the Soviet Union with the objective to accomplish *transfer of the construction bureaus as well as 2,000 German specialists til the end of 1946.*

The People's Commissariat for Internal Affairs commissioned Ivan Serov, Head of the Soviet Military Administration in Germany, with the secret preparations. The Soviet Union wanted to ensure full access to German technologies both through the transfer of expert knowledge and the dismantling of the production facilities and their reconstruction in the Soviet Union. In addition, according to the Potsdam Agreement of 2 August 1945, developing and manufacturing weapons in Germany was banned. With the decree of the Council of Ministers of the Soviet Union No. 1539-686 of 9 July 1946, Stalin laid 22 October 1946 as the start of the dismantling operations.

Operation Ossawakim was completely unprecedented in its dimensions: in a concerted, secret operation on 22 October 1946, employees of facilities within the entire Soviet zone of occupation were drafted within half a day, and 92 freight trains were made available for transport. In detail, for example, it was presented as follows: Days beforehand, Kurt Magnus noticed the unusual bustle of the Soviet military and the arrival of freight trains at the station in Bleicherode. A specialist from Dessau managed to escape hours beforehand. He could not manage to warn his colleagues by telephone, as the telephone network had been shut down. Public transport in Dessau had been suspended as well. A designer at Zeiss suffered a fatal heart attack when he was informed that he would be transported away.

The night of 21 October 1946, the day following the 1946 Soviet occupation zone state elections as well as the 1946 Berlin state election until 22 October 1946, soviet officers accompanied by a translator as well as an armed soldier stopped by the homes of German specialists, ordering them to pack their belongings. Trucks and trains had been prepared and were standing ready for the immediate transport of around 6,500 people against their will.

- 1,385 of these specialists had worked in the Ministry of Aviation developing aircraft as well as jet engines and Surface-to-air missiles.
- 515 in the Ministry of Armaments, primarily concerned with the development of liquid rocket engines.
- 358 in the Ministry of Telecommunications Industry (Radar and Telemetry).
- 81 in the Ministry of Chemical Industry.
- 62 in the Ministry of Shipbuilding (gyro and navigation systems).
- 27 in the Ministry of Agricultural Machinery (solid rocket engines).
- 14 in the Ministry of Cinema and Photographic Industry,
- 3 in the Ministry of Petroleum Industry.

- 107 in establishments of the Ministry of Light Industry.

On 22 October, the Berlin branch of the Social Democratic Party of Germany protested against the deportation. On 24 October, the Allied Control Council received a complaint from the British representative of the Allied Kommandatura, along with the consent of the American and French Representatives, condemning the transfer of 400 Berlin specialists, including residents of the British sector of Berlin, to the Soviet Union as a violation of valid labour laws as well as violations of human rights. A discussion of the Allied Control Council about this deportation was adjourned by its coordination committee on 29 October because of *strong differences about the voluntary or involuntary character of the transports* between the Soviet and the American and British representatives.

Inside the Soviet occupation zone of Germany and East Berlin all protests were silenced quickly following a short uproar of the Free German Trade Union Federation.

Both the German and Soviet factory management were surprised by this action. Days, even years later, more precise details of this large-scale, perfectly planned and at the same time carefully kept secret deportation operation leaked out.

Sudden attacks were made not only in Bleicherode but all over the entire Soviet occupation zone: In Halle, Leipzig and Dresden; in Dessau, Jena and Rostock; in Brandenburg, Potsdam and East Berlin. According to credible estimates, around twenty thousand Germans - fitters, foremen, technicians, engineers, designers and scientists, women and children – were picked up, loaded and transported in that one night. Ninety-two trains loaded with human loot passed through Frankfurt (Oder) at this time.

Despite this, the affected specialists and their families were doing well compared to citizens of the Soviet Union and the Soviet Zone, apart from the suffering of deportation and isolation. The specialists earned more than their Soviet counterparts. The scientists, technicians and skilled workers were assigned to individual projects and working groups, primarily in aeronautics and rocket technology, nuclear research, Chemistry and Optics. The stay was given for about five years.

In the following years, equipment from numerous high-tech companies, including

The first A-4/V-2 rocket from German stocks was transported to the launch site on a truck trailer by the Russians. It was launched on 18 October 1947 from the Kapustin Yar test site. It flew 206.7 kilometres and deviated left for 30 kkilometres.

A-4/V-2s were stored - and found, everywhere. Here one is being seemingly pulled out of a shed on a narrow gauage railway track. *[Photo: NARA]*

those from Carl Zeiss (Jena), Junkers (Dessau) and the Siebel works (Halle), were dismantled and shipped to the Soviet Union. It was part of the reparations payments agreed upon in the Potsdam Agreement. The deportation mentioned above secured the specialists needed for the operation and continuation of the Soviet Union in advance. Their goals were to advance the armaments industry's expansion and develop nuclear and rocket technology.

For strategic reasons, they also did not want to leave military research and development in the SBZ, especially since the Potsdam Agreement provided for the demilitarisation of Germany.

As one historian described it: *'The Soviets were only interested in skimming off the specialist knowledge of the technicians and engineers in order to be able to develop their own missile program on this basis. At the end of 1947, the German scientists had done their duty when these replica German V2 rockets were repeatedly successfully launched, and then the Soviets took matters into their own hands and a year later, in November 1948, they had the first launch of the Soviet ones.'*

Under the supervision of the Special Technical Commission (OTK) established by the Soviet Union to oversee rocketry operations in Germany, A-4s were assembled and studied. Eleven A-4/V-2s, six of them assembled at NII-88, the other five at Nordhausen, were launched from the Soviet launch site Kapustin Yar, the first taking to the skies on 18 October 1947. Only five of the rockets reached their target, roughly the same reliability the rocket had under the Germans during the war. The experience derived from assembling and launching A4 rockets was directly applied to the Soviet copy, called the R-1.

Kapustin Yar was a Russian military training area and a rocket launch complex in Astrakhan Oblast, about one hundred kilometres east of Volgograd. It was established by the Soviet Union on 13 May 1946. In the beginning, Kapustin Yar used technology, material, and scientific support gained from the defeat of Germany. Numerous launches of test rockets for the Russian military were carried out at the site, as well as satellite and sounding rocket launches. The towns of Znamensk and Kapustin Yar were built nearby to serve the missile test range.

Originally called NII-88 (Scientific-Research Institute No.88), the entity was established on 13 May 1946, located at what was then called Kaliningrad, Moscow Oblast (now Korolyov), northeast of Moscow. It was based at M.I. Kalinin Plant No. 88, that produced artillery and tanks during the Second World War and headed by Dmitriy Ustinov who had successfully lobbied to control post-war research and development of rockets in late 1945.

Impressed by his work in Germany on the analysis of the V-2, Ustinov appointed Sergei Korolev as chief designer of section 3 on long-range missiles, later called OKB-1. In 1956, OKB-1 was removed from NII-88 to become an independent bureau.

Helmut Gröttrup headed a group of German scientists working for the Soviets at Branch 1 of NII-88 on Gorodomlya Island. Their job was to help reconstruct a Russian version of the V-2, called the R-1, after which they were returned to Germany.

Partially in response to this drastic action, on 11 December, the Defence Committee of the UK Cabinet, chaired by the Prime Minister Clement Attlee, agreed that *it was necessary to deny to the Russians those German scientists and technicians, within our influence, who could contribute substantially to the building up of Russian war potential.*

Schemes were developed to facilitate this denial policy and they did have some

A partially complete A-4/V-2 is displayed to the people of France. It is thought that this picture was taken in Reims. *[Photo: NARA]*

Another partially complete A-4/V-2 displayed to the people of France - this one is thought that this picture was taken in Paris. Note the missing rudders *[Photo: NARA]*

successes. A team of six specialists who had worked during the war on German Vengence weapon production at the Linke - Hofmann - Busch firm were evacuated from Berlin to Britain, which was believed to have seriously affected Russian exploitation of German-guided missile research. Nonetheless, the resources available to the Soviet Union meant that these minor non-proliferation measures were likely to have only a limited effect. Indeed, the British authorities concluded that while the denial of experts to the Soviet Union *may have delayed Russian developments, it has hardly prevented them.'*

While this concerned the British, their main drive concerning German rocket expertise was to utilise it for their own ends, not to deny it to the Soviet Union. In Alwyn Crow's October 1945 report to the JTWC, he stated his belief that British rocket technicians"are equal and superior to those of USA, Russia and Germany. Given adequate facilities there is no reason to doubt that Britain could hold her own in the race for the development of these new weapons. Sharing Crow's optimism, the post-war British government decided to provide these inadequate facilities and ordered the creation of a Guided Projectiles Establishment (GPE) to be based at a former RAF aerodrome at Westcott, in Buckinghamshire.

The Westcott facility opened in the summer of 1946, although it remained incomplete for some time thereafter. The first group of ten German rocket experts, including Riedel and Schmidt, arrived in November. The reactions from local people were not wholly warm. A petition sent to the local MP read: *We very strongly object to this move, which would almost certainly result in many Germans living in the district and being free to mix with our people, and suggesting that they be housed in some place where they would not be able to exercise what might be a harmful influence on village life.*

Over time, opinions softened and when, a year after they had arrived, an explosion at the GPE claimed the life of Johannes Schmidt as well as two British personnel, there was an outpouring of grief in the area. The local newspaper even went as far as to say that the 'poignancy of the accident was heightened by the fact that a great German scientist whose knowledge and skill were being applied to British research work was among the three who lost their lives.' Even so, trust in the German recruits was not complete, as revealed when it was discovered in 1947 that caches of technical documents about rocketry had been hidden in Germany during the final days of the Third Reich, perhaps to secretly recreate a missile programme in Germany after the war. Under the so-called Operation Abstract', German rocketeers now in British or American employ were interrogated about these illicit stashes, and a spirit of suspicion returned to relations between the experts and their new employers, albeit briefly.

The work conducted at Westcott, and to which the German experts directly contributed, was dictated by the priorities of the Service departments. In early 1947, on the list discussed by the Guided Weapons Advisory Committee (GWAC), one of the 'Priority A' items was a strategical rocket codenamed 'Menace', in which the General Staff, the Air Staff and the Naval Staff were all interested.

The criteria for this weapon included suitability for launch from any part of the world, having a range from 400 to 2,000 miles, but with maximum ranges of 800 to 1,500 miles of operational value. It should also be 'Destructive'- that is, able to carry high explosive, or act as a 'Carrier', meaning it was able to uplift atomic or biological warheads as required.

It also needed to have a *50% zone of two miles at all ranges*, meaning that half of all rockets fired should land within two miles of the exact target. In addition, long-range rockets seemed a smart investment as they could act as a deterrent, thus minimising the chances of war and reducing the need for Britain to maintain a large and costly conventional army in a period of economic,

The Allies displayed a number of A-4/V-2 in liberated cities of Europe, this one in the Nederlands. *[Photo: NARA]*

not to mention geopolitical, decline. However, even at this point, there were concerns that the development work involved in such a weapon was also prohibitively expensive for cash-strapped post-war Britain, not least because the technology needed considerable improvement before it could serve as the primary form of long-range bombardment. In the autumn of 1947, the GWAC recommended that at the present time, the method to be adopted for long-range bombardment must be the manned subsonic bomber. In 1948, the Ministry of Supply decided to curtail research into a long-range strategic missile and focus efforts instead on jet-powered manned bombers and anti-aircraft projectiles. The result was five designs: the English Electric Canberra, the Shorts Sperrin, the Vickers Valiant, the Avro Vulcan and the Handley-Page Victor.

It was 1955 before Britain decided to pursue a long-range rocketry programme again, when it began work on the ultimately abortive Blue Streak medium-range ballistic missile. Britain's first entry into the missile age had been tentative and fleeting but it did lay the framework for future developments.

von Braun speaks out.

Years later, von Braun, by now the technical director of the Army Ballistic Missile Agency, Huntsville, Alabama, made a series of forthright comments in 1959 following the success of the Russians in impacting the Moon, which revealed much about the American mindset that went right back to Operation Backfire. The Soviet Union, he said, was far ahead of the United States in space projects, *'...and there is no amount of money which can buy back lost time.'*

Von Braun added that he was convinced that if Russia stopped immediately, the US could catch up with them in one, two, or three years. *We have the brains, the resources, the capability, but continuous evaluations hamper us. It is all justifications and rejustifications instead of progressing in our development of space projects* he said. He thought the United States needed to spend twice its present budget on space research and blamed 'red tape,' lack of funds and complacency for America lagging behind.

Dr. von Braun felt, however, that the United States might be on a par with Russia in developing ballistic missiles, particularly the ICBM. But. he said, he had been *'alarmed all along'* about Soviet progress in space projects and had not been surprised when the Russians hit the Moon with Lunik II.

With eight times the thrust of Jupiter or Thor, the US Saturn rocket could deliver a hefty payload to the Moon, but the first Saturn shot might be three years away.

'It is definitely possible that Russia will have advanced beyond the Saturn capabilities by the time we are ready. I am quite sure that when our young astronauts blast off into space, they will meet Russian Customs officers.

Chapter Six

The Launches

The work of the Germans was concluding with a total of eight V-2 rockets produced. The date of the first firing was announced to be on 27 September 1945. Everyone was striving to reach this high point; the first shot. Tension was in the air as the day approached. The first rocket was towed to the firing position a few days prior to launching. It was placed under a storage tent and protected by a British special guard.

Everything had been meticulously documented. Photographs of the installations, equipment, procedures, and launchings were taken by the British Army Film Photographic Unit (AFPU) using a Zeiss Super Ikonta with a six centimetres by six centimetres f2-8 Zeiss Tessar lens camera and by the US Army Signal Corps Photographic Unit using a Kodak Speed Graphic five-inch by four-inch camera.

The equipment used for the action sequences was three Newman cameras, one Mitchell camera, three Vinten cameras and one Eyemo camera.

For filming the launchings on 2 October, 4 October, and 15 October 1945, remotely controlled and manually operated cameras were used. The remote-controlled cameras were positioned on two gun shields erected on the launching site and started from the command post.

A detachment of the British Army Kinematograph Service was employed to take footage used to prepare a training film. The object of the film was not so much to record Operation Backfire but to show how the A-4 worked, its handling from railhead to firing point, and the process of launching. Shooting commenced on 12 September 1945 and was completed on 22 October 1945. All sequences were shot at Krupps or the firing site, except a few shots of German operational launching positions in The Hague area.

In later years, this led to the propagation of an urban legend that claimed that much of the film of the A-4/V-2 launches was actual wartime footage, especially as most of the Germans employed still wore wartime uniforms.

The first rocket was finally ready. 1 October 1945 dawned with grey skies and increased tension in the German camp. There were doubts whether the launch would occur, the but an attempt was mounted anyway.

During the main test, difficulty was experienced in getting the steam unit valves to open. It was eventually found to be due to a fault in the ground control equipment which had had to be wired from memory; the fault had not been discovered during the preliminary tests through two errors cancelling one another out. After the necessary repairs were done, an attempt was made to launch at 15:50 hours. The igniter functioned satisfactorily, and the flame pattern was good.

The Main Stage did not come on as the Stotz lugs (ground-connector plugs) did not automatically throw off. The flame in the venturi was immediately put out using foam extinguishers, and after preliminary examination, it was decided to make a second attempt to launch. German personnel stated that the failure of the lugs to throw off occurred in around one in every ten rocket

V 2 TO BE FIRED FROM GERMANY

FILLED WITH SAND

FROM OUR SPECIAL CORRESPONDENT

CUXHAVEN, SEPT. 24

A V 2 will be fired from Germany again in the near future, but this time it will not be aimed at London. It will be launched under British supervision, and the war-head will be filled, not with high explosive, but with sand.

In all other respects it will be the genuine rocket projectile which was the last and one of the worst terrors the people of London had to endure—weighing some 12½ tons when launched, rising 70 or more miles into the air, and moving faster than sound travels. It will be launched from the coast near here and directed out to sea. Its flight will be photographed by observers here and along its course. The purpose is to make certain that we have all the secrets of this projectile. Inevitably assembling one—it consists of 2,500 principal parts and, as well, special tools have had to be got together—has been a long and laborious task: and, moreover, assembling the fuel required to launch it presents its own difficulties and dangers.

Careful precautions, including the provision of shelters, are being taken to ensure that none of those working on the project is injured. The experiment is in the hands of S.P.O.G.—Special Projectiles Operations Group. It is a joint Anglo-American affair, with technicians and scientists working with military experts. Every German projectile—those in use and those projected—will be fully investigated.

SECRET WEAPONS

It is known that the Germans were working on newer, more powerful V 2 models and on versions to be launched by ship, aeroplane, and submarine. Right to the end they were busy on secret weapons, some fantastic in concept, such as giant mirrors miles above the surface of the earth which would collect and concentrate the rays of the sun on a target, burning everything within a given area, and some of which were impracticable, such as 100-ton tanks. It seems possible that their work on radioactivity was directed more to securing fuel of an altogether new performance than new explosives. Germans are employed in assembling the V 2 under British supervision.

Among those who will photograph and record the flight of the projectile are members of the A.T.S. who, within a few miles of the front line, did a similar job when V 2s were being fired on Antwerp. They came from The Hague.

Details of the Operation Backfire's launches from Cuxhaven were far from secret. News was reported in many British newspapers, providing a lot of information, including that every precaution was being taken to preserve everyone's safety!

launches. No fault could be found, and they believed it was worth making another attempt.

Before making this attempt, however, it was necessary to carry out certain work. The low melting point solder used to seal the thirty-six special alcohol cooling jets in the venturi had, in several cases, melted. Therefore, the alcohol was leaking away in the venturi. Sometimes, in field operations, it was possible to get over this by plugging the holes. However, it was ineffective, and removing and replacing sixteen of the jets was necessary. It was done by a man climbing up inside the venturi wearing a macintosh coat to protect him from the alcohol which was pouring down. Reports in the press that this man became *'drunk with alcohol fumes'* are not founded on fact. It is, however, understood that the man carrying out this operation usually wears a small face mask with breathing apparatus, as otherwise, it is impossible to stay in the venturi for long without being overcome by the fumes. Also, the venturi is uncomfortably hot.

A fresh set of paper-protecting cups for the oxygen jets was inserted, and a special sealing compound was smeared over the alcohol jets. A fresh igniter was inserted, and a second attempt was made to launch. As the batteries had run for only twenty seconds, changing them was not considered necessary. To prevent freezing up, the hot air blower was kept in operation most of the time before the second attempt to fire.

In the second attempt, the igniter lit correctly but was thrown out before it had time to light the fuel. It happened because

When not required for the launches, radar equipment was stored at Krupps, Cuxhaven. *[Photo: NARA]*

the sealing of the alcohol jets was not quite effective, and the free alcohol caused a slight explosion, which in turn expelled the igniter.

A further attempt to fire was not made owing to the lateness of the hour. The site was illuminated using searchlights, which had been held in readiness for such an eventuality, and the rocket was untanked. This proceedure took approximately two and a half hours. The rocket was returned to the Vertical Testing Chamber for overhaul.

It is worth noting that in the logs there appears the phrase 'X Minus' used as a warning. This was the early equivalent to the modern idiom of 'T Minus'.

The abortive First Launch. Log of Sequence of events for the launch on 1 October 1945.

09:30 Control point manned.

10:43 Fuel column left Krupps.

10:45 Setting up of rocket completed.

10:50 All kine sites manned.

I1:08 All kine lines tested.

12:09 All Kine Theodolite's collimated.

13:30 R1, R2 and R3 sites manned.

14:00 Watches synchronised with broadcast BBC time signal.

14:11 Rocket tests completed.

14:12 Fuel column arrived at launching site.

14:25 Tanking begun.

14:25 X-60 warning to recording sites.

14:33 All radars ready for action.

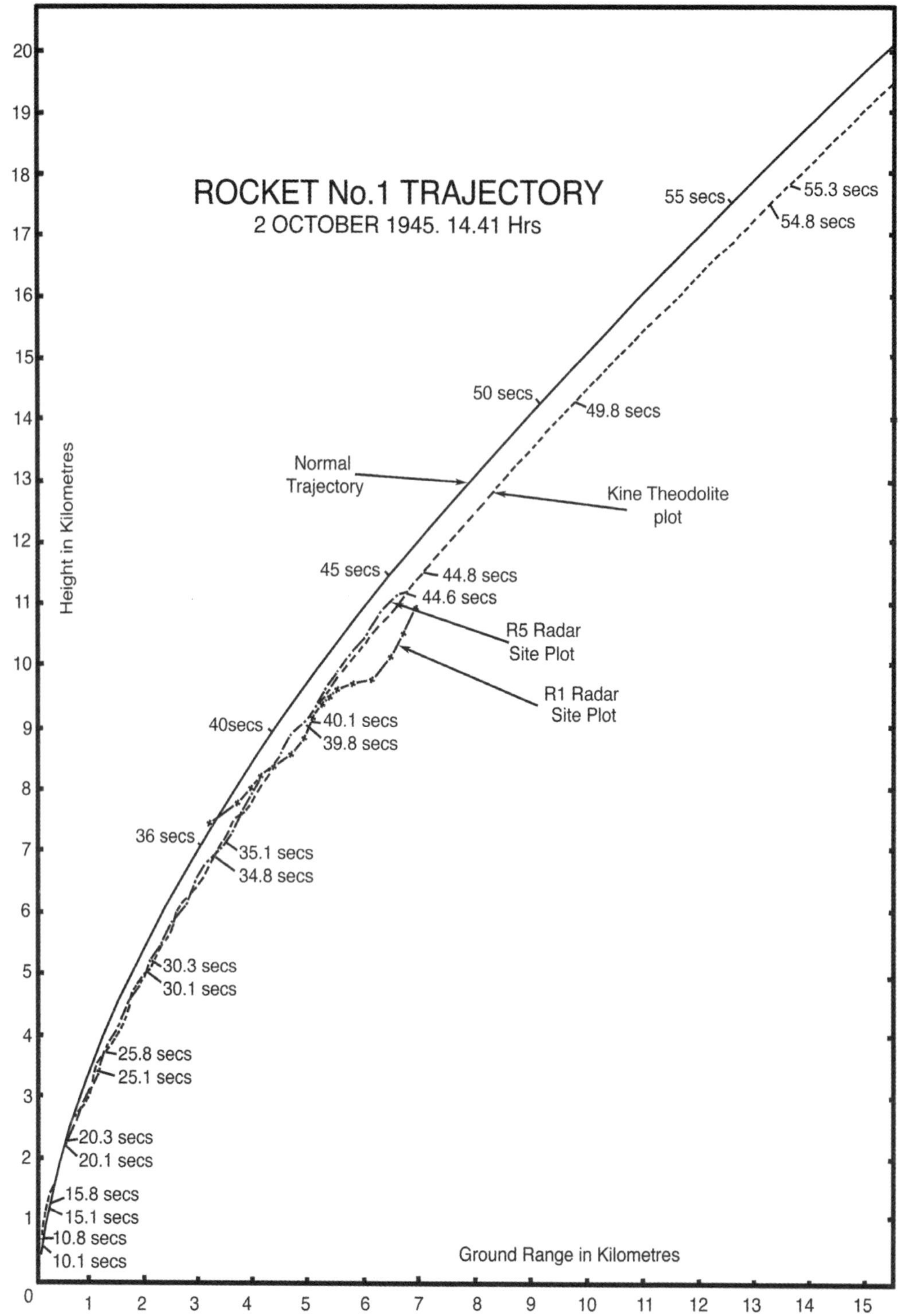
ROCKET No.1 TRAJECTORY
2 OCTOBER 1945. 14.41 Hrs
Height in Kilometres
Ground Range in Kilometres
Normal Trajectory
Kine Theodolite plot
R5 Radar Site Plot
R1 Radar Site Plot
55 secs
55.3 secs
54.8 secs
50 secs
49.8 secs
45 secs
44.8 secs
44.6 secs
40secs
40.1 secs
39.8 secs
36 secs
35.1 secs
34.8 secs
30.3 secs
30.1 secs
25.8 secs
25.1 secs
20.3 secs
20.1 secs
15.8 secs
15.1 secs
10.8 secs
10.1 secs
0
1
2
3
4
5
6
7
8
9
10
11
12
13
14
15
16
17
18
19
20

15:00 Time check.

15:22 Fuelling completed.

15:23 X-30 warning to recording sites.

15:27 Fuel column left launching site.

15:27 Commander, 307 Infantry Brigade reported 'All clear'.

15:41 Meilerwagen departed.

15:42 Orientating completed.

15:42 X-I5 warning to recording sites.

15:46 Insertion of Igniter.

15:49 Steering tests completed.

15:51 X-3 warning to recording sites.

15:52.5 Red Verey light fired.

15:54 Attempt to launch rocket.

17:51 X-15 warning to recording sites.

1800 All radars and kines ready for action.

18:00 Watches synchronised with broadcast B.B.C. time signal.

18:10 X-3 warning to recording sites.

18:12 Red 'Verey' light fired.

18:5 Attempt to launch rocket.

18:15 Stand down.

The First Successful Launch.

The next attempt was set up for firing on 2 October and was successfully launched at the first attempt at 14:41. It was the first A-4 launch to be observed by Allied personnel at close quarters. Weather conditions were ideal. There was little wind and a clear sky.

Only one fault was discovered during the main tests, which involved changing an alternator. The rocket's behaviour from the moment of take-off to the moment of fall was perfect. The take-off was steady, and the turn-over from vertical occurred at just the right moment. Brennschluss - meaning either the cessation of fuel burning in a rocket or the time that the burning ceases - occurred after sixty-five seconds. The error in line was 1.5 kilometres to the left, and the range error was 1.9 kilometres short. The length of time of the flight was four minutes and fifty seconds. The control method for the range of this rocket, and all others, was employing a time switch controlling the fuel cut-off. No form of radio control was used.

The rocket reached a maximum height: of 69.4 kilometres and flew a distance of 249.4 kilometres.

Log of Sequence of Events for the launch on 2 October 1945.

09:30 Control point manned.

09:50 Setting up of rocket completed.

10:16 Fuel column left Krupps.
10:50 Fuel coumn arrived at special vehicle park.

10:55 All kine sites manned.

10:55 Main rocket tests completed.

11:20 All kine lines tested.

12:00 Fuel column anives launching site.

12:45 Tanking procedure commences.

12:47 X-60 warning to recording sites.

12:49 All Kine Theodolite's collimated.

13:05 Radar R2 reported out of action. Radar N at R1, and Radar at R5 reported ready for action.

13:37 Kine at Site C out of action. Impulse line not working.

13:44 Commander, 307 Infantry Brigade reported 'All clear'.

13:55 Type 14 at R4 reported out of action.

14:00 Watches synchronised with broadcast BBC time signal.

14:06 Superfiuous personnel leave launching site.

14:08 X-30 warning to recording sites.

14:08 Tanking completed. Departure of fuel column.

14:10 All transport clear of temporary car park.

14:15 Igniter inserted.

14:25 X-15 warning to recording sites.

14:28 Orientating completed.

14:30 Departure of Meilerwagen.

14:32 Type 14 at R4 ready for action with modified range tube.

14:36 All Kine Theodolite's ready for action.

14:37 Test radar report.

14:37 Steering test completed. Launching troop take cover.

14:37 X-3 warning to recording sites.

14:41 Rocket launched.

Judging from the fall of the shot, this rocket behaved normally. Using a time switch to give fuel cut-off, a fifty per cent zone for a range of +/- ten kilometres should be expected of 'normal' shots since no allowance is made for variation in burner performance in the absence of an integrating accelerometer or radio fuel cut-off. The closeness of the fall of the shot to the point of aim about nineteen kilometres short is satisfactory evidence that the thrust unit behaved normally. Unfortunately, it was impossible to plot the exact position and time of fuel cut-off from the recorded results due to the unsteadiness of the velocity graph obtained from the kine theodolite records.

The velocity graph shows that the rocket had an acceleration of 0.89G rising to more than 3G in the region of fuel cut-off. The velocity at the fuel cut-off must have been of the order of 1,410 metres per second. to give the observed range. The inclination angle to the horizontal at fuel cut-oil was 39 degrees, and the observed time of flight 287 +/- 5 secs. The vertex height above ground was 69.4 kilometres.

The rocket fell 1.2 kilometres to the left of the line of fire, corresponding to an error in line of 0.28 degrees.

The weather was good, with an almost clear blue sky. All the kine theodolites functioned correctly. 'A' post lost the target before the others due to a small patch of cloud. Due to a fault in the cine camera in the R5 recording van which caused the film to blur, thus making the pulse counter illegible, it was impossible to tie these results with the radar results with any great accuracy. The exact time of take-off in relation to the theodolite records could, however, be obtained from the records of the 'B' post.

Radar Site R1 had only one SCR-584 in action, which followed the rocket for thirty-five seconds. The initial signal/noise ratio was 6:1 and range pickup was 65,000 yards. The aspect angle of the target lost was about one hundred degrees. The second SCR-584 here was out of action due to trouble with the long-range modification.

At the R2 radar site, the SCR-584 and GL2 failed to observe the rocket. It was later discovered that a longer spinner was necessary to work with the eight-foot paraboloid, and this had not been supplied. In the case of the G2, a fault was later discovered in the transmitter bandpass filter, which was causing a loss of power.

At Radar Site R3 the SCR-584 did not observe the rocket, probably due to the natural hazards of scanning the sky for a fast-moving target. The GL2 observed the target at one minute fifty-four seconds after launch at a range of 72,000 yards, bearing 217.8 degrees, A/S 45.7 degrees. The target was lost after 21 seconds. The radar track showed an apparent horizontal trajectory of the rocket at one-sixth of the true value. The angle of sight was nine degrees too low and the bearing rate of change six times too small. The slant range was about ten per cent too small.

Radar Site R4 suffered from having the Type 14 PPI being out of action. The radar observed a saturation break at 85,000 yard range. The range and amplitude was steady for thirty seconds, which the radar transmitter tripped. No target was seen on the GL2.

Meanwhile, at Radar Site R5 an immediate pickup was obtained. The signal faded and the radar ceased accurate following at 15,000 yards. The radar operator

BRITISH FIRE V2s 150 MILES, MISS BY THREE

BRITISH soldiers and technicians firing V2s have achieved greater accuracy than ever the Germans are believed to have obtained with the rockets.

So satisfactory were our new guiding devices that one of two rockets fired from Germany into the North Sea fell within three miles of the target point.

Faulty materials

On the dissolution of Shaef the Ministry of Supply appointed Sir Alwyn Crow to supervise experiments designed to test the statements of German scientists as to the way rockets were fired. The whole organisation was under the command of Maj.-Gen. Cameron.

No complete V2s were available, and components rejected by the Germans as scrap had to be used.

The Germans had discovered that if firing was long delayed the percentage of failures rose to as high as 40 per cent.

The British technicians, therefore, were dealing with an entirely new projectile and faulty materials.

New testing gear had to be devised, new guiding devices incorporated, and repairs carried out to each projectile.

German prisoners used

In six weeks, R.E.s constructed a launching site and large buildings for testing and assembling.

The rockets were removed to the launching site by German prisoners.

One rocket at first failed to rise. A technician who climbed into the combustion chamber to see what was wrong became drunk by inhaling the alcoholic fumes.

The second rocket was assembled, tested and launched with complete success at a target area 150 miles out in the North Sea.

Details of the Operation Backfire's launches from Cuxhaven were far from secret - they even reported the results!

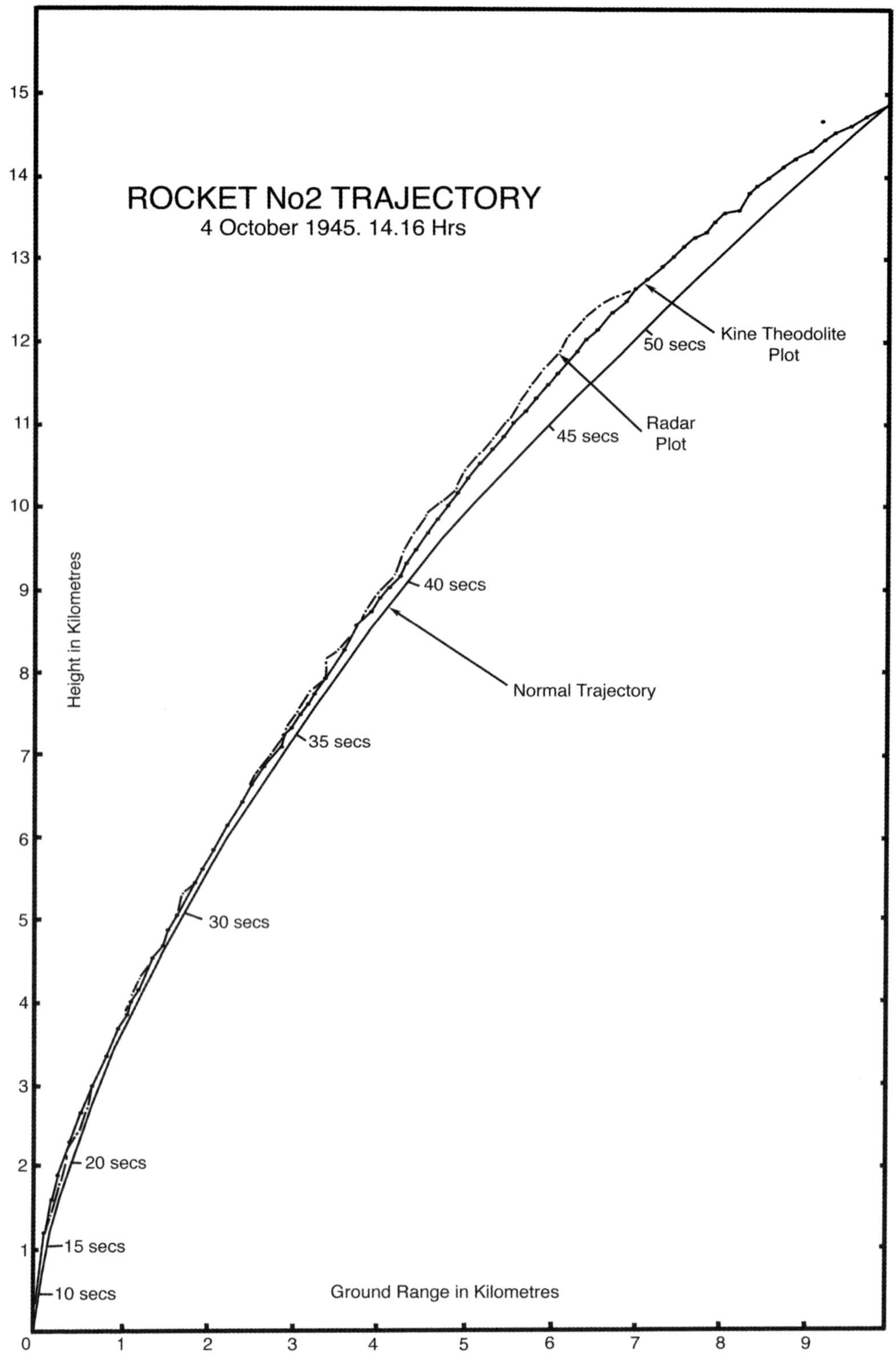

ROCKET No2 TRAJECTORY
4 October 1945. 14.16 Hrs
Height in Kilometres
Ground Range in Kilometres
15
14
13
12
11
10
9
8
7
6
5
4
3
2
1
0
1
2
3
4
5
6
7
8
9
10 secs
15 secs
20 secs
30 secs
35 secs
40 secs
45 secs
50 secs
Kine Theodolite Plot
Radar Plot
Normal Trajectory

tended to overrun in range by expecting a greater rate of increase of velocity than occurred. Film from the parabolid camera was useless due to over-exposure.

Launch Two.
The next missile launch took place on 4 October. Weather conditions were again ideal; there was no wind, and visibility was almost perfect. The missile, which had failed to fire on 1 October, was set up, having been checked over in the intervening period, and was launched at 15:15. Brennschluss seemed to occur after thirty-five seconds of burning, and the projectile fell 24.95 kilometres from the point of launch and 0.99 kilometres left of the line of fire. The flight was two minutes and sixteen seconds long.

It was initially thought that this failure was due to the turbine being overrun. If the turbine runs too fast, there is a danger of an explosion and a break up in the air. A centrifugal switch was installed to give a fuel cut-off if the turbine's revolution rate was excessive. So that the cut-off would not occur so soon that the missile would not land on friendly territory, this switch could not be energised until forty seconds after launch. The cut-off could then be given in the hope that the rocket would reach enemy territory in one piece, even if it did fall short.

Later examination of the Kine-Theodolite films - two stations followed the missile throughout its complete course - indicated that the thrust ceased after thirty-five seconds. No satisfactory explanation was discovered. While the rocket's behaviour was not satisfactory, its launch showed that it was possible to fuel and de-fuel a rocket and later launch it without carrying out a major overhaul.

09:15 Setting up rocket completed

10:06 Control Point manned - was delayed due to transport breakdown.

10:10 Fuel column leaves Krupps.

10:45 Fuel column arrives at special vehicle park.

10:49 All kine sites manned.

11:30 Main rocket tests completed.

12:25 Fuel column arrives at launching position.

12:54 Tanking commences.

12:54 X-60 warning to recording sites

12:55 Preliminary radar report. Only R5 completely ready for action.

13:02 All kine lines tested. The delay was due to fault an impulse line at site B.

13:02 All Kine Theodolite's collimated.

13:41 X-30 warning to recording sites.

13:45 Commander, 307 Infantry Brigade reported 'All clear'.

13:47 Tanking completed. Fuel column departed.

13:55 Superfiuous personnel warned off site.

13:56 All radars ready for action

14:00 Orientating completed.

14:00 Watches synchronised with broadcast BBC time signal.

14:01 X-I5 warning to recording sites

14:04 All transport clear of temporary car park.

14:04 Igniter inserted.

14:06 Departure of Meilerwagen.

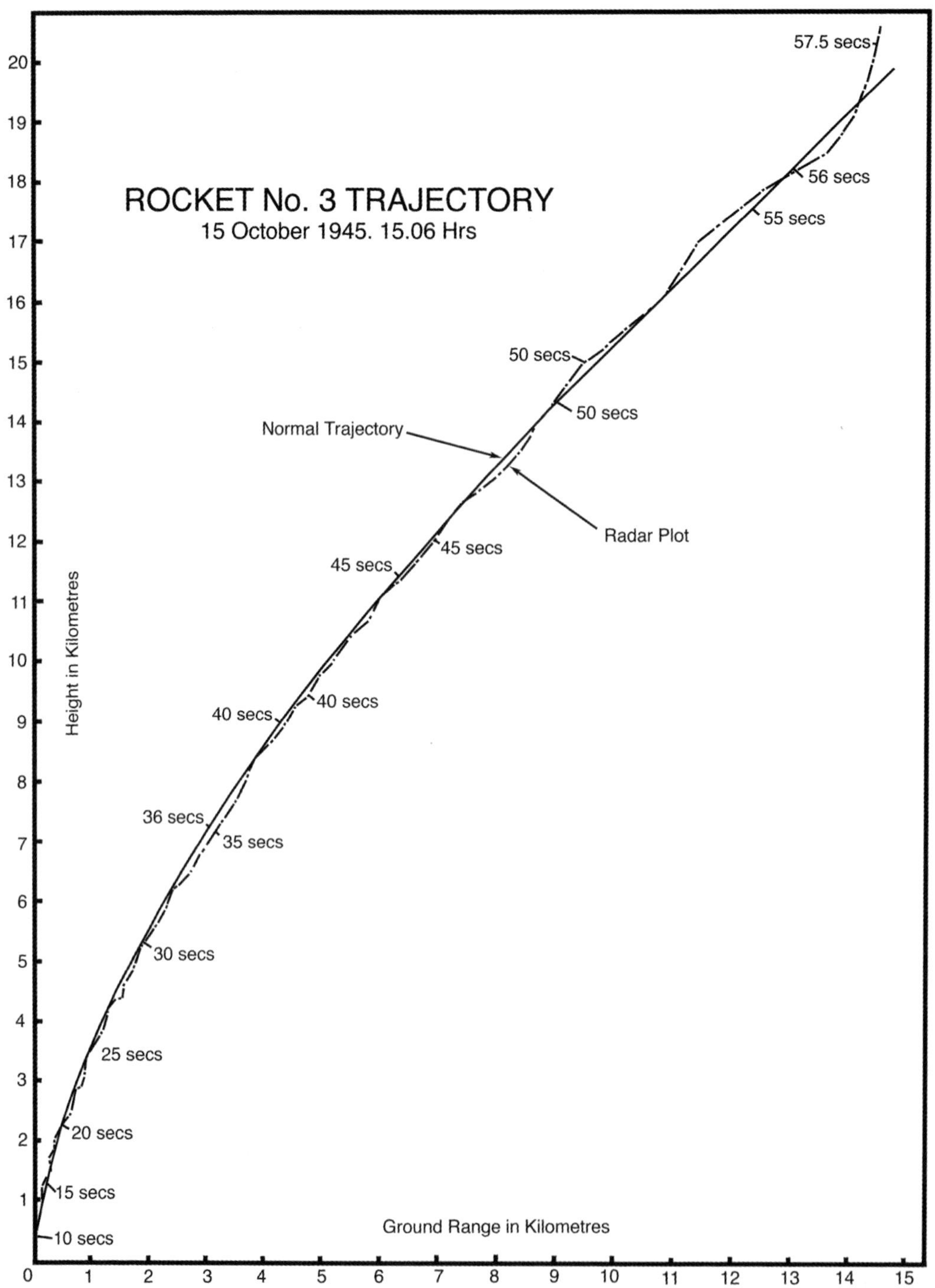
ROCKET No. 3 TRAJECTORY
15 October 1945. 15.06 Hrs
Height in Kilometres
Ground Range in Kilometres
Normal Trajectory
Radar Plot
10 secs
15 secs
20 secs
25 secs
30 secs
35 secs
36 secs
40 secs
40 secs
45 secs
45 secs
50 secs
50 secs
55 secs
56 secs
57.5 secs
0
1
2
3
4
5
6
7
8
9
10
11
12
13
14
15
16
17
18
19
20

14:09 Steering test completed. Launching Troop take cover.

14:10 Kine Site C out of action.

14:12 X-3 warning to recording sites.

14:14 Red 'Verey' light fired.

14:15 Rocket launched.

This rocket experienced fuel cut-off after 34.5 seconds, at which time it achieved a velocity of 520 metres per second and was at an inclination of 58 degrees to the horizontal. The range to the fall of the shot was 25 kilometres, the vertex height 17.4 kilometres and the total flight time 136 seconds. The rocket fell 1 kilometre to the left of the line of fire, corresponding to an error in line of 2.3 degrees.

The initial acceleration of the rocket was 1.02 G. Thus, the thrust of the missile was ten to fifteen per cent greater than for the first one, resulting in a greater acceleration than normal. This impression was also gained by experienced Germans who observed the take-off.

The reason for the early fuel cut-off was not clear. It could not have been fuel out-off due to the overrunning of the turbine (schnellsehluse) since the centrifugal switch, which gave the cut-off signal for this, was not energised until forty seconds after take-off. It is certain that no physical break-up of the rocket occurred, neither did it burst into flames, since the kine theodolite operators would have observed this. From the theodolite films it would appear that flames were still being emitted from the venturi for some six seconds after the rocket ceased to accelerate.

The weather was cloudless with a slight high haze. Kine Theodolites 'A' and 'B' posts functioned correctly. The 'C' post, due to line troubles, was only working locally and the 'D' Post was out of action due to a faulty camera motor. 'A' Post lost the target after

about fifty seconds due to haze. 'B' and 'C' Posts followed the projectile down to zero elevation at twenty-five kilometres from the firing point.

At Radar Site R1, one SCR-584 was working. The signal appeared as before but was lost after six seconds when the radar locked down to ground echoes. A fault was later discovered in the anti-lockdown modification. The second SCR-584 could not be used due to mutual interference.

Radar Site R2 had both radars in action, but both failed for the same reasons as with the previous launch.

Both SCR-584s were out of action at Radar Site R3 and, in any case, could not have observed the rocket since it fell short. The GL2 saw the target for one second, seventy seconds after launch at a range of 110,000 yards on a bearing of 214 degrees.

Radar Site R4 completely failed to pick up the target completely and Radar Site R5 saw the target being lost at 20,000 yards due to the fading signal. The camera on the paraboloid gave good results. Higher ratio gears were fitted to the range unit to allow higher rates to be produced.

The rocket reached a maximum height: of 17.4 kilometres and flew a distance of only 24 kilometres.

Third Launch

The third and final rocket was launched on 15 October as a demonstration to representatives from the USA, Russia, France, the Dominions, Whitehall and the press. Weather conditions were poor, with low clouds and a thirty mph surface wind, but the main objective of the launch was to demonstrate to the visitors that it was carried through despite the poor conditions.

When one looks at the log for this flight, there are seemingly 'gaps' in the timeline. This was done to accommodate the

Former Allied officers gathered at Cuxhaven to watch the third Operation Backfire launch

distinguished visitors, the normal time allowed for the procedure being extended by forty-five minutes.

The launch was made on time, and no hitch occurred in the preliminary proceedings. The rocket behaved normally, but it fell 18.6 kilometres short and 5.3 kilometres right of the point of aim. The flight time was four minutes and thirty-seven seconds.

09:00 Setting up of rocket completed. Preliminary work had been done ahead of schedule.

09:20 Control point manned.

10:30 All kine sites manned.

10:43 Fuel column left Krupps.

10:47 Main rocket tests completed.

11:20 All kine lines tested.

11:30 Fuel column arrived at special vehicle park.

11:50 Radar report : R1, R2, R4 and R5- ready for action. R3 - SCR-584 ready for action. GL2 High angle cams being fitted. Estimated ready for action at 12:30.

13:02 Fuel column arrived at launching sie.

13:30 Tanking procedure begins.

13:31 X-60 warning to recording sites.

14:00 Watches synchronised with broadcast BBC time signal.

14:30 Commander, 307 Infantry Brigade reported 'All clear'.

14:32 Tanking completed. Fuel column departed.

14:32 X-30 warning to recording sites.

14:50 All transport clear of car park.

14:52 Warning to clear launching site.

14:54 All radars on the air and ready for action.

14:55 Orienting completed.

14:55 Igniter inserted.

14:58 Departure of Meilerwagen.

15:00 Steering tests completed. Launching troop takes cover.

15:02 X-3 warning to sites.

15:04 Red 'Verey' light fired

15:06: Rocket launched

No visual results are available for the trajectory above two thousand feet. The acceleration at take-off was 1.02 G, which was greater than the expected value. It was confirmed by the radar results, which showed that although the trajectory was standard in space, the rocket climbed more rapidly up its trajectory than it should have done. It indicated that either the timing switch operated several seconds sooner than it should have done, the thrust deteriorated after forty-five seconds, or the fuel cut-off was given by the overrunning of the turbine (schnellschuss).

The flight time was 274 +/- 3 seconds, and the vertex height was estimated to have been sixty-four kilometres above the ground. The rocket fell 5.3 kilometres to the right of the line of fire, corresponding to an error of 1.3 degrees in the line of fire.

For this launch, low cloud blanketed the area. The target was lost in cloud at two thousand feet. Nevertheless, all theodolites functioned correctly.

Radar Site R1 was now at it's new site at Tonning. Increased spacing between radar units allowed both to operate simultaniously without any interferance. Both SCR-584s saw the rocket with full signal strenth and locked on. The signal faded rapidly after a few seconds. One radar attempted to lock on for a second time when the rocket was some twenty kilometres above the ground, at a range of 60,000 yards and aspect of 80 degrees, but the radar did not track and the signal faded.

The two SCR-584s (one with an eight foot paraboloid) saw the missile for a few seconds only. The signal/noise was 1.5/1 at each. The signals faded immediately, and no tracking was done. The rocket was not seen subsiquently. The GL2 followed in range only for eighteen seconds. The signal/noise ratio was 2:1, which was insufficient to allow constant following in bearing and angle.

At Radar Site G3, the GL2 was out of actin with valve and transformer defects. The SCR-584 picked up the missile unaided and tracked it for about fifteen seconds at a range of 83,000 yards. The Type 14 radar at Radar Site R4 saw the fall of shot at 78,000 yards, bearing 240 degreesThe signal was less strong than for the first rocket: the signal/noise ratio was initially1.5:1, becoming 4:1 almost inmmediately. The signal diminished to zero amplitude slowly - it was visible for sixty-eight seconds. The LW Radar (AA No.4, Mk.III) saw the break for one second, three seconds earlier than the Type 14, at a range of 79,200 yards, bearing 246 degrees. The GL2 failed to see any target.

At Radar Site R5 that target was lost at 29,000 yards. The camera on the parabaloid was useless due to the cloud cover.

The rocket reached a maximum height: of 64 kilometres and flew a distance of 233 kilometres.

Interestingly, amongst the guests watching the launch that day at Cuxhaven was Colonel Sergei Korolov ((*b.* 12 January1907, *d* 14 January 14, 1966). He was part of the Soviet intelligence team sent to investigate battered Peenemünde following its capture by Russian forces and was responsible for the exploitation of what remained at Nordhausen.

During World War II Korolev was held under technical arrest but spent the years designing and testing liquid-fuel rocket boosters for military aircraft. After the war he modified the German V-2 missile, increasing its range to about 426 miles. He also supervised the test firing of captured V-2 missiles at the Kapustin Yar proving ground in 1947. In 1953 he began to develop the series of ballistic missiles that led to the Soviet Union's first intercontinental ballistic missile. Essentially apolitical, he did not join the Communist Party until after Joseph Stalin's death in 1953.

Korolev would be championed as the Soviet Union's chief spacecraft designer and the grandee accountable for building the Vostok, Voshkod, and Soyuz spacecraft, which since the 1960s have carried all Soviet cosmonauts into orbit.

Chapter Seven

Conclusions

Drawing compelling conclusions about Operation Backfire is not easy because it can be viewed from two very different perspectives. The first would be a contemporary one 'of the time', and the other is a retrospective from eighty years in the future.

In my Introduction, I set myself three challenges. The first was to show that, despite popular belief, Great Britain did indeed show serious interest in developing a viable ballistic missile programme immediately after the war. In fact, in 1946, the British Interplanetary Society proposed an enlarged man-carrying version of the V-2, named Megaroc. It could have enabled sub-orbital spaceflight similar to, but at least a decade earlier than, the American Mercury-Redstone flights of 1961.

At the time, Operation Backfire primarily aimed to learn and record detailed information on specific aspects of the A-4/V-2 rocket. It was done by following the instructions issued by SHAFE. If any point was unknown to Britain and the United States after the investigations were concluded, the fault lay between those who drafted the instructions and those at SPOG who interpreted them. All were believed to be known, and others could use that knowledge.

The German V-1 and V-2 together were estimated to have cost about US$500 million. Given the relatively smaller size of the German economy, this represented an industrial effort equivalent to but slightly less than that of the U.S. Manhattan Project that produced the atomic bomb. The V-2 was something of a contradiction. In concept and design - which took the most time, effort and therefore money - it was very high-tech; in manufacture and production, it was almost the opposite - it used little to no advanced materials. Most of the construction was steel and light alloy, with plywood even used for some items! Control was what today would be called 'analogue', using servos gyroscopes and switches.

Supposedly just over six thousand V-2s were built, at a cost of approximately 100,000 Reichsmarks each; 3,225 were said to have been launched. Actual production was not that difficult, for SS General Hans Kammler originated the idea of using concentration camp prisoners as slave labourers for the rocket programme. It was later claimed that more people died manufacturing the V-2 than were killed by its deployment.

The V-2 consumed a third of Germany's fuel alcohol production and major portions of other critical technologies. Due to a shortage of explosive materials, some warheads were simply filled with concrete, using the kinetic energy alone for destruction, and sometimes the warhead contained photographic propaganda of German citizens who had died in Allied bombings.

The psychological effect of the V-2 was considerable, as it travelled faster than the speed of sound and gave no warning before impact, unlike conventional bombing aircraft or the V-1 flying bomb, which made a characteristic buzzing sound. There was no effective defence and no risk of pilot or crew casualties.

An example of the impression it made is in the reaction of American pilot, future nuclear strategist, and Congressional aide William Liscum Borden, who, in November 1944, while returning from a night time air mission over Holland, saw a V-2 in flight on its way to strike London. Borden became a pilot of the Consolidated B-24 Liberator, based in England with the Eighth Air Force. He flew thirty missions there, volunteering for service with a unit, the 856th Bombardment Squadron of the 492d Bombardment Group, that was part of Operation Carpetbagger and was based at USAAF Station 179 at RAF Harrington. As part of these operations, Borden flew specially equipped B-24s at night over Germany and Nazi-occupied Western Europe, dropping by parachute spies and Jedburgh saboteur teams as well as supplies to resistance groups.

Borden went on to describe the event in somewhat flowery terms: *'It resembled a meteor, streaming red sparks and whizzing past us as though the aircraft were motionless. I became convinced that it was only a matter of time until rockets would expose the United States to direct, transoceanic attack.'*

The method of attaining this objective was a meticulous process. It involved collecting individual parts and damaged rockets from fields, ditches, railway yards, canals, and factories, and then employing Germans to clean, repair, test, and assemble them into complete rockets. Eight rockets were built and tested as fit to fire. In proof of the correctness of the work, three of these were set up for firing, and all three were successfully launched. This process was a testament to the dedication and effort put into Operation Backfire.

At that time, the A-4/V-2 was a monumental achievement, being the only long-range rocket the world had ever produced. It was the first weapon to carry a payload of nearly one ton to a range of one hundred and eighty miles in a time of flight of five minutes, and that in any weather by night or day. Its capabilities were unprecedented, and it was clear that without air superiority, there was as yet no counter to it; once launched, nothing could be done. Its firing site required no preparation; all that it needed was a hard-standing, twenty-three feet square, with road access. It rose completely vertically and could be launched from the middle of a wood. Within two hours of the first arrival on site, the rocket could be fired, and the site cleared, leaving no visible trace. It can change its railhead every day. It possesses mobility and security to an unusual degree, and can only be countered by destruction of its factories or rail communications.

The disadvantage has been the enormous production effort required to achieve a relatively small and inaccurate result. However much it may be decried, though, its achievements have been by no means negligible. Of the 1,800 rockets launched against Antwerp in Belgium, forty-four per cent landed within a circle of ten kilometres radius. The military and civil effort put into defensive measures was considerable. The physical destruction and morale effects in both London and Antwerp had to be considered. These were the results of the first operational model of an entirely new type of weapon. The aircraft deployed in the early days of The Great War of 1914-15 hardly achieved as much.

As the Operation Backfire Report said: *'From such a start, the possibilities of development must be enormous—simplification of production, increased range, increased payload, and improved accuracy will magnify its effect. If an atomic bomb can replace the high explosive content of the warhead, its destructive ability will be colossal. The Germans looked still further ahead. They were planning an A-9 to carry a pilot in a pressure cabin, with retractable wings to put out at the height of its trajectory so that when it came back into the atmosphere, it could glide to earth in safety. A mail service which could bridge the Atlantic in forty minutes might be of more value than a weapon of war.*

Whatever the future may hold, the A-4 is

undoubtedly already a feasible weapon of war. Even if Britain and the United States do not wish to use it, they must, at all costs, be prepared to counter it. Efficient and up-to-date counter-measures cannot be produced without developing the weapon itself.

The lesson of operation "BACKFIRE" is that what Britain and the United States can do, other nations can do. No nation can afford to allow the development of long-range rockets to jog along as a matter of routine.

There is need of all the imagination, drive, and brains that can be mustered. For the sake of their very existence, Britain and the United States must be masters of this weapon of the future.

The second challenge was to correct the widespread assumption that the quickest and easiest way for Britain to obtain a missile capacity of its own would be to draw upon German technology and expertise once the Third Reich had collapsed.

It was done by locating German contributions to this process and thus reframing the narrative as transnational rather than solely Anglo-centric.

There can be little doubt that Britain, with its almost complete lack of wartime long-range rocket research, needed to rely heavily on German advances in creating a post-war missile programme. As Alwyn Crow reported to the JTWC in October 1945, *'the weapons V-1 and V-2 which Germany has produced represent considerable technical achievement, far beyond anything for which facilities and money have been made available in this country.*

These weapons have been developed with striking imagination [and] with drive and initiative.'

As such, the recruitment of German personnel was of great value - in 1949, it was noted that '*the Guided Weapons fields in which the Germans were so far ahead of us at the end of the war have been particularly carefully combed The result of this careful combing is that approximately one-third of our present ninety German scientists are working for us directly on guided weapon problems and a fair proportion of the remainder are on related work'.*

The other side of the story here was the fear that the German expertise the British sought might prove equally helpful to the Soviet Union. In May 1946, the Joint Intelligence Committee stated its anxious belief that 'the alliance of German brainpower and Russian resources may prove to be the most important outcome of the occupation of Germany.'

Every German rocket engineer employed in Britain was one fewer who could fall into Soviet hands, making the German involvement in the British missile programme doubly important.

Looking back on the episode from today's viewpoint, it is clear from this that Cameron and the Backfire team were officially very diplomatic - and virtually silent - regarding any internal problems and obstacles and also as to who the British saw as the real 'enemy' - Josef Stalin and the Soviets, although in many respects the Americans came a close second!

Finally, the third objective was to show that Britain and the United States did not always present a united front in the immediate post-war years and that the changing global power dynamics involved in this reconfiguration of the Anglo-American alliance led to competition as much as co-operation. The wrangling over the twenty-seven German missile experts during Backfire was one particularly glaring manifestation of this. Nonetheless, this transatlantic animosity could not last, especially under the shadow of the looming Soviet threat.

With the end of the war in Europe, the Allies descended on Germany and its previously occupied countries like a plague of locusts, searching out and stripping away every shred of German high technology under the guise of 'wartime reparations'. Indeed, before 6 June 1944, the USA created the 'Priority One List', a document issued to all technical officers to look out for and secure anything that remotely looked like anything appearing on it. The list contained hundreds of items. Behind the scenes and away from any public gaze, the French, the British, the Americans and the Russians were each straining to get their hands on the technology before the others. I covered this in detail in *'Operation Lusty: The Race For Hitler's Secret Technology'.* The frail coalition that created 'The Big Three' in Europe began to crumble as soon as, if not before, peace was declared in May 1945.

The Big Three leaders, Franklin D. Roosevelt, Winston Churchill, and Joseph Stalin, maintained a complex relationship. They frequently communicated via ambassadors, top generals, foreign ministers, and special emissaries such as the American Harry Hopkins. This 'Strange Alliance', as it was prophetically called, united, under fragile circumstances, the leaders of the world's greatest capitalist state (the United States of America), the greatest socialist state (the Soviet Union), and the greatest colonial power (the United Kingdom).

The three leaders played a pivotal role in shaping the war effort and the plans for the postwar world. Their co-operation, especially between the United Kingdom and the United States, was instrumental in forming the Combined Chiefs of Staff and making major decisions.

There were also numerous high-level conferences; Churchill attended fourteen meetings, Roosevelt twelve, and Stalin five. Most visible were the three summit conferences: The Tehran Conference, The Yalta Conference and the Potsdam Conference, which brought together the three top leaders. The Allied policy toward Germany and Japan evolved and developed at these three conferences.

Behind the scenes, there were many tensions among the Big Three leaders, although they were not enough to break the alliance during wartime. Division emerged over the time the Western Allies took to establish a second front in Europe. Stalin and the Soviets used the potential employment of the second front as an 'acid test' for their relations with the Anglo-American powers. The Soviets were forced to use as much manpower as possible in the fight against the Germans. In contrast, the United States had the luxury of flexing its industrial power but with the 'minimum possible expenditure of American lives'. Roosevelt and Churchill opened ground fronts in North Africa in 1942, Italy in 1943, and, with the build-up of the American Air Force in Great Britain, launched massive, almost round-the-clock air attacks on Germany, but Stalin kept wanting more.

Although the US had a strained relationship with the USSR in the 1920s, relations were normalised in 1933. The original terms of the Lend-Lease loan were amended towards the Soviets, to be put in line with British terms. The United States would now expect interest in the repayment from the Soviets following Operation Barbarossa's initiation at the war's end, the United States was not looking to support any 'postwar Soviet reconstruction efforts', which eventually manifested into the Molotov Plan. During the meetings from 1943 to 1945, there were disputes over the growing list of demands from the USSR.

The tension within the alliance escalated significantly when Roosevelt, a key figure in the Big Three, passed away. His successor, Harry Truman, took a different approach and rejected Stalin's demands, further straining the relationship.

Other long-standing issues were going on as well. Politicians, the media and historians have long discussed the much-vaunted 'Special Relationship' between the UK and the USA. Its origins can be traced back to well before the outbreak of World War Two, which provoked the rapid emergence of a seemingly unambiguously positive relationship between the two nations. The Fall of France in 1940 has been described as a decisive event in international relations, which led the Special Relationship to displace the Entente Cordiale as the pivot of the international system. During the war, one observer noted that *'...Great Britain and the United States integrated their military efforts to a degree unprecedented among major allies in the history of warfare'.*

On the other hand, Churchill is supposed to have shouted to General Charles de Gaulle, the leader of the Free French, in 1945, *'Each time I must choose between you and Roosevelt, I shall choose Roosevelt'.*

Between 1939 and 1945, Churchill and Roosevelt exchanged 1,700 letters and telegrams and met eleven times. Churchill estimated they had one hundred and twenty days of close personal contact.

Churchill's mother was a US citizen, and he keenly felt the links between the two English-speaking peoples. He first used the term 'special relationship' on 16 February 1944, when he said it was his 'deepest conviction that unless Britain and the United States are joined in a special relationship... another destructive war will come to pass'. He used it again in 1945 to describe not the Anglo–American relationship alone but Britain's relationship with both the Americans and the Canadians. *The New York Times Herald* quoted Churchill in November 1945: *'We should not abandon our special relationship with the United States and Canada about the atomic bomb and we should aid the United States to guard this weapon as a sacred trust for the maintenance of peace'.*

The intense level of military co-operation between the UK and the US began with the creation of the Combined Chiefs of Staff in December 1941, a military command with authority over all American and British operations. After the end of the Second World War, the joint command structure was disbanded, but close military co-operation between the nations resumed in the early 1950s with the start of the Cold War. The Tizard Mission catalysed Allied technological co-operation during World War Two.

Or did it?

Back in 2020, I wrote *'The Secret US Plan To Overthrow The British Empire: War Plan Red'.* It was a joint US Army and Navy War Plan; Red was one of a series of colour-coded war plans created by the United States armed forces in the late 1920s and early 1930s to estimate the requirements for a hypothetical or otherwise war with the United Kingdom.

The War Plan Red set of documents as promulgated by Admiral Charles F Hughes in May 1930, clearly demonstrated that there was a strong vein of belief existing within the American military establishment and within the wider USA that promoted the concept of American Imperialism and the desire to become what was later called a 'superpower'. This belief ran deep and wide and linked with other socio-political concepts.

American Imperialism was, and still is, a policy to extend the United States government's political, economic, and cultural control over areas beyond its boundaries. It could be accomplished in any number of ways: by military conquest, by treaty, by subsidisation, by economic penetration through private companies followed by intervention when those interests were threatened, or by regime change.

War Plan Red was just two more stages of this imperialist expansion - to annexe Canada and the whole of the Caribbean - the bonus was that it would destroy the British Empire and thus allow America to take up the mantle of being the world's only superpower!

By 1939, when the war broke out, War Plan Red was shelved, but certainly not scrapped, for as each day passed, it was becoming clearer that the British Empire was poorly equipped for the conflict that was seemingly bound to happen. Public opinion was against America being dragged into the war: accounts suggest that within 'the establishment' of the USA there was the growing thought that there was no need to go to war with the British Empire - the potential for war with Germany may have been increasing, but Hitler had never expressed any interest in the geopolitical importance of the USA and was downright dismissive of the country on racial grounds. He predicted that the country's downfall would be brought about by its racial diversity, not its purity.

Many in the military-industrial complex seemed to think it might be a good strategy to let the two protagonists slug it out, and then move in to pick up the pieces that included the technology!

Without a shadow of a doubt, the USA knew that Great Britain was on its knees, emotionally and financially. After six years of unrelenting conflict, the country was exhausted, its industrial complex was worn out, and its national infrastructure desperately needed rebuilding. The British Empire, already weak in the 1930s was also in turmoil. Despite the final victory of Britain and its allies, the damage to British prestige and the British economy helped accelerate the empire's decline. India, Britain's most valuable and populous possession, achieved independence in 1947 as part of a larger decolonisation movement, in which Britain granted independence to most territories of the empire. So, the American thought process went, why was Britain testing rockets they could not afford? Far better that they had it all!

So, the old thoughts of War Plan Red resurfaced. Once again, here was a chance for the Americans to 'stick the knife in'. American Imperialism would triumph, and the USA would start and eventually win the Space Race.

In September 1948, when the Guided Weapons Advisory Committee concluded that pursuing a long-range rocket programme was beyond British resources, they noted *'...that intensive work is in progress in the USA'*. They, therefore, recommended *'...that the closest co-operation be maintained with the USA in the development problems associated with long-range rocket bombardment '*.

Perhaps this was *'...the first steps to the realisation of a common policy on bombardment weapon development between the UK and USA.'* This suggestion became a reality with the bilateral military-technological sharing arrangements of the Burns-Templer Agreement in 1948 and the Sandys-Wilson Agreement of 1954, which led to a joint Anglo-American missile programme of Thor, Polaris and Trident.

Appendix One

Major-General A M Cameron's covering letter for the final 'Operation Backfire' report.

Headquarters, Special Projectile Operations Group,
B.A.O.R.

SPOG/500,12

7th November,1945

TO: Under Secretary of State,
The War Office.

Commanding General, United States Forces,
European Theatre.

Sir

1. I have the honour to submit my report on Operation " BACKFIRE."

2. On the 22nd June, 1945, I was instructed by the Supreme Commander, Allied Expeditionary Force, in "BACKFIRE " Instruction No. I , that the object of this operation was as follows :-

'The primary object of the operation is to ascertain the German technique of launching long range rockets and to prove it by actual launch. As complete, undamaged and fully-tested rockets are not available, it is necessary first to assemble rockets from the available components. In addition to the primary object, the operation will therefore provide opportunities to study certain subsidiary matters such as the preparation of the rocket and ancillary equipment, the handling of fuels, and control in flight.'

3. On the 11th August, 1945, after the W'ar Office had assumed responsibility for this operation on the dissolution of Supreme Headquarters, I was instructed by the Army Council in War Office letter 43/T'raining/3548(R.A.3) that the object of the operation was as follows:-

'The object of this operation is to obtain while the German technical staff originally employed on long range rockets are still available and the details are still fresh in their minds :-

(a) Information on the resting, assembly and filling of the German A-4 rocket.

(b) Detailed knowledge and experience of the German technique for launching long range rockets.'

'The intention is that you will collect information by carrying out the operation of assembly and filling in Germany, using German disarmed personnel supervised by British technical experts, and that the successful completion of the operation will be proved by the firing of a number of A-4 rockets. Observation of the trajectory and photographic records will be taken as far as possible and the drill employed for firing the rockets will be recorded in detail.'

4. The main text of my report describes the means by which these tasks were accomplished; my conclusions on the future of this weapon are stated in Section 8. Information which has been gathered on the preparation of the rocket and ancillary equipment and on testing and assembly is recorded in Volume 2. The technique of launching is described, and the drill is recorded in detail in Volume 3. It was proved by actual launches on the 2nd, 4th and 15th October, 1945. The results of observations of the trajectory and photographic records are set out in Volume 5. Section 5, and Volume 5 contains information on the handling of fuels and filling of the rocket. As no equipment for the remote control of the rocket in flight was uncovered, I have been unable to study this subject.

5. At a later date I was instructed by the War Oflice to make certain film records. These have been made and a brief description is given in Volume 5.

6. At Section 9 is a list of officers who have acquired special knowledge through participation in this operation.

I have the honour to be,

Sir,
Your obedient servant,
(Sgd) A. M. Cameron,
Major General,
Commander, Special Projectile Operations Group.

Copy to : The Secretary, The Ministry of Supply.

Appendix Two

Officers who have acquired special knowledge through participation in Operation Backfire.

HEADQUARTERS	**NAME**	**REMARKS**
H.Q. SPOG	Maj.-Gen. A. M. Cameron	Commander.
	J/Comd. J. C. C. Bernard, A.T.S.	P.A. to Commander.
	Col. W. S. J. Carter	Colonel G.S., and responsible for complete field operation and flight recording.
	Lt.-Col. F. Seebohm, R.A.	G.S.O. I.
	Maj. C. W. Lloyd, R.A.	G.S.O. 2 (Technical), responsible for collection of equipment and provision of fuel; also for technical reports on auxiliary equipment.
	Maj. B. H. F. Fehr, R.A.	S.I.G.; responsible for supervision of field work and recording of complete field procedure.
	Mai. R. T. H. Redpath, Int. Corps	G.S.O. 2 (Intelligence); responsible for all intelligence work in connection with the operation.
	S/Ldr. H. M. Stokes, R.A.F.	Technical Interrogator; responsible for technical interrogation and translation
	Capt. M. W. S. Meyer, Int. Corps	Interrogation Officer.
	Capt. J. L. Robertson, R.A.	G.S.O. 3; responsible for collection of equipment under G.S.O. 2
	Capt.]. F. Mills, Gen. List	A.O.R.G.; responsible for all technical recording and rocket ballistics
	Capt. W. N. Ismay, Gen. List	Ministry of Supply Liaison Officer, attached to H.Q. SPOG.
	Capt. D. Baldie, R.A.	I.G.; assistant to SIG.
307 Bde.	Brig. L. K. Lockhart	Commander, 307 Bde. ; responsible for all installations, British troops and German personnel employed on the operation.
	Mai. E. H. B. Greenfield, R.A.	B.M.
	Capt. D. K. Wood, R.A.	I.O.
	Maj. G. H. Smith-Parr, R.E.M.E.	Bde. E.M.E.
	Capt. J. R. Brough, R.E.M.E.	Tele-communications Officer.
	Capt. D. S. Clarke, R.A.	Interpreters Pool.
	Capt. P. Markstein, Pioneer Corps	Interpreters Pool.
	Capt. W. Game, R.A.O.C.	Ordnance Section.
'X' Radar Bty. R.A.	Maj. A. M. H. Jones, R.A.	O.C. and technical adviser on Radar.
20 Special Svy. Det. R.A.	Capt. N. Chaskins, R.A.	O.C. and responsible for all survey
Westex Recording Unit, R.A.	Lt. G. P. James, R.A.	Recording & evaluation of Radar data.
	Lt. R. Henry, R.A.	Recording & evaluation of Radar data.
	Lt. P. Humphrey, R.A.	Recording & evaluation of Radar data.
	Lt. P. W. T. Vint, R.A.	Recording & evaluation of Radar data.
	Lt. G. R. Hatcher, R.A.	Recording & evaluation of Radar data.

	Lt. P. M. Goffey, R.A.	Recording & evaluation of Radar data.
	Lt. H. W. Thomas, R.A.	Recording & evaluation of Radar data.
2 A.A. (A.T.S.) KT. Det.	Sub. R. Nicholson, A.T.S.	O.C. and responsible for all Kine operations and evaluation.
Ministry of Supply	Col. G. W. Raby	Chief Technical Superintendent
	W/Cdr. L. W. T. Newman	Deputy Chief Technical Superintendent.
	Lt.-Col. H. W. Goodger, R.A.	Inspection Staff.
	Lt.-Col. J. S. Brown	Chief Fuel Adviser.
	Maj. L. R. Targett	Technical Equipment Officer.
	Maj. C. Black, R.E.M.E.	Superintendent on mechanical constructlon.
	Maj. P. A. Cittenden	Superintendent of Electrical and Electronic Assembly.
	Brig. W. H. Wheeler	Represented D.G.P.
Military Gov.	Mr. J. Wortley	Assistant Fuel Adviser
United States Forces	Col. W. I. Wilson	U.S.A. Ordnance Dept.
	Col. J. H. Weber	U.S.A. Ordnance Dept.
	Lt.-Col. L. Ballard	U.S.A. Ordnance Dept.
	Maj. L. D. Rockwell	U.S.A. Ordnance Dept.
	1st Lt. H. S. Hochmuth	U.S.A. Ordnance Dept.
		Present as observers and generally to represent the interests of Commanding General, United States Forces, European Theatre

Appendix Three

German prisoners interrogated directly by Operation Backfire.

Name	Rank/Position	Remarks
Oberst Lt. Weber.	Acting Commander Div, z.V.	No specialised technical knowledge.
Maj. Thomschke	Reserve RegtCommander, 902 Regt.	Provided no useful information.
Maj. Schlesiger.	O.C. 901 Regt.	Information on targets and Order of Battle.
Hptm Bauch.	O.C. Fuk Horch Abt 1192.	General picture of functions of Unit.
Hptm Mueller.	c/o Ver. U Lehr Batt. 444	Details of battery movements and rocket setting up proceedure.
Hptm von Chilingsperg.	Staff of 902 Abt.	Questioned on site locations and supply.
Oblt. Graetz.	I.a.Tech at Div.z.V.	Covered all questions of the rocket and its controls.
Oblt. Ralle.	O.C. Technical Battery.	Details of employment in Grupe Sued.
Oblt. Bader.	O.C.Technical Battery.	Details of employment in Grupe Sued.
Lt. Lohmann.	Resp for Optical Measurement.	Located at Hachenburg. Provided knowledge of the proceedure used.
Lt. Pils	Resp for Direction Finding systems.	Provided details of 'Toscana' and other systems.
Lt. Thies	Resp for Optical Measurement.	Provided nothing additonal to Lt. Lohmann's statement.
Lt. Dietriech	Resp for Optical Measurement.	Provided nothing additonal to Lt. Lohmann's statement.
Lt. Lucke.	i/c Sendezug Lucke.	Gave details of activity.
Lt. Zimmerman.	Leading engineer at The Hague.	Provided details of rocket performance.
O. Faehnr Simon.	Mobile L/S Monitoring equipment.	Provided details of activity.
O. Faehnr Priesner.	B/S Monitoring.	Provided details of activity.
Fhj. Wacht. Brink.	Maintenance Eng. for Tarnsender.	Provided information on D/F methods and enemy coding principals.
Wachtmstr. Belwe.	Asst. Maintenance Eng. for Tarnsender.	Provided no additional information.
Wachtmstr. Baass.	Surveyor.	Questioned on aiming points.
Gefr. Blasche.	Operator of Companie L/S Monitoring.	Provided details and use of monitoring equipment.
Gefr. Dankwerts	Operator of Salerno Monitoring equip.	Provided details and use of monitoring equipment.

Appendix Four

Explanation.

Parts of this appendix have appeared elsewhere in this book, but the entire document is shown here for context and completeness. As with many documents, the item I have in my possession, dated 4 July 1945, was a poor-quality carbon copy that had been microfilmed. It had then been digitised and finally transcribed by myself. I suspect that the errors it contains, such as the language and spelling, suggest it was written by someone for whom English was not their first language. This I have left uncorrected, so as to maintain the accuracy of the primary source documentation. The document has been reproduced as verbatim as possible.

A report by the Scientific Advisors of the Air Defence Division, SHAEF on operational aspects of the German A-4 rocket organisation, as submitted on 20 July 1945 by Colonel W S J Carter, GS, Special Projects Operations Group.

SECRET

Some Operational Aspects of the German A-4 Rocket Organisation.

All information in this report has been obtained from Prisoners of War and should therefore be read with the usual caution.

<u>Introduction</u>

1. This report is based on the interrogation of a number of prisoners held in preparation for operation BACKFIRE there is reason to believe that most of the information obtained is substantially correct, and that the errors lie only in the detailed figures and date. The interrogation was conducted in order to assist in the interpretation of the findings of various teams, which had been studied the CROSSBOW operations in the UK and on the continent. For this reason, only certain selected topics were discussed, and then often only in outline much more information on these and other topics could undoubtedly be acquired by further interrogation.

<u>The A-4 Rocket</u>

2. Only one kind of A4 rocket has been used in operations. Any differences between rockets were only differences of content, (e.g. control apparatus) and not in external dimensions. Similarly, only one type of warhead was fitted containing 60/40 mixture. (amatol?) No aluminised fillings were used in operations, although they may have been during trials work. Oblt RALLE (Chief of a Technical Battery) stated that it had been the practice to pack extra explosive charges into the empty GERAETRAUME when radio control was not used, it was the general opinion however, that until more sensitive or proximity fusing could be developed. No advantage would accrue from increase in explosive effect. Since only increased crater size would result. Only one basic fusing system had been used although minor adjustments have been made to the sensitivity.

<u>Launch and Burning.</u>

3. During launch and burning, the rocket goes through the following stages:-

i. VORSTUFE. Fuel is descending to the burner and the gravity only and our ignited this stage last 3 to 5 seconds. Turbines are then set running.

ii. 8-TONNESTUFE (8-ton stage). Lasts 1/10th sec, occurs only as a result of the order in which switching is carried out.

iii. HAUPTSTUFE (25 ton stage). Full thrust operation. Rocket takes off. Operative until about three seconds before fuel cut off. (BRENNSCHLUSS).

iv. 8-TONNESTUFE (8-ton stage). Reduce thrust operative for the three seconds prior to BRENNSCHLUSS. Change over from HAUPTSTUFE is operated by the I-GERAET or by radio from the radio BRENNSCHLUSS ALANGE (B/S).

v. BRENNSCHLUSS. Fuels are either shut off by I-GERAET or B/S.

For ignition, a chemical igniter was first used this was later replaced by the PYRO ZEUNDUNG (a type of Catherine Wheel). The turbine takes about two seconds to reach full power. After starting the function of the final 8-ton stage is to give more accurate control of velocity at BRENNSCHLUSS. The rocket did not and has never taken off in the 8-ton stage. According to Prisoner of War Lt ZIMMERMANN this would be impossible since the thrust at that stage is not sufficient.

4. Acceleration at takeoff is roughly 1G and it rises to about 5G just before BRENNSCHLUSS. For the first 40 seconds after takeoff, the alcohol tank is pressurised by air flowing through the pipe, leading from the warhead. After 40 seconds, the source of pressure is insufficient and compressed air stored in the GERAETRAUM is used. After BRENNSCHLUSS the tabs on the fins are held centrally. It was not intended that the rocket should spin after BRENNSCHLUSS.

<u>Flight Path Controls.</u>

5. HORIZONT (pitch) and VERTIKANT (line and roll) Gyros.

Two types of gyros were used in the field. These were made by. SCHULTZ and LUFTWAFFE GERAET WERKE (LGW). Oblt GRAETZ considered that the LGW type was inferior. There were no great differences in the performance of the two products, the use of two varieties, was due to production difficulties due to bombing.

6. PROGRAMALZ

The PROGRAM for pitch was as follows:

Vertical climb - 4 seconds

Curved path - 47 seconds

Rocket held at constant inclincation until BRENNSCHLUSS.

No attempt had been made to control the PROGRAM from the ground (eg by control of the ratchet motor or by I/S beam modulations).

7. I-GERAET

Two types were used in operations, mechanical (gyro) and electro-mechanical (electrolytic cell). They were fired. Indiscriminately, either type of I-GERAET being used with LEITSTRAHL (L/S). Trials had shown the electro-mechanical to be better, but Oblt GRAETZ was critical of the way in which the trial had been conducted. The method of assessment had been by proximity of pairs of rounds, and a somewhat arbitrary elimination of rounds had been made. The electro-mechanical variety required more careful handling, and its performance was probably not so good in the hands of operational troops. Three types of the No.1 I-GERAET (gyro) had existed. The Mk.I was only designed for up to 250kms, and was therefore useless against LONDON. The Mk.II uncluded a few modifications, details of which were not sought from prisoners. In the beginning the I-GERAET gave trouble, but latterly they were perfectly and almost none were rejected. The tolerances were never reduced.

8. Radio BRENNSCHLUSS (B/S)

The B/S ALANGE consisted of two vans. The original siting requirements were that it should be within 500 metres of a point 12 km behind the firing position on the line of fire later. This was extended to a square 2 x 4 km with centre 5 km behind the firing site. Operation was entirely automatic.

9. LEITSTRAHL (L/S)

The L/S ALANGE consisted of two aerial arrays served by a single transmitter van (HAWAI). The van must be situated 8 to 16 km behind the firing line dead on the line of fire. No tolerance was allowed the distance between the areas have a tolerance of 6 mm and the height difference was not to exceed 20 cm. This latter tolerance could be exceeded if the dipoles were set slightly askew to the perpendicular to the line of fire. The original requirement was for flat ground in a 600 x 800 metres square. This was later reduced to a flat rectangle of 100 x 300 metres about each dipole.

A L/S reciever was situated 1 km in the rear of the firing site and used to align the L/S beam. This was referred to as KOBLENZ. The only siting requirement was a free radio path from the L/S ALANGE clear from obstructions such as walls, trees or HT cables that would interfere with receiption.

10. The general principal of the L/S is to use the two dipoles energised with a phase difference of about 120º. When at the correct distance, apart, these produce single astrometrical forward and backward looking lobes by altering the phase relations between the dipoles, the load may be switched on either side of a line perpendicular to the line joining the two dipoles. In one position, the carrier frequency is modulated at 5 kcs and in the other at 7 kcs. The pulse with an interval between pulses are both 1/50 seconds the L/S receiver (VICTORIA GERAET) receives these pulses and controls the rocket, so as to keep the signal strength received from either lobe equal.

11. The troops in the field disliked using radio controls as they greatly complicated the organisation and procedure due both to the number of extra personnel required and to the difficult siting requirements. Oblt GRAETZ said that both Gen. DORNBERGER and H.A.P. 11 preferred radio controls. He said that they had played a large part in the case of DORNBERGER'S opinion and H. A. P. 11 were enthusiastic because it kept another side of their establishment in touch with the weapon.

<u>Range Capabilities.</u>

12. Originally methyl alcohol was used as fuel. The average maximum range with all full fuel burn was 295 km with a 100% zone of +/-35 km. Hence, for the rocket to reach the target in 100% of cases without having run out of fuel before BRENNSCHLUSS the target must not be more than 260 km away from the fire in the site, allowing a 10 km safety factor. This fix is the maximum operational range at 250 km. Faulty rounds are neglected and the range distribution is assumed to be Gaussian.

13. Originally the minimum operational range was 120 km being determined solely by the fact that the range tables (compiled by Oblt GRAETZ) did not go below this range. Since the range between THE HAGUE and ANTWERP was less than this, the range tables were prepared for ranges down to 80 kms. These ranges were never in fact used. 80 kms is the absolute minimum for the rocket in its present form sincethe minimum burning time is fixed at 45 seconds by the existing switching motor (ZEITSCHALTWERKE).

14. The use of ethyl instead of methyl alcohol adds 17 km to the maximum range. With a full alcohol 50% of rockets aimed at a range of 312 km will achieve the required velocity before expending the available fuel the range to the STADTMITTE of LONDON was of this order. Eythl alcohol was used in all rockets fired against LONDON from early in October onwards. In order further to improve the maximum range performance of the rocket, it was decided at the beginning of December to increase the trust by increasing turbine speed. This was accomplished by alteration of the setting of the pressure reducing valve of the turbine to raise the pressure by 4 atmospheres above the normal value (varied 25 to 36 ata). The expected increase in range was approximately a further 18 km. This from THE HAGUE the average maximum range was up to 330 km with this system roughly 60 to 70% of rockets should before running out of fuel achieve the necessary velocity to arrive at the LONDON aiming point. Rockets may go as far as 360 to 380 km, allowing all fuel to burn and ranges as high as 425 km are on record. So far as is known optimum range considerations were not taking into account in choosing firing areas.

<u>Effect of increase in turbine speed on misfires.</u>

15. In practice the increase of 4 atm at the turbine seriously increased the proportion of rounds which disintegrated or otherwise failed during the period of burning. The cause of this

was not cleared until the beginning of February, and for 2 to 3 weeks during January, the additional pressure applied was 2 atmospheres instead of 4. The range table data used however assumed the full increase and therefore these rounds may be expected to have fallen short.

16. In the rocket, there is a centrifugal switch attached to the turbine, which will cause BRENNSCHLUSS if that if the turbine races racing will occur, if theA-STOFF should vaporise in the pipe, leading to the turbine, owing to the decreasing resistance, offered to the pumps. Increase in the rpm of the turbine, increased the chance of this happening, and hence of misfires. To correct there is the pressure in the a staff tank was increased from 2 to 2.1 atmospheres. Attached to the rocket is a relay which can be operated to shut off. the fuel while the rocket is still on the table if it is seen that the flame is not burning correctly. Increased vibration due to the increased rpm of the turbine caused this relay to operate from vibrations alone after takeoff. An arrangement was therefore made to de-energised the relay on takeoff. In general increased vibrations, probably gave rise to, or at least aggravated several other causes of misfire, of which about 11 are known to Oblt GRAETZ.

17. Effect of increased thrust on trajectory.

Originally before the rpm of the turbine was increased the angle at all burns was 47° to the vertical. Increase in the rpm decrease the angle to about 42° using the PROGRAM. This resulted in a much higher trajectory and the range tables were therefore re-computed as noted above in order to decrease the number of misfires, the turbine was not given the full pressure increase during January. The new range tables were, however, used to compute the I-GERAET and B/S settings. The fall of shot during this period would therefore be biased short. Oblt. GRAETZ estimated that the angle at all burnt would have a 100% zone of +/- 5° about the mean. Variations were generally thought by the prisoners of war, to be due to variations in the trust performance, rather than in the functioning of the PROMRAMALZ.

<u>Accuracy of Performance.</u>

18. Thrust and BRENNSCHLUSS

Kine-theodolites had been deployed at THE HAGUE towards the end of the operation. Only a cursory investigation of the results was undertaken. The Kine-theodolites were deployed by HAUPTM. BECK and he was assisted by Lt. THIES. The latter knew nothing of the results. Oblt GRAETZ had visited THE HAGUE and seen the results. He had noted that in line the rockets tended to follow on a sinusoidal course, with roughly a half period of 40 seconds, and an amplitude of about 300 metres. In good visibility rockets could be followed out to about 150 km. Lt. LOHMANN, who was in charge of KTs at AHAUS, said, however, that the films were not readable beyond BRENNSCHLUSS, although visual following was possible. Oblt GRAETZ would not say whether the sinusoidal path was indeed a fact, and not merely a function of the recording. It was also found that BRENNSCHLUSS showed considerable spatial dispersion, which was considered was due to variation in thrust performance. Low trajectories were due to low thrust performance. Thrust, varied between rockets, and also during the burning of individual rockets. This situation mught be improved by having proper regulation of A and B STOFF supply. There was a kink in the acceleration curve due to the changeover to supersonic speeds.

Fall of Shot.

19. The German ballisticians had considered the fall of shot pattern woud be Gaussian, but Oblt GRAETZ considered that it would be platykurtic. He gave the following estimates of performance:-

	Type of Control	50% zone @ 250kms
From Line	Mechanical	+/- 8 kms
From Line	L/S	+/- 2 kms
From Range	I-GERAET I	+/- 8kms
From Range	I-GERAET II	+/-8 kms

H.A.P. 11 claimed that B/S what is the most accurate method of range control, but it was considered that the limited nature of their trials did not make their results significan. The regiment commander of GRUPPE SUED, Maj.

SCHLESIGER, estimated that the proportion of shots which had fallen in the neighbourhood of the launching site at 8 to 9%, he thought GRUPPE SUED was better in this respect than GRUPPE NORD.

Airburst and Air Break-up.

20. Three type of events were recognised:

1. Deep crater - due to faulty fuze-action.
2. Small crater - correct fuse-action.
3. Air burst and air break-up.

Air break-up was considered to be partly due to weakness in the region of the GERAETRAUME and of the conical part of the front of the B-STOFF tank. This becomes critical when the rocket strikes the atmosphere on descent, the structure collapsing in the air and cover being stripped off. To overcome this. The relevant parts were strengthened.

21. Because of their detonation were not properly known. OBLT GRAETZ suggested that the causes were:

(a) Shattering of the glass nose and consequent operation of the fuse
(b) Inability of the exploder.
(c) Spontaneous ignition of the explosive how into high temperatures 600 to 700°C.

He gave us his estimate as performance against the UK

25% air break-up
5% airburst
60 to 70% in London.

The glass wool was introduced by HIP 11th to reduce their break up but Oblt GRAETZ did not consider it to have been of much use.

<u>Suggestions for improvement of the A-4 - Oblt GRAETZ.</u>

22. <u>Range Accuracy.</u>

(1) Minor improvesments to the I-GERAET.
(2) Making the PROGRAM a function of time and distance (double integration). This would make the rocket follow a single trajectory independant of variations in thrust. No attempt at double integration has yet appeared in practival form. (Note: Wachm BRINK had a proposal for improvement in this direction).
(3) More accurate thrust control.
(4) More satisfactory regulation of the supply of A and B STOFF to the burner.

<u>Line Accuracy.</u>

(1) Development of an integrator for yaw which would correct the rocket on to the required path.
(2) Improvement in roll control. roll in the first vertical part of the trajectory is a major source of error.
(3) Maintenance of flight control after BRENNSCHLUSS.

<u>Increased Range.</u>

(1) By regulation of the supply of A and B STOFF (see para 18). This would ensure more efficient burning and would both increase the maximum range and by decreasing the range scatter of burn-outs, increase the accuracy.
(2) By use of bigger fuel tanks.
By these means a range of 400 kms could probably be satisfactorily reached.

<u>General.</u>

(1) Reduction of misfires and airburst/air break-ups.
(2) Increase in explosive effect by use of a more sensitive fuse.

<u>General.</u>

C.C.C.S. Air Defence Division SHAEF has found that the concentration of fall of shot showed a statistically significant decrease for all firing units during March as compared with previous result. No technical reason could be advanced by prisoners to explain this. Oblt RALLE (O.C. Tech Bty, Gr SUED) suggested that decreased efficiency and application of servicing and firing troops as a reason. He said he had noticed some signs of a decline in the efficiency of his men, but considered the steps he had taken to stop this were effective. He considered that his men were as good as could be expected, although his various shifts varied widely in their enthusiasm and efficiency. If this was the reason he wouldexpect the effect to have been less marked in his Bty than in others.

Firing the A-4 from trains.

24.Hptm MUELLER stated that work had been done on this project which was Gen. KAMMLER's idea. The advantages were:

(1) All fue1s and GERAETE could be stored in the train.

(2) Rockets could be set up and prepared in the tunnel and wheeled out when ready to fire.

No such scheme was ever put into operation of the heavy concrete installation at SAINT OMER in the PAS DE CALAIS was to have operated in this manner but when almost complete it was destroyed by bombing

25.Firing an A-4 from submersible platforms at sea.

Work had been done on this scheme according to Oblt GAETZ. The principal was the large platform carrying all necessary equipment and fuel was to be towed into position by U-boat. The whole platform would would submerge after firing. Oxygen was to have a separate container. It was hoped to fire at NEW YORK in this manner. Work on this project was broken off in the summer of 1944 by order of Gen. KAMMLER.

26.Vapour Trails

Oblt GAETZ considered the wavy disorganisation of vapour trails, after formation to be due to meteorological effects. No attempts have been made to suppress vapour trail formation. The enemy had apparently not envisaged the trails, being to be used to pinpoint sites by ground observation, and since they only form above normal operational heights for aircraft, it was considered that they should not be used to find launching sites from the air.

Miscellaneous weapons.

27.HOCHDRUCHHPUMPE (TAUSENDFUSSLER) - 75 Bty

This batterie was on the command of Div z.V and was attached to 901 Regt. The weapon consisted of a tube, some 30 metres length along which were four or five chambers. The tube was aligned on the target at a Q. E. of approximately 40°, being supported on the reverse slope of a hill. The shell is of ordinary artillery shape with no fins and a calibre, roughly 150 mm. The chamber contain propellant and as the projectile passes up the tube, the chambers fire in turn. It was used in operations from the TRIER area (L22) against LUXEMBOURG. Preparations had been made to use it against MULHOUSE during January and February. Oblt. GRAETZ confirmed that this weapon on a larger scale was t have been used from an underground installation in the PAS DE CALAIS (MIMOYECQUES).

28.RHEINBOTE - 709 Bty.

This batterie was on the command of Div z.V and was attached to 902 Regt. It was a three-stage rocket fired from a MEILERWAGEN with the cradle elevated to the required Q.E. The projectile was roughly 12 metres long calibre about 200 mm. During flight the powder containers are dropped off when they are used up. It was described by as a wildly inaccurate weapon capable of falling at any range from 30 to 320 km. It had been fired at LIEGE and BRUSSELS.

Organisation.

29.Division z.V. evolved over time. Experience in the field showed that three batteries were too great a responsibility for a single ABTEILUNG and on 20 January 1945, the division was re-organised. The former ABTEILUNGEN became REGIMENTEN and the BATTERIEN ABTEILUNGEN.

Movements of firing units.

30. LEHR and VERSUCHSBATTERIE 444

Firng was opened by thisbatterie on 8 September 1944, when two rounds were fired against PARIS from FRACTURE (P.5885) in the ARDENNES. While here the batterie was under the control of 836 ABTEILUNG and was supplied by road from EUSKIRCHEN. The batterie was then moved to SEROOSKERBE (D.1336) on WALCHEREN ISLAND. The batterie occupied this position from 16-18 September. Six rounds were fired at LONDON, one of which fell in the sea. Rockets came by road from BERGEN OP ZOOM (D.6027) and fuels from GOES (D.3329) and ZUID BEVELAND.

31. Following the air landings at ARNHEM the batterie withdrew to RIJS (Z.4975), a position it occupied from 21 September until 20 October 1944. About 80 rounds were fired in all. 10 or 12 were aimed at ANTWERP 3 or 4 at GREAT YARMOUTH and the remainder at NORWICH. There is no basis in the suggestion that any trials were being undertaken during the firing at NORWICH. The first two rounds fired at ANTWERP was aimed at the town, subsiquent rounds at the docks. Both rockets and fuels were originally supplied from STEINWIJK (Z.9167) and latterly from SNEEK (Z.6095).

32.The batterie then moved to THE HAGUE and occupied positions there from 23 October to 27 January. During the period 1 November to 2 December the batterie was alone in THE HAGUE. During this period it was strengthened by the attachment on one firing troop all-rounds fired were aimed at a single point in London. Great uncertainty seem to exist as to the geographical position of this aiming point, while most prisoners interrogated considered the STADMITTE [city centre] to have been the point of the aim, one prisoner said it was the dock area.

33. At the end of January, the batterie withdrew to KARLSHAGEN to undertake trial firings designed to remove minor faults from the equipment. No firings took place as Gen. KAMMLER had ordered that all rockets produced must be used operationally.

1/485 later became I/902.
34.This batterie deployed to THE HAGUE at the beginning of operations and fired on LONDON. On 18 September it withdrew to LEGDEN (A.5782) and fired at TOURNAI, HASSELT, CHARLEROI and ANTWERP until 17 December when the unit returned to THE HAGUE. It remained there until thegeneral withdrawal at the end of March 1945.

2/485 later became II/902.
35.This batterie also deployed to THE HAGUE and withdrew on 18 September to AHAUS (A.5087) where for ten days itfired at TOURNAI, HASSELT, CHARLEROI and MASSTRIGHT. At the beginning of October it returned to THE HAGUE where it remained until the beginning of November. During this period LONDON was the only target. In early November the batterie withdrew to BURGSTEINFURT (A.7395) and remained there until the end of active operations, firing at ANTWERP.

3/485 later became III/902.
36. This batterie was originally deployed in the AHAUS area and moved to THE HAGUE about the middle of January. It remained there until the end of operations.

SS WERFER ABT. 500.
37.This batterie deployed at OMMEN (V.1135) about the middle of November 1944 and remained there until the conclusion of the operation all round is fine were against ANTWERP except for 11 fired against REMARGEN all supplies pass through OMMEN but towards the end oxygen was being brought by road all the way to the firing positions as bombing was seriously interfering with rail communications. The order to fire at REMARGEN came from HITLER one days firing being sanctioned, the target was the area of the crossing and not necessarily the bridge itself. The exact timing point was not known

1/836 later to be I/901
38. At the beginning of the operation this batterie was firing in trials at TUCHEL. It was first deployed operationally about 23 October 1944 at REINSFELD with its firing site near L.3621 and TECHNISCHE Batterie deployed near L.3926. Rockets were unloaded at POELERT (L.4625). ANTWERP was the only target engaged.

39. About 1 December 1944 the batterie moved

to MONTABAUR occupying the firing positions along the road between G.009012 and G.018009. The technical battery was situated along the road between F.997053 and 991028. Rockets were originally unloaded at GOLDHAUSEN ((G.0906) and later, after an air attack on HADAMAR (G.2206) and RANSBACH (F.9907). Oxygen was unloaded at WIRGES (G.0307). The fuel batterie was located at first at VIELBALCH (G.0211) and after 1 February at DERNBACH (G.0306).

2/836 and 3/836 became II/901 and III/901.
40. These batterien were first deployed together near ROTTGEN, the firing sites being near F.5328 and TECHNISCHE batterie at F.5231. Rockets were unloaded at HEIDGEN (F.4932. From this position the batteries fire at ANTWERP, LILLE, TOURCOING, ROUBAIX, CAMBRAI, ARRAS, LIEGE and HASSELT. After three weeks the two batteries moved to HACHENGURG and fired from platform along the road G.023226 - 033028. The TECHNISCHE batterie was situated at G.060205 and all equipment was unloaded at SELTERS. ANTWERP was the only target engaged from now on after about five days, during which time 30 rockets were fired. Both batteries moved to GREIMEPATH. The firing platforms were in the vicinity of L.2107 and the TECHNISCHE batterie L..2309. All stores were unloaded at NIEDER ZERF (L.2412). 2/836 left towards the end of this period for KARLSHAGEN and 3/836 moved to HEMERSKEIL where it had firing platforms in the area of L.5730. The TECHNISCHE batterie was situated near L.5227. Rockets were unloaded at DHRONECHEN (L.4625).

41. About 4 December the batterie moved to HACHENGURG and operated from firing platforms along the road G.047243 - 055270. The TECHNISCHE batterie was along the road G.090267 -080280. Rockets were unloaded at KORB (G.1028) and taken on VIDALWAGGEN to the TECHNISCHE batterie by way of ALPENROD (G.0926). In snow, and when the raods were bad the crane which moved the rockets from the VIDALWAGGEN to the MEILERWAGGEN was moved from the vicinity of the TECHNISCHE batterie (G.078283) to the firing site (G.053269) so that the rockets could be carried further on the lighter transporter. A route through HACHENGURG instead of ALPENROD was used. Movement of rockets along roads by day was concealed by a smokescreen. Oxygen was loaded at HACHENGURG and alcohol at SELTERS. The unit remained in the area until the end of the operation.

42. II/902 returned to GRUPPE SUED in January but it did not commence firing until the middle of February. Their sites were on the roads running northwest from KENSBURG (G.1330). The batterie shared technical and supply facilities with III/901.

Aiming Points
43. Only two aiming points in ANTWERP were used after the first weeks. These were the docks and the STADTMITTE [city centre]. Aiming points were normally past as coordinates from Division and the computing section of the battery converted these to range and line, including the necessary corrections for earth's rotation et cetera. The range ordered was then corrected for the constants of the individual rocket (KINDERKRANK). According to Major SCHLESIGER the aiming points for 836 ABTEILUNG was the town from 25 October to 1 December. He estimated that after 1 December, 700 rounds were fired, of which 500 were aimed at the docks. The aiming point in LONDON is discussed in para 32 above.

44. Organisation of the technical batteries.
The main function of the technical batteries was to inspect the rockets before firing. Inspection was carried out on the VIDEL waggon and after inspection the rocket was moved on to the MEILERWAGEN by crane and taken to the firing site. The technical battery was organised in two shifts, while the firing battery had only one. 20 rockets came in each train together with warheads and carbon vanes. When GRUPPE SUED was in the COBLENZ area. The control of the rocket trains went to the two technical batteries alternately. While normally I-GERAET

were fitted at MIDDLEWERK, supply often lagged behind and they were fitted by the technical battery.

Filling the rocket with fuel.

45. The first operation is to fill the alcohol tank. This process takes 20 minutes. While this is going on the tubes necessary for oxygen filling are attached to the rocket, a process taking about 10 minutes, and the T-STOFF (hydrogen peroxide) is measured out, a process also taking about 10 minutes. After measuring the T-STOFF tank is filled. After some alcohol had been put in the tank, the sealing of all pipes and joints is checked. If this is found to be satisfactory oxygen filling can commence. Originally two oxygen carrying vehicles were used and the process of filling took 20 minutes. Latterly a single larger tanker was used and the filling time was reduced to 10 minutes. Finally the Z-STOFF tank is filled.

46. The proceedure by night was the same as that employed by day, but if camouflage were good the rocket might be set up and checked by day and fuelled and fired by night. Towards the end of the operation, when fuels were much delayed in transit, rockets were often set up and inspected so that they could be fired as soon as possible after the arrival of the fuel. This was, however, only done if it was considered that there would be little or no likelihood of air attack.

Utilisation of Operational Data.

47. Very little appears to have been made of data accumulated during the operation. The methods of trajectory measurement described below (para 63) were largely regarded as checks on performance. While it was nominally the duty of W A PRUEF 10 to study operational performance, they appear to have done very little. Some investigations were, however, undertaken under the direction of 1aTech at Division. There is no suggestion that the operation was in any way regarded as a large scale trial.

Anti-Jamming.

48. Attached to Div.z.V was FUNK HORCH ABEILUNG 1192. At the beginning of the operation this had its headquarters at UEDEM (E.9843) and moved on 23 September 1944 to BRECKERFELD (A.8296). This unit had originally two functions:-

(1) To report and examine any jamming or interference that occurred on operational frequencies.

(2) To transmit camouflage signals in the hope that any jamming would be directed against threse rather than any genuine signals.

Frequency Monitoring.

49. Frequency monitoring receivers were situated at Headquarters - COMPANIE. Communications between firing positions and COMPANIE were by W.T. Three monitoring receivers were used. One for the L. S. reciever, one for the VERDOPPLER and one for the control reciever (HONNEF).

50. On the receipt of a report of interference from listening posts at headquarters, the MODESENDER which was a copy of the LEITSTRAHL transmitter was switched on. The MODESENDER and VICTORIA GERAET could be tuned to the range of 9 operational frequencies. Any interference, together with the normal signal, passed through the VICTORIA GERAET. Observation of the micrometer showed wether the unwanted signal would result in deflexion being orderd by the L/S receiver. The character of interference could be studied with the oscillograph and associated equipment, Operational Frequency 3 was always used.

51. The fundamental and doubled frequencies were both checked. The effect of the noise on SALERNO could be directly observed and its character examined using the cathode ray tube and ancilliary equipment. A similar arrangement was used to study the effect of interference on HONNEF, the audio tone filters being altered to agree with those in the particular control receiver to be used by the battery about to fire. The usual operational frequency for the VERDOPPLER and HONNEF was No.5.

52. The firing batteries would transmit through

GEIGAND or LUCKE (see para 55) information about the controls to be used. The reports to COMPANIE were in the following terms:-

Message No.	**Comment**
1 X-90	90 minutes before firing.
Batterie Rot 5	HONNEF freq 5
Batterie Gruen 5	VERDOPPLER freq 5
Batterie +Gelb 3	LEITSTRAHL freq 3
Gruppennummer	Indications of audio freq
Schluesselstecker	filters for HONNEF
Target No.	
2 Batterie X-10	10 minutes before firing.
3 Batterie X-5	5 minutes before firing.
4 Shot	Transmitted as long dash.
5 Firing time	
Batterie Rot 5	HONNEF freq 5
Batterie Gruen 5	VERDOPPLER freq 5
Batterie Gelb 3	LEITSTRAHL freq 3

53. The times X-90 etc correspond to the following physical events:-

X-120	Rocket brought to firing position.
X-90	Rocket erect.
X-60	Completion of inspection. Beginning of fuelling.
X-30	End of fuelling.
X-15	Lining up on table.
X-5	End of final inspection.
X-1	Firing connections made.

54. The deployment at BRECKERFELD was augmented by mobile vans built to monitor the performance of the VERDOPPLER and the L/S apparatus. The former (Ofahn SIMON) was deployed in January at DEDEMSVAART (V.1345) near ZWOLLE and then moved to THE HAGUE. Oscillograph records were taken. The L/S monitoring equipment (Ofahn WROOST) was depoloyed for a short time near ZWOLLE and then moved to THE HAGUE. No oscillograph records were made. Interference reports for both monitoring untils went back to COMPANIE by the usual channels and not by W.T. Despite the many elaborate precaustions interference was never a serious operational problem.

Camouflage transmissions.

55. In order to sidetrack Allies jamming efforts, two stations transmitting special signals were set up. These operated on frequencies slightly removed from the correct operational frequencies and the signals were differently modulated at the beginning of the operation one TARNSENDER station was employed with each GRUPPE. The TARNSENDER for GRUPPE NORD (Lt. GEIGAND) was originally deployed near HAARLAM (Y.8825). About the middle of September the station was moved to BILLERBECK (V.6975) and remained there till the end of the operation. The station with GRUPPE SUED (Lt. LUCKE) was initially at WEILER (L.5690) in the EIFEL, it moved about 20 September to RUESCHEID (F.8714) where it remained until 7 October. The station then moved to OTTWEILER (Q.5889) until the 3 December when it returned to RUESCHEID where itremained until the end of January. It was then decided to move the station forward to THE HAGUE as it was considered possible that the transmissions were not being heard. The station arrived at THE HAGUE on 4 February and remained there until the end of the operation. When the TARNSENDER moved from GRUPPE SUED to THE HAGUE, a WT station was left behind for communication with COMPANIE.

56. Each station normally consisted of four transmitters, two sets of transmitters were deployed at THE HAGUE to correspond with the two main launching areas as it was considered that agent reports of a single set of transmitters might have given a clue to the real function.

57. Add each station, one transmitter was supposed to resemble the one VERDOPPLER, the one HONNEF and the LEITSTRAHL transmission, the three transmitters broadcast at the appropriate times for approximately the correct interval.

The fourth transmitter gave signals which were intended to correspond approximately to the last 10 seconds of flight. For this purpose the firing battery had to pass the TARNSENDER the extended time of flight. The character of the broadcast was invariant for all transmissions being made regardless of the type of control gear in the rocket. The frequencies used by the GRUPPE SUED transmitters were changed only once, namely, when they were moved to THE HAGUE. The GRUPPE SUED transmitter is originally transmitted for every rocket fired, but latterly, for only about one in three transmissions, and unaccompanied by rockets, were also made so that they could not be used as a form of early warning, this practice was discontinued when the transmitters were deployed at THE HAGUE.

58. Communication was normally by W.T., but at THE HAGUE where the transmitters were sited at WASSENAAR and SCHEVENINGEN, line was used. Continuous warning messages of time from fire in the form of X – 90 X – 60 et cetera were passed from the battery. Latterly these messages were omitted as there were many other things to do. It is not clear whether this refers to transmissions from Batterie to TARNSENDER, or from there to companie.

59. The powers of the transmitters were as follows:

Type of Transmitter	Power (watts) (normal)	Power (watts) (at THE HAGUE)
LEITSTRAHL	100-120	100-120
HONNEF	800	100-120
VERDOPPLER	100-120	100-120
4th	800	100-120

60. For fall of shot location (see para 68) the VERDOPPLER what is sometimes modified to transmit during the whole time of flightt. The type of camouflage transmission was not altered in these circumstances if two sites were launching it, nearly the same time, the second rocket was not covered by transmission so the observation of the signals for the first rocket would not be disturbed. The transmission is well made only for whichever Batra reported X – 10 first.

61. An investigation was made at THE HAGUE by Lt. LUCKE to see whether there was any interference on his camouflage frequencies. The interference was reported by W.T. to company in the following form.

Frequency	30.4 M Htz.
Frequency covered	29.8 - 31.2 M Htz
No modulation	
1012 - 1125 hrs	
Not deliberate	
Signal strength 5	

Some interference was detected, but the sounce was not known.

62. Every evening a summary was given by station GEIGAND and LUCKE on their activities. This was made by W.T. if possible. Conditions for transmission in GRUPE SUED were generally unfavourable and line was used instead.

<u>Observation of fall of shot.</u>

63. Information on fall of shot was sought by the following methods.

(a) Agents.
(b) Photo Reconnaissance.
(c) Optical methods
  (i). Director
  (ii) Kine Theodolites.
(d) Electrical methods
  (i). Use of ORTLER to D/F rocket in. flight.
  (ii) Use of ORTLER to obtain several relative velocities on the same rocket - the TOSCANA system.

No attempt what is made at Sound ranging the use of radar had been considered by the G.A.F, but they were of the opinion that none of their sets were sufficiently powerful.

64. All methods used to study in fall of shot were only checks on performance. No attempt was made, except in one case (see para 66) to correct either range or line settings on the basis of observations made.

65. Agents were only used against LONDON. Time, date and place of fall were recorded agents were not employed in ANTWERP, where it was considered photo-reconnaissance gain better results.

66. Reconnaissance flights were flown every 14 days over ANTWERP; attempts were made to fly over London as well. G.A.F. photographic, interpretation experts annotated the cover distinguishing between V-1 and V-2, and also between old and new craters. No attempts appear to have been made to use spoil patterns to determine the direction of flight of individual rounds in February. DIVISION ordered an increase in range of about 2 km for all ABELEILUNGEN firing against ANTWERP for photographs had shown the majority of rounds falling short. The clear clips one corresponding to GRUPPE NORD and the other corresponding to GRUPPE SUED were recognised short of the aiming point.

Optical methods.

67. The first optical method introduced in January 1945 involve the use of one director only. This was set up 3 to 4 km behind the launching position and on the line of fire. The director was laid on a predetermined low elevation such that the rocket would pass through the field of the director, nine seconds after launch. When the rocket was first observed, the liar gave a signal and a stopwatch was started. The rocket was followed by the director and the azimuth was read at regular intervals. Deviation in line could be calculated using the data for horizontal distance, travelled in the given time which was shown in the range tables. In good visibility, the rocket could be followed for 80 to 90 seconds by day and for about 100 seconds by night elevation was not recorded.

68. The use of line theodolites was developed by Hptm BECK. They were installed in THE HAGUE towards the end of February, and at AHAUS at the beginning of March. Two instruments were used being sited behind and either side of the firing position. Normal method of calculation were used to, and from the observations, velocity, trajectory, inclination, and position at BRENNSCHUSS could be determined by parabolic extrapolation. The position of full of shot could be estimated no corrections were made for retardation or meteorological conditions. Beyond that, the instruments could be delayed an approximate measurements taken by night the rocket could be followed to position slightly beyond BRENNSCHUSS. Oblt GRAETZ stated, however, that the rocket could be followed to 150 km by the theodolites in good weather conditions. (Comment. These statements are not necessarily contradictory for Oblt GRAETZmay have only had a laying in mind if this is so it seems probable that the same riddle ground plan track described in Para 17 is probably a laying effect and not something inherent in the rocket.) Lt. LOHMANN estimated the accuracy of the procedure to be 200 to 300 m. The fire plan was not altered in order to permit optical measurement if the weather was cloudy.

Electrical methods.

69. A modification to the VERDOPPLER will allow it to transmit during the whole time of the flight of the rocket. This modified transponder is referred to as ORTLER. In the spring of 1944, experiments were carried out on the Pomeranian coast to develop the suitable message to find direction using this signal. the siting of equipment on the channel coast was then in mind. FUNK HORCH ABTILUNG 1192 were trained in the use of this method at BLIZA in POLAND in November and December 1944.

70. The equipment finally used consisted of 3 G.A.F. HEILERGAETE Type 80 B2 and two WEHRMACHT mock ups. The sets were deployed in January. The associated WT station is being deployed earlier so that they might undertake training and attempt was made to use the set during the last week of operations, but no success was achieved. Only shots fired at Antwerp were followed.

71. The deployment of the equipment was as follows:-

Locality	Comment
STAVOREN (z.3979)	These two stations
REES (A.5307)	came into action first.
BRECKERFELD (F.8296)	Army type.
KOENIGSWINTER (F.6131)	Never worked
KAUB (M6503)	

The deployment of a station at THE HAGUE

was under consideration, the equipment had a simple Adcock array with an acoustic presentation. The operator were to obtain minimum signal readings of bearings were taken while the rocket was in flight. These were recorded against an arbitrary zero obtained from the relayed shot. Signal passed from the batteries to company to check the timing. Another signal might be sent out by company five minutes after the first.

72. The observations made were passed back as times and bearings. They were, then plotted and smooth curtains drawn from the intersections of the bearings from several stations. At the same time, the path and point of full could be ascertained. (Comment: presumably the time at which the signal stopped, was also noted.)

73. On the basis of the trials in POLAND, it was estimated that 80% elipse of error had a 7 to 10 km axis in range and a 3 to 6 km axis in line.

74. The TOSCANA system was developed by Prof. WOLMAN of DRESDEN. This system used 3 or 4 SALERNO units. The exact method of deployment is uncertain. The beat notes from the units were taken on to a single strip of film on which was also printed a 100 cycle note a reference. This latter signal was produced by equipment known as KLEIN FLORENZ. By an examination of the 3 or 4 beat frequencies the trajectory of the rocket could be determined. This system was only deployed in the last weeks of the operation by SS WERFER ABTEILUNG 500.

75. The interference monitoring van deployed at THE HAGUE was literally used to check the accuracy of rocket carrying I-GERAETE. Oscillograph records were taken of rockets carrying ORTLER and I-GERAET. Disallowed timer flight velocity at all, burnt and burning time to be measured, accurately but the fall of shop measurements were only rough as they were partly depending on the range table data. SIMON put the accuracy as low as +/- 50 km.

Tailpiece.

76. Oblt GRAETZ often said to Gen. Kammler that the potatoes used in making alcohol would be better used in feeding the population.

Appendix Five

Correspondence between Dir Hans Lindenberg and the Project Backfire team.

1. Proposal for face-to-face meetings.

Altenwalde, Aug 28 1945.

To: Major TARGETT

Concerns Technical reasons for my propsal to visit camp C. personally, in order to clear, with Dipl. Ing. ZANGL, Dipl. Ing. HELLER, Ing. BIPPART and Werkemeister KONIG, questions which have to guarantee the security of function of rockets, built by us.

In every rocket, there exists parts tuned upon and adjusted with each other, as f. i. burner, turbine, vapour unit, pipes assembly. The pressure losses of the single parts determine the diameter of the fuel and oxygen restricting plate. As the documents of the parts and spares in this place are not at all complete, certain parts have to be exchanged and no expedients (tables and formulas) for computation are available, I have to refer to the experience of Dipl. Ing ZANGL in this matter, in order to ascertain these values. That is not possible by a written communication, but has to be performed by personal contact.

There has to cleared similar questions with respect to the fuel what, if it should be useful for the exercise BACKFIRE were to be done by personal contact.

To gain information, if and how far the turbines and pumps under consideration are safe, it will be necessary to take to pieces each pump and turbine. For the critical examination, discussion and, in this case, even the presence of Werkemeister KONIG is urgent.

With regards, the rigidity of the whole body frame, a critical consultation of Ing. BIPPART is necessary. This, too, is not possible by letter and such a matter can be handled more successful by a personal discussion.

(signed)
LINDENBERG

2. Technical report dated 30 August 1945 on the testing and matching of assemblies of rockets arising from the proposal from Herr Lindenberg on 28 August 1945

Present:
Major TARGETT, L R.
Mr. WORTLEY
Lt. MEYER
Herr LINDENBERG
Ing ZANGL

Place of meeting - British Technical Office, KRUPPS.

1. Following discussions with Herr LINDENBERG and his suggestion outlined in copy of his letter of Aug 28, a meeting was held in order to clarify the position regarding the fundamental data relating to test equipment and matching.

2. A preliminary survey of various assemblies and components was made in the workshops and stores. The purpose of this survey was to:-

a. Allow ZANGL to get an appreciation of the condition of assemblies from deterioration point of view.

b. To endeavour to locate test sheets and data for individual assemblies.

3. The rockets on which work is processing have been damaged and exposed to adverse conditions. This necessitates, the replacement of either components or assemblies, which may be found defective on the elementary tests which are capable of being carried out at KRUPPS. This replacement raises the question of the characteristics of components and assemblies, and whether the tolerances and specifications laid down, are either fine or wide. Both LINDENBERG and ZANGL confirmed that the characteristics would vary considerably in some cases as much as + or - 10% and therefore, in order to match components accurately at KRUPPS, special tables would be required which may take any time from 2 to 2½ years to compute. The following notes were taken in conference after examination outlined above.

4. LINDENBERG asked if ZANGL was in a position to give the matching values. If one part of the rocket had to be removed and replaced by another i.e. if the venturi was removed owing to damage, and another venturi, of which the characteristics were unknown was put in its place whether ZANGL would be in a position to calculate the adjustments needed for matching purposes. The same would obviously apply to the turbine pumps and steam unit. ZANGL answered that these values were obtained by means of tables and nomographs. These nomographs were composed from theoretical calculations, and, partly from practical deductions. From these nomographs a set of reference figures were

evolved such that each individual piece of apparatus could be given a code number indicating its performance figures. This method of testing was also an indication that unskilled or sem-skilled inspection could be employed and the tables were such that large tolerances in manufacture could be allowed. It is interesting to know that these individual values and tables are calculated from 25 variables.

5. ZANGL stated that each component test and data sheets were made out giving the relative performance figures. These data sheets were placed in the assembly cases and should always have been with the particular unit concerned. And examination of the equipment at KRUPPS have shown that few datasheets were available. Mainly concerned with the steam units and the pumps. No data sheets have been found for the venturi, and therefore owing to the lack of these figures, and what is more important, the lack of nomographs, no interchangeability values can be given for each separate assembly.

6. The practical conclusion was therefore as follows that the firing of rockets from KRUPPS from the manufacturing standpoint must be dealt with under two headings:-

a. the examination of complete, but damaged rockets requiring no interchanging of combustion components.

b. Rockets in which individual components must be interchanged.

7. The following notes were made on (a).

Complete rockets have obviously, before passing from works, had their assemblies and such assemblies matched; for instance, the orifices needed to balance and match pumps and venturis and the setting of the reducing valve for these particular values would have been fitted. Therefore, if these rockets are stripped and subject to pressure test and they are found to require no further changing of components, the orifices installed could be replaced and the reducing valve set to the figures which are shown painted on the tail unit. It is most important that when these rockets are reassembled, and the orifice plates are replaced, the reducing valve must be set to the exact value stated.

8. The following notes were made on (b)

Small faults in the calibration of components affect the trajectory of the rocket in so much as they alter the thrust, and therefore the initial acceleration. In affect the rate of inclination, during the initial trajectory may be influenced thus affecting height at the point of cut-off for an equivalent duration of thrust.

9. Two other important factors arising from inaccurate matching are variation in fuel ratio and in steam unit pressure. The matching of orifices is made by initially installing one standard restricting throat in either the alcohol or oxygen pump delivery. Final matching is carried out by the insertion of a sharp edged orifice into whichever delivery pump is found to require reduction in pressure. The predetermined value of this standard restricting throat was given by ZANGL as 125mm. If the manufacture of the pumps were such that the performance could be kept within close limits, then standard throats could be predetermined for both pumps.

10. Arising from the notes on (b) above, it was agreed that in order to carry out exercise BACKFIRE, the inclusion of two standard restricting throats was thought to be the best arrangement in order to take the minimum amount of risk. It would also be proposed that in the case of be the reducing valve controlling pressure on the steam unit should be set at the average value of 32.5 atmospheres. It was disclosed that for each atmosphere dropped on the setting of the reducing valve, the revolution of the turbine, and therefore pumps is decreased by 100 per minute. The working revolution of the turbine was stated to be approx [remainder of sentance illegible on the microfilm copy].

GENERAL
11. With regard to the cleaning of the venturi, ZANGL stated that wash through with water under pressure was the best method of cleaning any foreign matter. The use of rust removing fluids is not advisable owing to the restrictions and corners which are inherent in the manufacture of this part. There was also the possibility of chemical reaction between the fluid and the fuel is used.

12. LINDENBERG asked if by using the two standard restriction throats, there would be a danger for the venturi to burn through. Basing his answer on experience, ZANGL that only trial would prove this point, and that there is a danger of burning through the venturi. If this content contained foreign matter or if loosened foreign matter, is passed through onto the jets, thus blocking them and upsetting the fuel ratio.

13. The attached appendix gives some idea of the type of nomograph which the Germans involved and the general conclusion reached after this meeting was that no guarantee of matching and therefore fuel ratio can be given that all components must be pressure tested that as far as possible. Complete assemblies should be used, since to introduce new components will upset the values and that the flame pattern check may be necessary before actual firing is contemplated. It would therefore be noted that so far as operation BACKFIRE is concerned, concentration will have to be made on the rockets that were recently chosen from CUXHAVEN railway yard since from the every outward appearance, these are in a fair state of preservation.

signed
L R TARGETT. Major.

J WORTLEY (C.T.A)

NOTE

Nomograph = a Nomograph is a graph, usually containing three parallel scales graduated for different variables so that when a straight line connects values of any two, the related value may be read directly from the third at the point intersected by the line.

Inexpensive scientific and engineering calculators eliminated the need for nomographs that embody complicated relationships that would prove cumbersome or difficult to calculate otherwise.

Bibliography

A4 - Fibel, German Field Technical Manual - German Army 1944 - Redstone Arsenal, Alabama, John A. Bitzer & Ted A. Woerner, 1957 (ISBN 0-9696169-5-X)

Agoston, Tom. **BLUNDER! How the U.S. Gave Away Nazi Supersecrets to Russia.** London: William Kimber, 1986..

Baker, David, Ph.D. **The Rocket: The History and Development of Rocket and Missile Technology.** London: Crown Publishers, 1979.

Barber, Murray and Michael Keuer, **Hitler's Rocket Soldiers.** West Sussex, UK: Tattered Flag, 2011.

Barber, Murray. **V2: The A4 Rocket from Peenemunde to Redstone.** Manchester, UK: Crecy Publishing, 2017.

Bode, Volkhard and Gerhard Kaiser. **Raketenspuren Peenemünde 1936-1996.** Bechtermunz Verlag, ISBN 3-86047-584-3.

Boer, J. F. A. **Raketten Over Den Haag.** Amsterdam: Die Haeghe Jaarboek, 1948.

Boer, J. F. A. **V-weapons in Overijssel.** Amsterdam: Die Haeghe Jaarboek, 1951.

Cabell, Craig, and Graham A Thomas. **Operation Big Ben: The Anti-V2 Spitfire Missions 1944–1945**. Kent: T. J. International Ltd., 2004.

Collier, Basil. **The Battle of the V-Weapons.** London: Hoddler and Stoughton, 1964.

Culver, Bruce. **"The A4/V2 Missile."** *Allied-Axis Photo Journal No. 1* (2000)

De Maeseneer, Guido. **Peenemünde: The Extraordinary Story of Hitler's Secret Weapons V-1 and V-2.** Vancouver: AJ Publishing, 2001.

Dornberger, Walter. **"Can Russian Missiles Strike the United States?"** *Collier's Magazine* (January 1955)

Dornberger, Walter. **V-2: The Nazi Rocket Weapon.** Translated by James Cleugh and Geoffrey Halliday. New York: Viking Press, 1954.

Dungan, T. Dwayne. **V-2: A Combat History of the First Ballistic Missile**. Yardley, PA: Westholme Publishing, 2005.

Engelmann, Whriter Joachim. **Geheime waffenschmiede Peenemünde. V-2 /Wasserfall / Schmetterling,** Podzun- pallas-Verlag Friedberg, ISBN 3-7909- 0118-8

Franssen, Theo and Captain Wood. **The Battle of Antwerp, 'City of Sudden Death...'** Antwerp: De Sleutel, 1945

Galván, J. Manuel Ramírez. **V2, La Venganza de Hitler.** Spanish language only, Rústica, Melusina, 2012.

Garlinski, Jozef. **Hitler's Last Weapons: The Underground War Against the V1 and V2.** ISBN 0904014231

Glass, A., S. Kordaczuk, and D. Stepniewska. **Wywiad Armii Krajowej W Walce Z V-1 / V-2 (Polish Home Army Intelligence Service Against the V-1 and V-2).** Warszawa: Mirage Hobby, 2000

Grailet, Lambert. **Première Mondiale Pour le V-2 sur Paris.** Tongeren: George Michiels, 1996.

Gruen, Adam L. **Preemptive Defense, Allied Air Power Versus Hitler's V-Weapons 1943–1945.** United States Air Force Historical Studies Office, 1991.

Gückelhorn, Wolfgang, and Detlev Paul. **V2 gefrorene Blitze (V2 Frozen Lightning): Einsatzgeschichte der V2 aus Eifel, Hunsrück und Westerwald 1944/45.** Aachen: Helios Verlags- und Buchvertriebsgesellschaft, 2007.

Hautefeuille, Roland. **Constructions Spéciales.** Detailed description with original drawings about the blockhaus buildings for V-weapons in France. Paris: Selbstverlag, 1985.

Hearn, Major Bunn (Headquarters, U.S. War Department Memorandum). **V-Weapon Activity Report.** April 7–8, 1945.

Hechler, Ken. **The Bridge at Remagen: The Amazing Story of March 7, 1945 - The Day the Rhine River was Crossed.** 1957. Reprint, Missoula, Montana: Pictorial Histories Publishing Company, 1993

Heitmann, Jan. **The Peenemünde Rocket Centre.** *After the Battle Magazine,* no. 74 (1991)

Helfers, Lieutenant Colonel M.C. **The Employment of V-Weapons by the Germans During World War II.** Washington D.C.: Department of the Army, Office of the Chief of Military History, 1954
Hindriks, Klaas Jan and Rudolf Spoor. **Wernher von Braun; één van de 118.** Amsterdam: 1977.
Hölsken, Dieter. **V-Missiles of the Third Reich: The V-1 and V-2.** Sturbridge, Massachusetts: Monogram Aviation Publications, 1994.
Howard, Michael. **British Intelligence in the Second World War**. New York: Cambridge University Press, 1990
Huzel, Dieter K. **Peenemünde to Canaveral.** New Jersey: Prentice-Hall, 1962.
Johnson, David. **V-1, V-2: Hitler's Vengeance on London.** New York: Stein and Day Publishers, 1981.
Johnson, David. **V for Vengeance: the Second Battle of London.** London : Kimber, 1981.
Jones, R. V. **Most Secret War.** London: Hamish Hamilton, 1978.
Jungbluth, Uli. **Wunderwaffen im KZ Rebstock, Zwangsarbeit in Dernau/Rheinland-Pfalz und Artern/Thüringen im Dienste der V-Waffen.** Briedel/Mosel: Rhein-Mosel-Verlag, 2000
Jungbluth, Uli. **V1,2,3: Hitler's Geheimwaffen im Westerwald.** Montabaur/Westerburg: Werkstatt-Beiträge zum Westerwald, 1996.
Kennedy, Gregory P. Germany's **V-2 Rocket.** Atglen, PA: Schiffer, 2006.
Kennedy, Gregory P. **Vengeance Weapon 2: The V-2 Guided Missile.** Washington, D.C.: Smithsonian Institution Press, 1983.
King, Benjamin, and Timothy J. Kutta. **Impact: The History of Germany's V-Weapons in World War II.** New York: Sarpedon, 1998.
Klee, Ernst, and Otto Merk.**The Birth of the Missile: The Secrets of Peenemünde.** Hamburg: Gerhard Stalling Verlag, 1963
Klee, Ernst, and Otto Merk. **Damals in Peenemünde.** Oldenburg: Gerhard Stalling Verlag, 1963.
Koopman, Henk. **Vergeltungswaffen in the Nederland (V-weapons in the Netherlands).** Utrecht: Uitgeverij Flying Pencil BL B.V., 2018 (Dutch language).
Lampton, Christopher. **Wernher Von Braun.** New York: Franklin Watts, 1988.
Longmate, Norman. **Hitler's Rockets: The Story of the V-2s.** London: Hutchinson Publishing, 1985
Margry, Karel. **Nordhausen.** *After the Battle Magazine,* no. 101 (1998)
McElheran, Brock. **V-Bombs and Weathermaps.** London: McGill-Queen's University Press, 1995.
McGovern, James. **Crossbow and Overcast.** New York: William Morrow and Co., 1964.
Michels, Jürgen. **Peenemünde und seine Erben in Ost und West, Entwicklung und Weg deutscher Geheimwaffen.** Bonn: Bernard and Graefe Verlag, 1997.
Middlebrook, Martin. **The Peenemünde Raid.** London: Penguin Books, Ltd., 1982 highly recommended *
Miranda, J. and P. Mercado. **Secret Wonder Weapons of the Third Reich: German Missiles 1934-1945.** Schiffer, (ISBN 0-7643-0086-5).
Neufeld, Michael J. **The Reichswehr, the Rocket, and the Versailles Treaty: A Popular Myth Reexamined.** *Journal of the BIS,* Vol. 53 (2000).
Neufeld, Michael J. **The Rocket and the Reich**. New York: The Free Press, 1995 highly recommended *
Neufeld, Michael J. **Von Braun: Dreamer of Space, Engineer of War.** New York: Random House, Knopf, 2007.
Ogley, Bob. **Doodlebugs and Rockets.** Kent: Froglets Publications, 1992.
Ordway, Frederick I., III, and Mitchell Sharpe. **The Rocket Team**. New York: Thomas Y. Crowell, 1979.
Palinckx, Koen. **Antwerpen Onder De V-Bommen 1944–1945.** Antwerpen: Pandora, 2004
Porezag, Karsten. **Geheime Kommandosache: Geschichte der V-Waffen und geheimen Militäraktionen des Zweiten Weltkrieges an Lahn.** Dill und im Westerwald: Verlag Wetzlardruck GmbH, Wetzlar, 1996.
Raiber, R, M.D. **The Führerhauptquartiere.** *After the Battle Magazine,* no. 19 (1977).
Ramsey, Winston G., and Robert Collis. **The Blitz Then and Now, Vol. 3. London**: Battle of Britain Prints International, Ltd., 1990.
Ramsey, Winston G**. The V-Weapons.** *After the Battle Magazine*, no. 6 (1974).
Ranstead, Chris. **Disarming Hitler's V Weapons: Bomb Disposal - The V1 & V2 Rockets.** Pen and Sword, Barnsley, S. Yorkshire, 2013.
Rely, Achiel, and Winston Ramsey. **Antwerp: City of Sudden Death.** *After the Battle Magazine,* no. 57 (1987).

Reuter, Claus. **The V2 and the Russian and American Rocket Program.** New York: S. R. Research and Publishing, 2000.

Ruff, Volker. **Der Strabokran. 15t and 16t Gantry Crane Variants Used in Tiger, Panther, Elefant & V-2 Rocket Units.** Buchdorf, Germany: Volker Ruff, 2011

Ruff, Volker. **Spezialfahrzeuge 1 Peenemünde 1942-45 (Peenemünde Special Vehicles 1). Design, Production and Deployment of Division z.V., the A-4 Rocket Units.** Buchdorf, Germany: Volker Ruff, 2025.

Russell, John, with R. De Norman. **No Triumphant Procession: The Forgotten Battles of April 1945.** London: Arms and Armour, 1994

Sellier, André. **Histoire du Camp de Dora**. Paris: La Découverte, 1998

Sellier, André, and Ives Le Maner. **Images De Dora 1943–1945.** Centre d'Histoire de la Guerre et des Fusées, Saint-Omer, 1999.

Serrien, Pieter. **Overzicht V-inslagen op België (Overview of V-bomb attacks on Belgium).** Uitgever: Horizon, 2016,

Simpson, Bill. **Spitfire Dive-Bombers Versus The V2.** South Yorkshire: Pen & Sword Books, 2007.

Speer, Albert. **Inside the Third Reich.** New York: Avon, 1970.

Stine, G. Harry. **ICBM: The Making of the Weapon that Changed the World.** New York: Orion Books, 1991.

Tinschert, Carlo. **Boodschap aan de Bevolking van Den Haag (Message to the People of The Hague: The bombing of Bezuidenhout).** Den Haag: Sdu Uitgevers, 2005 highly recommended *

United States Army Ordinance. **The Story of Peenemünde: What Might Have Been.** Washington D.C.: United States War Department, 1945.

Van der Boom, B. **Den Haag in de Tweede Wereld Oorlog (The Hague in the Second World War)**

Van Valkenburgh, Christopher. F**ifty Years of Silence; Ordnance Technical Intelligence Team Depot O-644,** Paris, France, 1944-1945. Independent: Amazon, 2020

Von Braun, Wernher, and Frederick I. Ordway, III. **History of Rocketry and Space Travel.** London: Thomas Nelson and Sons, Ltd., 1967

Von Braun, Wernher, and Frederick I. Ordway, III. **The Rockets' Red Glare.** New York: Doubleday, 1976

Wagner, Jens-Christian. **Produktion des Todes - Das KZ Mittelbau Dora.** Göttingen: Wallstein Verlag, 2001.

Ward, Bob. Dr. Space: **The Life of Wernher von Braun.** Annapolis, MD: US Naval Institute Press, 2005

The War Office. **Report on Operation Backfire.** London: January 1946.

Volume 1 - Scope and Organisation of the Operation; Sections 1 to 9.

Volume 2 - Technical Report; Sections 1 to 7.

Volume 3 - Field Proceedure; Sections 1 to 6.

Volume 4 - Descriptions of Equipment and Special Vehicles; Sections 2 to 38.

Volume 5 - Recording and Analysis of the trajectory. Sections 1 to 3.

Weber, Lieutenant Colonel Wolfgang and Dr. Merz, Dr. Priesner, **Altenwalder Versuchkommando. Die Fernrakete, Gerät und Zubehör, AVKO (From Fehrbellin to Altenwalde, AVKO): The history of the Div. z.V.- Cuxhaven/Altenwalde: 1945-46.**

Wegener, Peter P. **The Peenemünde Wind Tunnels: A Memoir.** New Haven: Yale University Press, 1996

Williams, Alan. **Operation Crossbow: The Untold Story of Photographic Intelligence and the Search for Hitler's V Weapons.** London: Cornerstone Publishing, 2013

Williams, Major C. R. **"V-Weapons: Crossbow Campaign."** U.S. Strategic Bombing Survey, Report No. 60 (1945)

Index

A4/V-2 rockets being prepared for shipment from Antwerp Docks to the USA. *(NARA)*